THE
SACRED BOOKS OF THE EAST

Translated by
VARIOUS ORIENTAL SCHOLARS

Edited by
F. MAX MÜLLER

Vol. 9

SACRED BOOKS OF THE EAST

(50 VOLUMES)

Series Editor : *F. Max-Müller*

ISBN: 978-81-208-0101-1 (Set) Rs. 15000 (Each Vol. Rs. 350)

These volumes of the Sacred Books of the East series include translations of all the most important works of the seven non-Christian religions that have exercised a profound influence on the civilisations of the continent of Asia. The Vedic Brahmanic system claims 21 volumes, Buddhism 10, and Jainism 2; 8 volumes comprise Sacred Books of the Parsis; 2 volumes represent Islam; and 6 the two main indigenous systems of China. Translated by twenty leading authorities in their respective fields, the volumes have been edited by the late F. Max Müller. The inception, publication and the compilation of these books cover almost 34 years.

I. BUDDHISM

Vol. 49: Buddhist Mahayana Texts (2 Parts)
Vol. 11: Buddhist Suttas
Vol. 10: The Dhammapada and Sutta Nipata
Vols. 35 & 36: The Questions of King Milinda (2 Parts)
Vol. 21: The Saddharma Pundarika or the Lotus of the True Law
Vols. 13, 17 & 20: Vinaya Texts (3 Parts)

II. CHINESE

Vol. 19: The Fo-Sho-Hing-Tsan-King
Vols. 3, 16, 27, 28, 39 & 40: The Sacred Books of China (6 Parts)

III. A GENERAL INDEX

Vol. 50: A General Index to the Names and Subject-matter of the Sacred Books of the East

IV. ISLAM

Vols. 6 & 9: The Qur'an (2 Parts)

V. JAINISM

Vols. 22 & 45: The Jaina Sutras (2 Parts)

VI. PARSIS

Vols. 5, 18, 24, 37 & 47: Pahlavi Texts (5 Parts)
Vols. 4, 23 & 31: The Zend-Avesta (3 Parts)

VII. VEDIC-BRAHMANIC SYSTEM

Vol. 8: The Bhagavadgita with the Sanatsujatiya and the Anugita
Vols. 29 & 30: The Grihya-Sutras: Rules of Vedic Domestic Ceremonies (2 Parts)
Vol. 42: Hymns of the Atharva Veda together with Extracts from the Ritual Books and the Commentaries
Vol. 7: The Institutes of Vishnu
Vol. 25: The Laws of Manu
Vol. 33: The Minor Law Books
Vols. 2 & 14: The Sacred Laws of the Aryas as Taught in the Schools of Apastamba, Gautama, Vasishtha and Baudhayana (2 Parts)
Vols. 12, 26, 41, 43 & 44: The Satapatha Brahmana According to the Text of the Madhyandina School (5 Parts)
Vols. 1 & 15: The Upanishads (2 Parts)
Vols. 34 & 38: The Vedanta Sutras (2 Parts)
Vol. 48: The Vedanta-Sutras (with the commentary by Ramanuja)
Vols. 32 & 46: Vedic Hymns (2 Parts)

THE QUR'ÂN

CHAPTERS XVII TO CXIV

Translated by

E.H. PALMER

PART II

MOTILAL BANARSIDASS PUBLISHERS
PRIVATE LIMITED • DELHI

7th Reprint: Delhi, 2012
First Published by the Clarendon Press, 1880

ISBN: 978-81-208-0110-3

MOTILAL BANARSIDASS
41 U.A. Bungalow Road, Jawahar Nagar, Delhi 110 007
8 Mahalaxmi Chamber, 22 Bhulabhai Desai Road, Mumbai 400 026
203 Royapettah High Road, Mylapore, Chennai 600 004
236, 9th Main III Block, Jayanagar, Bangalore 560 011
Sanas Plaza, 1302 Baji Rao Road, Pune 411 002
8 Camac Street, Kolkata 700 017
Ashok Rajpath, Patna 800 004
Chowk, Varanasi 221 001

UNESCO COLLECTION OF REPRESENTATIVE WORKS— Indian Series
This book has been accepted in the Indian Translation Series of the UNESCO Collection of Representative Works, jointly sponsored by the United Nations Educational Scientific and Cultural Organization (UNESCO) and the Government of India

Printed in India

By Jainendra Prakash Jain at Shri Jainendra Press,
A-45 Naraina, Phase-I, New Delhi 110 028
and Published by Narendra Prakash Jain for
Motilal Banarsidass Publishers Private Limited,
Bungalow Road, Delhi 110 007

RASHTRAPATI BHAVAN,
NEW DELHI-4
June 10, 1962

I am very glad to know that the Sacred Books of the East, published years ago by the Clarendon Press, Oxford, which have been out-of-print for a number of years, will now be available to all students of religion and philosophy. The enterprise of the publishers is commendable and I hope the books will be widely read.

S. RADHAKRISHNAN

PREFATORY NOTE TO THE NEW EDITION

Since 1948 the United Nations Educational, Scientific and Cultural Organisation (UNESCO), upon the recommendation of the General Assembly of the United Nations, has been concerned with facilitating the translation of the works most representative of the culture of certain of its Member States, and, in particular, those of Asia.

One of the major difficulties confronting this programme is the lack of translators having both the qualifications and the time to undertake translations of the many outstanding books meriting publication. To help overcome this difficulty in part, UNESCO's advisers in this field (a panel of experts convened every other year by the International Council for Philosophy and Humanistic Studies), have recommended that many worthwhile translations published during the 19th century, and now impossible to find except in a limited number of libraries, should be brought back into print in low-priced editions, for the use of students and of the general public. The experts also pointed out that in certain cases, even though there might be in existence more recent and more accurate translations endowed with a more modern apparatus of scholarship, a number of pioneer works of the greatest value and interest to students of Eastern religions also merited republication.

This point of view was warmly endorsed by the Indian National Academy of Letters (Sahitya Akademi), and the Indian National Commission for UNESCO.

It is in the spirit of these recommendations that this work from the famous series "Sacred Books of the East" is now once again being made available to the general public as part of the UNESCO Collection of Representative Works.

PUBLISHER'S NOTE

First, the man distinguished between eternal and perishable. Later he discovered within himself the germ of the Eternal. This discovery was an epoch in the history of the human mind and the *East was the first to discover it.*

To watch in the Sacred Books of the East the dawn of this religious consciousness of man, must always remain one of the most inspiring and hallowing sights in the whole history of the world. In order to have a solid foundation for a comparative study of the Religions of the East, we must have before all things, complete and thoroughly faithful translation of their Sacred Books in which some of the ancient sayings were preserved because they were so true and so striking that they could not be forgotten. They contained eternal truths, expressed for the first time in human language.

With profoundest reverence for Dr. S. Radhakrishnan, President of India, who inspired us for the task; our deep sense of gratitude for Dr. C. D. Deshmukh & Dr. D. S. Kothari, for encouraging assistance; esteemed appreciation of UNESCO for the warm endorsement of the cause ; and finally with indebtedness to Dr. H. Rau, Director, Max Müller Bhawan, New Delhi, in procuring us the texts of the Series for reprint, we humbly conclude.

CONTENTS.

		PAGE
XVII.	The Chapter of the Night Journey (Mecca) .	1
XVIII.	The Chapter of the Cave (Mecca) . . .	13
XIX.	The Chapter of Mary (Mecca)	27
XX.	The Chapter of *T.* H. (Mecca)	34
XXI.	The Chapter of the Prophets (Mecca) . .	46
XXII.	The Chapter of the Pilgrimage (Mecca) . .	56
XXIII.	The Chapter of Believers (Mecca) . . .	65
XXIV.	The Chapter of Light (Medînah) . . .	73
XXV.	The Chapter of the Discrimination (Mecca) .	83
XXVI.	The Chapter of the Poets (Mecca) . . .	90
XXVII.	The Chapter of the Ant (Mecca) . . .	99
XXVIII.	The Chapter of the Story (Mecca) . . .	107
XXIX.	The Chapter of the Spider (Mecca) . .	117
XXX.	The Chapter of the Greeks (Mecca) . .	124
XXXI.	The Chapter of Loqmân (Mecca) . . .	131
XXXII.	The Chapter of Adoration (Mecca) . .	135
XXXIII.	The Chapter of the Confederates (Medînah) .	138
XXXIV.	The Chapter of Sheba (Mecca)	150
XXXV.	The Chapter of the Angels, or, the Creator (Mecca)	157
XXXVI.	The Chapter of Y. S. (Mecca)	162
XXXVII.	The Chapter of the Ranged (Mecca) . .	168
XXXVIII.	The Chapter of S. (Mecca)	175
XXXIX.	The Chapter of the Troops (Mecca) . .	182
XL.	The Chapter of the Believer (Mecca) . .	190
XLI.	The Chapter 'Detailed' (Mecca) . . .	199
XLII.	The Chapter of Counsel (Mecca) . . .	205

		PAGE
XLIII.	The Chapter of Gilding (Mecca)	211
XLIV.	The Chapter of Smoke (Mecca)	218
XLV.	The Chapter of the Kneeling (Mecca) . .	220
XLVI.	The Chapter of El A'hqâf (Mecca) . . .	224
XLVII.	The Chapter of Mohammed, also called 'Fight' (Medînah)	229
XLVIII.	The Chapter of Victory (Medînah) . . .	233
XLIX.	The Chapter of the Inner Chambers (Medînah)	238
L.	The Chapter of Q. (Mecca)	241
LI.	The Chapter of the Scatterers (Mecca) . .	245
LII.	The Chapter of the Mount (Mecca) . . .	248
LIII.	The Chapter of the Star (Mecca) . . .	251
LIV.	The Chapter of the Moon (Mecca) . . .	254
LV.	The Chapter of the Merciful (Mecca) . .	258
LVI.	The Chapter of the Inevitable (Mecca) . .	262
LVII.	The Chapter of Iron (Medînah) . . .	266
LVIII.	The Chapter of the Wrangler (Medînah) . .	270
LIX.	The Chapter of the Emigration (Medînah) .	273
LX.	The Chapter of the Tried (Medînah) . .	277
LXI.	The Chapter of the Ranks (Mecca) . . .	280
LXII.	The Chapter of the Congregation (Medînah) .	282
LXIII.	The Chapter of the Hypocrites (Medînah) .	284
LXIV.	The Chapter of Cheating (place of origin doubtful)	286
LXV.	The Chapter of Divorce (Medînah) . . .	288
LXVI.	The Chapter of Prohibition (Medînah) . .	290
LXVII.	The Chapter of the Kingdom (Mecca) . .	292
LXVIII.	The Chapter of the Pen, also called Nûn (Mecca)	295
LXIX.	The Chapter of the Infallible (Mecca) . .	298
LXX.	The Chapter of the Ascents (Mecca) . .	300
LXXI.	The Chapter of Noah (Mecca)	302
LXXII.	The Chapter of the *G*inn (Mecca) . . .	304
LXXIII.	The Chapter of the Enwrapped (Mecca) . .	306
LXXIV.	The Chapter of the Covered (Mecca) . .	308
LXXV.	The Chapter of the Resurrection (Mecca) . .	310

		PAGE
LXXVI.	The Chapter of Man (Mecca)	312
LXXVII.	The Chapter of those Sent (Mecca)	314
LXXVIII.	The Chapter of the Information (Mecca)	316
LXXIX.	The Chapter of those who Tear Out (Mecca)	318
LXXX.	The Chapter 'He Frowned' (Mecca)	320
LXXXI.	The Chapter of the Folding up (Mecca)	321
LXXXII.	The Chapter of the Cleaving asunder (Mecca)	323
LXXXIII.	The Chapter of those who give short Weight (Mecca)	323
LXXXIV.	The Chapter of the Rending asunder (Mecca)	325
LXXXV.	The Chapter of the Zodiacal Signs (Mecca)	326
LXXXVI.	The Chapter of the Night Star (Mecca)	327
LXXXVII.	The Chapter of the Most High (Mecca)	328
LXXXVIII.	The Chapter of the Overwhelming (Mecca)	329
LXXXIX.	The Chapter of the Dawn (Mecca)	330
XC.	The Chapter of the Land (Mecca)	332
XCI.	The Chapter of the Sun (Mecca)	333
XCII.	The Chapter of the Night (Mecca)	333
XCIII.	The Chapter of the Forenoon (Mecca)	334
XCIV.	The Chapter of 'Have we not expanded?' (Mecca)	335
XCV.	The Chapter of the Fig (place of origin doubtful)	335
XCVI.	The Chapter of Congealed Blood (Mecca)	336
XCVII.	The Chapter of 'Power' (place of origin doubtful)	337
XCVIII.	The Chapter of the Manifest Sign (place of origin doubtful)	337
XCIX.	The Chapter of the Earthquake (place of origin doubtful)	338
C.	The Chapter of the Chargers (Mecca)	339
CI.	The Chapter of the Smiting (Mecca)	339
CII.	The Chapter of the Contention about Numbers (place of origin doubtful)	340

		PAGE
CIII.	The Chapter of the Afternoon (Mecca) . . .	340
CIV.	The Chapter of the Backbiter (Mecca) . . .	341
CV.	The Chapter of the Elephant (Mecca)	341
CVI.	The Chapter of the Qurâis (Mecca)	342
CVII.	The Chapter of 'Necessaries' (place of origin doubtful)	342
CVIII.	The Chapter of El Kâuthar (Mecca)	342
CIX.	The Chapter of the Misbelievers (Mecca) . . .	343
CX.	The Chapter of Help (Mecca)	343
CXI.	The Chapter of Abu Laheb (Mecca)	343
CXII.	The Chapter of Unity (place of origin doubtful) .	344
CXIII.	The Chapter of the Daybreak (place of origin doubtful)	344
CXIV.	The Chapter of Men (place of origin doubtful) .	345
Index	. . . .	347

Transliteration of Oriental Alphabets adopted for the Translations of the Sacred Books of the East 359

THE QUR'ÂN.

THE CHAPTER OF THE NIGHT JOURNEY[1].

(XVII. Mecca.)

In the name of the merciful and compassionate God.

Celebrated be the praises of Him who took His servant a journey by night from the Sacred Mosque[2] to the Remote Mosque[3], the precinct of which we have blessed, to show him of our signs! verily, He both hears and looks.

And we gave Moses the Book and made it a guidance to the children of Israel: 'Take ye to no guardian but me.'

Seed of those we bore with Noah (in the ark)! verily, he was a thankful servant!

And we decreed to the children of Israel in the Book, 'Ye shall verily do evil in the earth twice[4], and ye shall rise to a great height (of pride).'

---

[1] Also called 'The Children of Israel.' The subject of Mohammed's miraculous journey in one night from Mecca to Jerusalem, and his ascent into heaven, will be found discussed in the Introduction.

[2] The Kaabah at Mecca. [3] The Temple at Jerusalem.

[4] The Mohammedan commentators interpret this as referring the first to either Goliath, Sennacherib, or Nebuchadnezzar, and the latter to a second Persian invasion. The two sins committed by the Jews, and for which these punishments were threatened and executed, were, first, the murder of Isaiah and the imprisonment of Jeremiah, and the second, the murder of John the Baptist. Mohammedan views of ancient history are, however, vague.

[5] And when the threat for the first (sin) of the two came, we sent over them servants of ours, endued with violence, and they searched inside your houses; and it was an accomplished threat.

Then we rallied you once more against them, and aided you with wealth and sons, and made you a numerous band.

'If ye do well, ye will do well to your own souls; and if ye do ill, it is against them!

'And when the threat for the last came[1]—to harm your faces and to enter the mosque as they entered it the first time, and to destroy what they had got the upper-hand over with utter destruction.'

It may be that thy Lord will have mercy on you;—but if ye return we will return, and we have made hell a prison for the misbelievers.

Verily, this Qur'ân guides to the straightest path, and gives the glad tidings to the believers [10] who do aright that for them is a great hire; and that for those who believe not in the hereafter, we have prepared a mighty woe.

Man prays for evil as he prays for good; and man was ever hasty.

We made the night and the day two signs; and we blot out the sign of the night and make the sign of the day visible, that ye may seek after plenty from your Lord, and that ye may number the years and the reckoning; and we have detailed everything in detail.

And every man's augury[2] have we fastened on

---

[1] Supply, 'we sent foes.'

[2] I.e. 'fortune' or 'fate,' literally, 'bird;' the Arabs, like the ancient Romans, having been used to practise divination from the flight of birds.

his neck; and we will bring forth for him on the resurrection day a book offered to him wide open. [15] 'Read thy book, thou art accountant enough against thyself to-day!'

He who accepts guidance, accepts it only for his own soul: and he who errs, errs only against it; nor shall one burdened soul bear the burden of another.

Nor would we punish until we had sent an apostle. And when we desired to destroy a city we bade[1] the opulent ones thereof; and they wrought abomination therein; and its due sentence was pronounced; and we destroyed it with utter destruction.

How many generations have we destroyed after Noah! but thy Lord of the sins of his servant is well aware, and sees enough.

Whoso is desirous of this life that hastens away, we will hasten on for him therein what we please,—for whom we please. Then we will make hell for him to broil in—despised and outcast.

[20] But whoso desires the next life, and strives for it and is a believer—these, their striving shall be gratefully received.

To all—these and those—will we extend the gifts of thy Lord; for the gifts of thy Lord are not restricted.

See how we have preferred some of them over others, but in the next life are greater degrees and greater preference.

Put not with God other gods, or thou wilt sit despised and forsaken.

Thy Lord has decreed that ye shall not serve other than Him; and kindness to one's parents,

[1] Bade them obey the Apostle.

whether one or both of them reach old age with thee; and say not to them, 'Fie!' and do not grumble at them, but speak to them a generous speech. [25] And lower to them the wing of humility out of compassion, and say, 'O Lord! have compassion on them as they brought me up when I was little!' Your Lord knows best what is in your souls if ye be righteous, and, verily, He is forgiving unto those who come back penitent.

And give thy kinsman his due and the poor and the son of the road; and waste not wastefully, for the wasteful were ever the devil's brothers; and the devil is ever ungrateful to his Lord.

[30] But if thou dost turn away from them to seek after mercy from thy Lord[1], which thou hopest for, then speak to them an easy speech.

Make not thy hand fettered to thy neck, nor yet spread it out quite open, lest thou shouldst have to sit down blamed and straitened in means. Verily, thy Lord spreads out provision to whomsoever He will or He doles it out. Verily, He is ever well aware of and sees His servants.

And slay not your children[2] for fear of poverty; we will provide for them; beware! for to slay them is ever a great sin!

And draw not near to fornication; verily, it is ever an abomination, and evil is the way thereof.

[35] And slay not the soul that God has forbidden you, except for just cause; for he who is slain unjustly we have given his next of kin authority; yet

[1] I.e. if you are compelled to leave them in order to seek your livelihood; or if your present means are insufficient to enable you to relieve others.

[2] See Part I, p. 256, note 2.

let him not exceed in slaying; verily, he is ever helped.

And draw not near to the wealth of the orphan, save to improve it, until he reaches the age of puberty, and fulfil your compacts; verily, a compact is ever enquired of.

And give full measure when ye measure out, and weigh with a right balance; that is better and a fairer determination.

And do not pursue that of which thou hast no knowledge; verily, the hearing, the sight, and the heart, all of these shall be enquired of.

And walk not on the earth proudly; verily, thou canst not cleave the earth, and thou shalt not reach the mountains in height.

[40] All this is ever evil in the sight of your Lord and abhorred.

That is something of what thy Lord has inspired thee with of wisdom; do not then put with God other gods, or thou wilt be thrown into hell reproached and outcast. What! has your Lord chosen to give you sons, and shall He take for Himself females from among the angels? verily, ye are speaking a mighty speech.

Now have we turned it in various ways in this Qur'ân, so let them bear in mind; but it will only increase them in aversion.

Say, 'Were there with Him other gods, as ye say, then would they seek a way against the Lord of the throne.'

[45] Celebrated be His praises, and exalted be He above what they say with a great exaltation!

The seven heavens and the earth celebrate His praises, and all who therein are; nor is there aught but what celebrates His praise: but ye cannot understand their celebration;—verily, He is clement and forgiving.

And when thou readest the Qur'ân we place between thee and those who believe not in the hereafter a covering veil. And we place covers upon their hearts, lest they should understand, and dulness in their ears.

And when thou dost mention in the Qur'ân thy Lord by Himself they turn their backs in aversion.

[50] We know best for what they listen when they listen to thee; and when they whisper apart —when the wrong-doers say, 'Ye only follow a man enchanted.'

Behold, how they strike out for you parables, and err, and cannot find the way!

They say, 'What! when we have become bones and rubbish are we to be raised up a new creature?' Say, 'Be ye stones, or iron, or a creature, the greatest your breasts can conceive—!' Then they shall say, 'Who is to restore us?' Say, 'He who originated you at first;' and they will wag their heads and say, 'When will that be?' Say, 'It may, perhaps, be nigh.'

The day when He shall call on you and ye shall answer with praise to Him, and they will think that they have tarried but a little.

[55] And say to my servants that they speak in a kind way[1]; verily, Satan makes ill-will between them; verily, Satan was ever unto man an open foe.

Your Lord knows you best; if He please He will have mercy upon you, or if He please He will

[1] I.e. they are not to provoke the idolaters by speaking too roughly to them so as to exasperate them.

torment you: but we have not sent thee to take charge of them.

And thy Lord best knows who is in the heavens and the earth; we did prefer some of the prophets over the others, and to David did we give the Psalms.

Say, 'Call on those whom ye pretend other than God;' but they shall not have the power to remove distress from you, nor to turn it off.

Those on whom they call[1], seek themselves for a means of approaching their Lord, (to see) which of them is nearest: and they hope for His mercy and they fear His torment; verily, the torment of thy Lord is a thing to beware of.

[60] There is no city but we will destroy it before the day of judgment, or torment it with keen torment;—that is in the Book inscribed.

Naught hindered us from sending thee with signs, save that those of yore said they were lies; so we gave Thamûd the visible she-camel, but they treated her unjustly! for we do not send (any one) with signs save to make men fear.

And when we said to thee, 'Verily, thy Lord encompasses men!' and we made the vision which we showed thee only a cause of sedition unto men, and the cursed tree[2] as well; for we will frighten them, but it will only increase them in great rebellion.

---

[1] Sale interprets this to mean 'the angels and prophets.' Rodwell remarks that it is an 'obvious allusion to the saint worship of the Christians.' As, however, precisely the same expression is used elsewhere in the Qur'ân for the false gods of the Arabs, and the existence of those ginns and angels whom they associated with God is constantly recognised, their divinity only being denied, I prefer to follow the Moslem commentators, and refer the passage to the gods of the Arabian pantheon at Mecca; cf. Part I, p. 127, note 2.

[2] The Zaqqûm; see Chapter XXXVII, verse 60. The vision

And when we said to the angels, 'Adore Adam;' and they adored, save Iblîs, who said, 'Am I to adore one whom Thou hast created out of clay?'

Said he, 'Dost thou see now? this one whom Thou hast honoured above me, verily, if Thou shouldst respite me until the resurrection day, I will of a surety utterly destroy his seed except a few.'

[65] Said He, 'Begone! and whoso of them follows thee—verily, hell is your recompense, an ample recompense. Entice away whomsoever of them thou canst with thy voice; and bear down upon them with thy horse and with thy foot; and share with them in their wealth and their children; and promise them,—but Satan promises them naught but deceit. Verily, my servants, thou hast no authority over them; thy Lord is guardian enough over them!'

It is your Lord who drives the ships for you in the sea that ye may seek after plenty from Him; verily, He is ever merciful to you. And when distress touches you in the sea, those whom ye call on, except Him, stray away from you; but when He has brought you safe to shore, ye turn away; for man is ever ungrateful.

[70] Are ye sure that He will not cleave with you the side of the shore, or send against you a heavy sand-storm? then ye will find no guardian for yourselves.

Or are ye sure that He will not send you back therein another time, and send against you a violent wind, and drown you for your misbelief? then ye will find for yourselves no protector against us.

---

referred to is the night journey to heaven, although those commentators who believe this to have been an actual fact suppose another vision to account for this passage.

But we have been gracious to the children of Adam, and we have borne them by land and sea, and have provided them with good things, and have preferred them over many that we have created.

The day when we will call all men by their high priest; and he whose book is given in his right hand—these shall read their book, nor shall they be wronged a straw. But he who in this life is blind shall be blind in the next too, and err farther from the way.

[75] They had well-nigh beguiled thee from what we inspired thee with, that thou shouldst forge against us something else, and then they would have taken thee for a friend; and had it not been that we stablished thee, thou wouldst have well-nigh leant towards them a little: then would we have made thee taste of torment both of life and death, then thou wouldst not have found against us any helper[1].

And they well-nigh enticed thee away from the land, to turn thee out therefrom; but then—they should not have tarried after thee except a little.

[This is] the course of those of our prophets whom we have sent before thee; and thou shalt find no change in our course.

[80] Be thou steadfast in prayer from the declining of the sun until the dusk of the night, and the reading of the dawn; verily, the reading of the dawn is ever testified to.

---

[1] The commentators say that this refers to a treaty proposed by the tribe of *TH*aqîf, who insisted, as a condition of their submission, that they should be exempt from the more irksome duties of Muslims, and should be allowed to retain their idol Allât for a certain time, and that their territory should be considered sacred, like that of Mecca.

And for the night, watch thou therein as an extra service. It may be that thy Lord will raise thee to a laudable station.

And say, 'O my Lord! make me enter with a just entry; and make me come forth with a just coming forth; and grant me from Thee authority to aid.'

And say, 'Truth has come, and falsehood has vanished! verily, falsehood is transient.'

And we will send down of the Qur'ân that which is a healing and a mercy to the believers, but it will only increase the wrong-doers in loss.

[85] And when we favour man he turns away and retires aside, but when evil touches him he is ever in despair. Say, 'Every one acts after his own manner, but your Lord knows best who is most guided in the way.'

They will ask thee of the spirit[1]. Say, 'The spirit comes at the bidding of my Lord, and ye are given but a little knowledge thereof.'

If we had wished we would have taken away that with which we have inspired thee; then thou wouldst have found no guardian against us, unless by a mercy from thy Lord; verily, His grace towards thee is great!

[90] Say, 'If mankind and *g*inns united together to bring the like of this Qur'ân, they could not bring the like, though they should back each other up!'

We have turned about for men in this Qur'ân every parable; but most men refuse to accept it, save ungratefully.

---

[1] According to some, the soul generally; but according to others, and more probably, the angel Gabriel as the agent of revelation.

And they say, 'We will by no means believe in thee, until there gush forth for thee a fountain from the earth; or there be made for thee a garden of palms and grapes, and rivers come gushing out amidst them; or thou make the sky to fall down upon us in pieces; or thou bring us God and the angels before us; [95] or there be made for thee a house of gold; or thou climb up into the heaven; and even then we will not believe in thy climbing there, until thou send down on us a book that we may read!'

Say, 'Celebrated be the praises of my Lord! was I aught but a mortal apostle?'

Naught prohibited men from believing when the guidance came to them, save their saying, 'God has sent a mortal for an apostle.'

Say, 'Were there angels on the earth walking in quiet, we had surely sent them an angel as an apostle.'

Say, 'God is witness enough between me and you; verily, He is ever of His servants well aware, and sees.'

He whom God guides, he is guided indeed; and he whom God leads astray, thou shalt never find patrons for them beside Him; and we will gather them upon the resurrection day upon their faces, blind, and dumb, and deaf; their resort is hell; whenever it grows dull we will give them another blaze!

[100] That is their reward for that they disbelieved in our signs, and said, 'What! when we are bones and rubbish, shall we then be raised up a new creation?'

Could they not see that God who created the

heavens and the earth is able to create the like of them, and to set for them an appointed time; there is no doubt therein, yet the wrong-doers refuse to accept it, save ungratefully!

Say, 'Did ye control the treasuries of the mercy of my Lord, then ye would hold them through fear of expending; for man is ever niggardly!'

And we did bring Moses nine manifest signs; then ask the children of Israel (about) when he came to them, and Pharaoh said to him, 'Verily, I think thee, O Moses! enchanted.'

He said, 'Well didst thou know that none sent down these save the Lord of the heavens and the earth as visible signs; and, verily, I think thee, O Pharaoh! ruined.'

[105] And he desired to drive them out of the land; but we drowned him and those with him, one and all.

And after him we said to the children of Israel, 'Dwell ye in the land; and when the promise of the hereafter comes to pass, we will bring you in a mixed crowd (to judgment).

'In truth have we sent it down, and in truth has it come down; and we have not sent thee as aught but a herald of glad tidings and a warner.

'And a Qur'ân which we have divided, that thou mayst read it to mankind leisurely, and we sent it down, sending it down[1].'

Say, 'Believe ye therein, or believe not; verily, those who were given the knowledge before it, when it is read to them fall down upon their beards adoring! and they say, "Celebrated be the praises

---

[1] As occasion required.

of our Lord! verily, the promise of our Lord is ever fulfilled"—they fall down upon their beards weeping, and it increases their humility.'

[110] Say, 'Call on God, or call on the Merciful One, whichever ye may call on Him by; for His are the best of names[1].'

And do not say thy prayers openly, nor yet murmur them, but seek a way between these.

And say, 'Praise belongs to God, who has not taken to Himself a son, and has not had a partner in His kingdom, nor had a patron against (such) abasement.' And magnify Him greatly[2]!

The Chapter of the Cave.

(XVIII. Mecca.)

In the name of the merciful and compassionate God.

Praise belongs to God, who sent down to His servant the Book. and put no crookedness therein, —straight, to give warning of keen violence from Him; and to give the glad tidings to the believers, who do what is right, that for them is a goodly reward wherein they shall abide for ever and for

---

[1] The Arabs whom Mohammed addressed seem to have imagined that he meant by Allâh and Ar-ra'hmân (the Merciful One) two separate deities. The various epithets which are applied to God in the Qur'ân, such as 'kind,' 'seeing,' 'knowing,' &c., are called by the Muslims al 'asmâ'u 'l'husnâ, 'the best of names,' and are repeated in telling the beads of their rosary.

[2] This command is obeyed by the Muslims frequently pronouncing the phrase Allâhu akbar, especially as an expression of astonishment. It is the same expression as that used by the Egyptian women concerning Joseph, in Chapter XII, verse 31.

aye; and to give warning to those who say, 'God hath taken to Himself a son.'

They have no knowledge thereof, nor their fathers; a serious word it is that comes forth from their mouths! verily, they only speak a lie!

[5] Haply thou wilt grieve thyself to death for sorrow after them, if they believe not in this new revelation. Verily, we have made what is on the earth an ornament thereof, to try them, which of them is best in works; but, verily, we are going to make what is thereon bare soil.

Hast thou reckoned that the Fellows of the Cave and Er-raqîm were a wonder amongst our signs[1]?'

When the youths resorted to the cave and said, 'O our Lord! bring us mercy from Thee, and dispose for us our affair aright!'

[10] And we struck their ears (with deafness) in the cave for a number of years. Then we raised them up again, that we might know which of the two crews[2] could best calculate the time of their tarrying. We will narrate to thee their story in truth. Verily, they were youths who believed in their Lord, and we added to their guidance, and we braced up their hearts, when they stood up and said, 'Our Lord is the Lord of the heavens and the earth, we will not call upon any god beside Him, for then we should have said an extravagant thing.

[1] This is the well-known story of the Seven Sleepers of Ephesus. What is meant by Er-raqîm no one knows. The most generally accepted Mohammedan theory is that it was a dog belonging to the party; though some commentators take it to be the name of the valley or mountain in which the cave was situated; others again say that it was a metal plate inscribed with the name of the Sleepers.

[2] That is, the youths themselves or the people they met on their awakening.

These people of ours hav- taken to other gods beside Him. Though they do not bring any manifest authority for them. And who is more unjust than he who forges against God a lie?

[15] 'So when ye have gone apart from them and what they serve other than God, then resort ye to the cave. Our Lord will unfold His mercy to you, and will dispose for you your affair advantageously.'

And thou mightst have seen the sun when it rose decline from their cave towards the right hand, and when it set leave them on the left hand, while they were in the spacious part thereof. That is one of the signs of God. Whom God guides he is guided indeed, and whom He leads astray thou shalt surely find for him no patron to guide aright. Thou mightst have reckoned them waking though they were sleeping, as we turned them towards the right and towards the left; and their dog spreading out his fore-paws on the threshold. Hadst thou come suddenly upon them thou wouldst surely have turned and fled away from them, and wouldst surely have been filled by them with dread.

Thus did we raise them up that they might question each other. Spake a speaker amongst them, 'How long have ye tarried?' They said, 'We have tarried a day or part of a day.' They said, 'Your Lord knows best your tarrying; so send one of you with this coin of yours to the city, and let him look which of them has purest food, and let him bring you provision thereof; and let him be subtle and not let any one perceive you. Verily, they—should they perceive you—would stone you, or would force you back again unto their faith, and ye would never prosper then.'

[20] Thus did we make their people acquainted with their story, that they might know that God's promise is true; and that the Hour, there is no doubt concerning it. When they disputed amongst themselves concerning their affair, and said, 'Build a building over them, their Lord knows best about them;' and those who prevailed in their affair said, 'We will surely make a mosque over them.'

They will say, 'Three, and the fourth of them was their dog:' and they will say, 'Five, and the sixth of them was their dog:' guessing at the unseen: and they will say, 'Seven, and the eighth of them was their dog.' Say, 'My Lord knows best the number of them; none knows them but a few.'

Dispute not therefore concerning them save with a plain disputation, and ask not any one of them[1] concerning them.

And never say of anything, 'Verily, I am going to do that to-morrow,' except 'if God please;' and remember thy Lord when thou hast forgotten, and say, 'It may be that my Lord will guide me to what is nearer to the right than this[2].'

They tarried in their cave three hundred years and nine more. [25] Say, 'God knows best of their tarrying. His are the unseen things of the heavens and the earth—He can see! and hear[3]!'

---

[1] That is, the Christians.

[2] Mohammed being asked by the Jews concerning the number of the Seven Sleepers, had promised to bring them a revelation upon the subject on the morrow: this verse is a rebuke for his presumption.

[3] This expression Sale takes to be ironical, and translates, 'make thou him to see and hear;' Rodwell renders it, 'look thou and hearken unto him:' both translators having missed both the force

They have no patron beside Him, nor does He let any one share in His judgment. So, recite what thou art inspired with of the Book of thy Lord; there is no changing His words; nor shalt thou ever find a refuge beside Him; and keep thyself patient, with those who call upon their Lord morning and evening, desiring His face; nor let thine eyes be turned from them, desiring the adornment of the life of this world; and obey not him[1] whose heart we have made heedless of remembrance of us, and who follows his lusts, for his affair is ever in advance (of the truth).

But say, 'The truth is from your Lord, so let him who will, believe; and let him who will, disbelieve.' Verily, we have prepared for the evildoers a fire, sheets of which shall encompass them; and if they cry for help, they shall be helped with water like molten brass, which shall roast their faces:—an ill drink and an evil couch!

Verily, those who believe and act aright,—verily, we will not waste the hire of him who does good works.

[30] These, for them are gardens of Eden; beneath them rivers flow; they shall be adorned therein with bracelets of gold, and shall wear green robes of silk, and of brocade; reclining therein on

of the idiom and the explanation given by the commentators Al Bâi*dh*âvî and Jalâlâin, to whom Sale refers. The meaning is that which I have given, and the idiom is equivalent to that which occurs in a passage of Harîrî, Maqâmah 3 (p. 30, De Sacy's first edition), akrim bihi, 'how noble it is!' abzar bihi being equivalent to mâ abzarahu, 'how observant He is!'

[1] Said to refer to Ommâiyet ibn '*H*alf, who had requested Mohammed to give up his poorer followers to please the Qurâi*s*; see Chapter VI, verse 52.

thrones;—pleasant is the reward, and goodly the couch!

Strike out for them a parable: Two men, for one of whom we made two gardens of grapes, and surrounded them with palms, and put corn between the two. Each of the two gardens brought forth its food and did not fail in aught. And we caused a river to gush forth amidst them; and he had fruit, and said unto his fellow, who was his next-door neighbour, 'I am more wealthy than thee, and mightier of household.'

And he went in unto his garden, having wronged himself: said he, 'I do not think that this will ever disappear; and I do not think that the hour is imminent; and if even I be sent back unto my Lord, I shall find a better one than it in exchange.'

[35] Said unto him his fellow, who was his next-door neighbour, 'Thou hast disbelieved in Him who created thee from earth, and then from a clot, then fashioned thee a man; but God, He is my Lord; nor will I associate any one with my Lord. Why couldst thou not have said, when thou didst go into thy garden, "What God pleases[1]! there is no power save in God,"—to look at, I am less than thee in wealth and children; but haply my Lord will give me something better than thy garden, and will send upon it thunder-claps from the sky, and it shall be on the morrow bare slippery soil; or on the morrow its water may be deeply sunk, so that thou canst not get thereat!'

[40] And his fruits were encompassed, and on the

[1] In the original Mâ sâ' allâh; this is the usual formula for expressing admiration among Muslims.

morrow he turned down the palms of his hands[1] for what he had spent thereon, for it was fallen down upon its trellises. And he said, 'Would that I had never associated any one with my Lord!' And he had not any party to help him beside God, nor was he helped. In such a case the patronage is God's, the true; He is best at rewarding and best at bringing to an issue.

Strike out for them, too, a parable of the life of this world; like water which we send down from the sky, and the vegetation of the earth is mingled therewith;—and on the morrow it is dried up, and the winds scatter it; for God is powerful over all.

Wealth and children are an adornment of the life of this world; but enduring good works are better with thy Lord, as a recompense, and better as a hope.

[45] And the day when we will move the mountains, and thou shalt see the (whole) earth stalking forth; and we will gather them, and will not leave one of them behind. Then shall they be presented to thy Lord in ranks.—Now have ye come to us as we created you at first! nay, but ye thought that we would never make our promise good!

And the Book shall be placed[2], and thou shalt see the sinners in fear of what is in it; and they will say, 'Alas, for us! what ails this Book, it leaves neither small nor great things alone, without numbering them?' and they shall find present what they have done; and thy Lord will not wrong any one.

And when we said to the angels, 'Adore Adam,'

[1] I.e. wrung his hands. [2] In the hand of each.

they adored him, save only Iblîs, who was of the *g*inn, who revolted from the bidding of his Lord. 'What! will ye then take him and his seed as patrons, rather than me, when they are foes of yours? bad for the wrong-doers is the exchange!'

I did not make them witnesses of the creation of the heavens and the earth, nor of the creation of themselves, nor did I take those who lead astray for my supporters.

[50] On the day when He shall say, 'Call ye my partners whom ye pretend:' and they shall call on them, but they shall not answer them; and we will set the vale of perdition between them; and the sinners shall see the fire, and shall think that they are going to fall therein, and shall find no escape therefrom. We have turned about in this Qur'ân for men every parable; but man is ever at most things a caviller.

Naught prevented men from believing when the guidance came to them, or from asking pardon of their Lord, except the coming on them of the course of those of yore, or the coming of the torment before their eyes[1].

We sent not prophets save as heralds of glad tidings and as warners; but those who misbelieve wrangle with vain speech to make void the truth therewith; and they take my signs and the warnings given them as a jest.

[55] Who is more unjust than he who, being

---

[1] This passage is aimed at the Qurâis. The 'course of those of yore' is the punishment inflicted on the 'people of Noah, Lot,' &c. for similar acts of misbelief, and 'the torment' is said to refer to their losses at the battle of Bedr.

reminded of the signs of his Lord, turns away therefrom, and forgets what his hands have done before? verily, we will place veils upon their hearts lest they should understand, and dulness in their ears!

And if thou shouldst call them to the guidance, they will not be guided then for ever.

But thy Lord is forgiving, endowed with mercy; were He to punish them for what they have earned He would have hastened for them the torment. Nay rather, they have their appointed time, and shall never find a refuge beside Him.

These cities, we destroyed them when they were unjust; and for their destruction we set an appointed time.

And when Moses said to his servant, 'I will not cease until I reach the confluence of the two seas, or else I will go on for years[1].'

[60] But when they reached the confluence of the two[2] they forgot their fish, and it took its way in the sea with a free course.

And when they had passed by, he said to his servant, 'Bring us our dinners, for we have met with toil from this journey of ours.' Said he, 'What thinkest thou? when we resorted to the rock, then, verily, I forgot the fish, but it was only Satan who made me forget it, lest I should remember it; and it took its way in the sea wondrously!'

Said he, 'This is what we were searching for[3].' So they turned back upon their footsteps, following them up.

---

[1] The word used signifies a space of eighty years and upwards.

[2] Literally, 'of their intermediate space.'

[3] See Part II, note 3, p. 23.

Then they found a servant of our servants, to whom we had given mercy from ourselves, and had taught him knowledge from before us. [65] Said Moses to him, 'Shall I follow thee, so that thou mayest teach me, from what thou hast been taught, the right way?' said he, 'Verily, thou canst never have patience with me. How canst thou be patient in what thou comprehendest no knowledge of?' He said, 'Thou wilt find me, if God will, patient; nor will I rebel against thy bidding.' He said, 'Then, if thou followest me, ask me not about anything until I begin for them the mention of it.'

[70] So they set out until when they rode[1] in the bark, he scuttled it.

Said he, 'Hast thou scuttled it to drown its crew? Thou hast produced a strange thing.'

Said he, 'Did I not tell thee, verily, thou canst never have patience with me?'

Said he, 'Rebuke me not for forgetting, and impose not on me a difficult command.' So they set out until they met a boy, and he killed him. And he (Moses) said, 'Hast thou killed a pure person without (his killing) a person? thou hast produced an unheard-of thing.'

Said he, 'Did I not tell thee, verily, thou canst not have patience with me?'

[75] Said he, 'If I ask thee about anything after it, then do not accompany me. Now hast thou arrived at my excuse.' So they set out until when they came to the people of a city; and they asked

---

[1] That is, embarked. All nautical metaphors in Arabic being taken from camel riding. The Arabs do not call the camel 'the ship of the desert,' but they call a ship 'the riding camel of the sea.'

the people thereof for food; but they refused to entertain them. And they found therein a wall which wanted[1] to fall to pieces, and he set it upright. Said (Moses), 'Hadst thou pleased thou mightst certainly have had a hire for this.'

Said he, 'This is the parting between me and thee. I will give thee the interpretation of that with which thou couldst not have patience. As for the bark it belonged to poor people, who toiled on the sea, and I wished to damage it, for behind it was a king who seized on every bark[2] by force. And as for the youth, his parents were believers, and we feared lest he should impose upon them rebellion and misbelief. [80] So we desired that their Lord would give them in exchange a better one than him in purity, and nearer in filial affection. And as for the wall, it belonged to two orphan youths in the city, and beneath it was a treasure belonging to them both, and their father was a righteous man, and their Lord desired that they should reach puberty, and then take out their treasure as a mercy from thy Lord; and I did it not on my own bidding. That is the interpretation of what thou couldst not have patience with[3].'

---

[1] The expression wanted to fall is colloquial in Arabic as well as in English. Bâi*dh*âvî says, 'the expression wanting to is in this case figuratively used for being on the point of.'

[2] That is, every whole or sound ship.

[3] For this legend there appears to be no ancient authority whatever; the Mohammedan commentators merely expand it, and say that El '*Hidh*r (a mythical personage, who is identified with the prophet Elias, St. George, and the prime minister of Alexander the Great) had disappeared in search of the water of immortality. Moses was inspired to search for him, and told that he would find him by a rock where two seas met, and where he should lose a fish

And they will ask thee about Dhu 'l Qarnâin[1], say, 'I will recite to you a mention of him; verily, we stablished for him in the earth, and we gave him a way to everything; and he followed a way until when he reached the setting of the sun, he found it setting in a black muddy spring[2], and he found thereat a people.'

[85] We said, 'O Dhu 'l Qarnâin! thou mayest either torment these people, or treat them well.' Said he, 'As for him who does wrong, I will torment him, then shall he be sent back to his Lord, and He will torment him with an unheard-of torment; but as for him who believes and acts aright, for him is an excellent reward, and we will tell him our easy bidding.'

Then he followed a way until when he reached the rising of the sun, he found it rise upon a people to whom we had given no shelter therefrom.

[90] So! And we comprehended the knowledge of what (forces) he had with him.

Then he followed a way until when he reached the point between the two mountains, he found below them both a people who could scarcely under-

which he was directed to take with him. Moses' servant in the legend is Joshua, and the mysterious young man who guided him is generally supposed to be El '*H*id*h*r himself, rendered immortal and supernaturally wise by having found and drunk of the water of life.

[1] Literally, 'the two horned;' this personage is generally supposed to be Alexander the Great, who is so represented on his coins. The Mohammedan histories of him, however, contain so many gross anachronisms, making him, for instance, a contemporary with Moses, Abraham, &c., that it is probable they may have confused him with some much more ancient traditional conqueror.

[2] Probably, as Bâi*d*hâvî suggests, the ocean, which, with its dark waters, would remind an Arab of such a pool.

stand speech. They said, 'O Dhu 'l Qarnâin! verily, Yâgûg and Mâgûg[1] are doing evil in the land. Shall we then pay thee tribute, on condition that thou set between us and them a rampart?' He said, 'What my Lord hath established me in is better; so help me with strength, and I will set between you and them a barrier.

[95] 'Bring me pigs of iron until they fill up the space between the two mountain sides.' Said he, 'Blow until it makes it a fire.' Said he, 'Bring me, that I may pour over it, molten brass[2].'

So they[3] could not scale it, and they could not tunnel it.

Said he, 'This is a mercy from my Lord; but when the promise of my Lord comes to pass, He will make it as dust, for the promise of my Lord is true.'

And we left some of them to surge on that day[4] over others, and the trumpet will be blown, and we will gather them together.

---

[1] Gog and Magog. The people referred to appear to be tribes of the Turkomans, and the rampart itself has been identified with some ancient fortifications extending from the west coast of the Caspian to the Pontus Euxinus. The word translated mountains is the same as that translated rampart a little further on. I have, in rendering it mountains, followed the Mohammedan commentators, whose view is borne out by the subsequent mention of mountain sides.

[2] The process here described for repressing the incursions of Gog and Magog is the building of a wall of pig iron across the opening between the two mountains, fusing this into a compact mass of metal, and strengthening it by pouring molten brass over the whole.

[3] Gog and Magog.

[4] On the day of judgment, or, as some think, a little before it.

[100] And we will set forth hell on that day before the misbelievers, whose eyes were veiled from my Reminder, and who were unable to hear. What! did those who misbelieve reckon that they could take my servants for patrons beside me? Verily, we have prepared hell for the misbelievers to alight in!

Say, 'Shall we inform you of those who lose most by their works? those who erred in their endeavours after the life of this world, and who think they are doing good deeds.'

[105] Those who misbelieve in the signs of their Lord and in meeting Him, vain are their works; and we will not give them right weight on the resurrection day. That is their reward,—hell! for that they misbelieved and took my signs and my apostles as a mockery.

Verily, those who believe and act aright, for them are gardens of Paradise[1] to alight in, to dwell therein for aye, and they shall crave no change therefrom.

Say, 'Were the sea ink for the words of my Lord, the sea would surely fail before the words of my Lord fail; aye, though we brought as much ink again!'

[110] Say, 'I am only a mortal like yourselves; I am inspired that your God is only one God. Then let him who hopes to meet his Lord act righteous acts, and join none in the service of his Lord.'

---

[1] Here the Persian word Firdâus is used, which has supplied the name to the abode of the blessed in so many languages.

The Chapter of Mary.

(XIX. Mecca.)

In the name of the merciful and compassionate God.

K. H. Y. *'H.* Z. The mention of thy Lord's mercy to His servant Zachariah, when he called on his Lord with a secret calling. Said he, 'My Lord! verily, my bones are weak, and my head flares with hoariness;—and I never was unfortunate in my prayers to Thee, my Lord! [5] But I fear my heirs after me, and my wife is barren; then grant me from Thee a successor, to be my heir and the heir of the family of Jacob, and make him, my Lord! acceptable.'

'O Zachariah! verily, we give thee glad tidings of a son, whose name shall be John. We never made a namesake of his before[1].'

Said he, 'My Lord! how can I have a son, when my wife is barren, and I have reached through old age to decrepitude?'

[10] He said, 'Thus says thy Lord, It is easy for Me, for I created thee at first when yet thou wast nothing.'

Said he, 'O my Lord! make for me a sign.' He said, 'Thy sign is that thou shalt not speak to men for three nights (though) sound.'

Then he went forth unto his people from the

[1] Cf. Luke i. 61, where, however, it is said that none of Zachariah's kindred was ever before called by that name. Some commentators avoid the difficulty by interpreting the word samîyyun to mean 'deserving of the name.'

chamber, and he made signs to them: 'Celebrate (God's) praises morning and evening!'

'O John! take the Book with strength;' and we gave him judgment when a boy, and grace from us, and purity; and he was pious and righteous to his parents, and was not a rebellious tyrant.

[15] So peace upon him the day he was born, and the day he died, and the day he shall be raised up alive.

And mention, in the Book, Mary; when she retired from her family into an eastern place; and she took a veil (to screen herself) from them; and we sent unto her our spirit; and he took for her the semblance of a well-made man. Said she, 'Verily, I take refuge in the Merciful One from thee, if thou art pious.' Said he, 'I am only a messenger of thy Lord to bestow on thee a pure boy.'

[20] Said she, 'How can I have a boy when no man has touched me, and when I am no harlot?' He said, 'Thus says thy Lord, It is easy for Me! and we will make him a sign unto man, and a mercy from us; for it is a decided matter.'

So she conceived him, and she retired with him into a remote place. And the labour pains came upon her at the trunk of a palm tree, and she said, 'O that I had died before this, and been forgotten out of mind!' and he called[1] to her from beneath her, 'Grieve not, for thy Lord has placed a stream beneath thy feet; [25] and shake towards thee the trunk of the palm tree, it will drop upon thee fresh dates fit to

[1] Either the infant himself or the angel Gabriel; or the expression 'beneath her' may be rendered 'beneath it,' and may refer to the palm tree.

gather; so eat, and drink, and cheer thine eye; and if thou shouldst see any mortal say, "Verily, I have vowed to the Merciful One a fast, and I will not speak to-day with a human being."'

Then she brought it to her people, carrying it; said they, 'O Mary! thou hast done an extraordinary thing! O sister of Aaron[1]! thy father was not a bad man, nor was thy mother a harlot!'

[30] And she pointed to him, and they said, 'How are we to speak with one who is in the cradle a child?' He said, 'Verily, I am a servant of God; He has brought me the Book, and He has made me a prophet, and He has made me blessed wherever I be; and He has required of me prayer and almsgiving so long as I live, and piety towards my mother, and has not made me a miserable tyrant; and peace upon me the day I was born, and the day I die, and the day I shall be raised up alive.'

[35] That is, Jesus the son of Mary,—by the word of truth whereon ye do dispute!

God could not take to himself any son! celebrated be His praise! when He decrees a matter He only says to it, 'BE,' and it is; and, verily, God is my Lord and your Lord, so worship Him; this is the right way.

And the parties have disagreed amongst themselves, but woe to those who disbelieve, from the witnessing of the mighty day! they can hear and they can see[2], on the day when they shall come to us; but the evildoers are to-day in obvious error!

[40] And warn them of the day of sighing, when

---

[1] See Part I, note 1, p. 50. [2] See Part II, note 3, p. 16.

the matter is decreed while they are heedless, and while they do not believe.

Verily, we will inherit the earth and all who are upon it, and unto us shall they return!

And mention, in the Book, Abraham; verily, he was a confessor,—a prophet. When he said to his father, 'O my sire! why dost thou worship what can neither hear nor see nor avail thee aught? O my sire! verily, to me has come knowledge which has not come to thee; then follow me, and I will guide thee to a level way.

[45] 'O my sire! serve not Satan; verily, Satan is ever a rebel against the Merciful. O my sire! verily, I fear that there may touch thee torment from the Merciful, and that thou mayest be a client of Satan.'

Said he, 'What! art thou averse from my gods, O Abraham? verily, if thou dost not desist I will certainly stone thee; but get thee gone from me for a time!'

Said he, 'Peace be upon thee! I will ask forgiveness for thee from my Lord; verily, He is very gracious to me: but I will part from you and what ye call on beside God, and will pray my Lord that I be not unfortunate in my prayer to my Lord.'

[50] And when he had parted from them and what they served beside God, we granted him Isaac and Jacob, and each of them we made a prophet; and we granted them of our mercy, and we made the tongue of truth lofty for them [1].

And mention, in the Book, Moses; verily, he was sincere, and was an apostle,—a prophet. We called

[1] That is, 'gave them great renown.'

him from the right side of the mountain; and we made him draw nigh unto us to commune with him, and we granted him, of our mercy, his brother Aaron as a prophet.

[55] And mention, in the Book, Ishmael; verily, he was true to his promise, and was an apostle,—a prophet; and he used to bid his people prayers and almsgiving, and was acceptable in the sight of his Lord.

And mention, in the Book, Idrîs[1]; verily, he was a confessor,—a prophet; and we raised him to a lofty place.

These are those to whom God has been gracious, of the prophets of the seed of Adam, and of those whom we bore with Noah, and of the seed of Abraham and Israel, and of those we guided and elected; when the signs of the Merciful are read to them, they fall down adoring and weeping.

[60] And successors succeeded them, who lost sight of prayer and followed lusts, but they shall at length find themselves going wrong, except such as repent and believe and act aright; for these shall enter Paradise, and shall not be wronged at all,—gardens of Eden, which the Merciful has promised to His servants in the unseen; verily, His promise ever comes to pass!

They shall hear no empty talk therein, but only 'peace;' and they shall have their provision therein, morning and evening; that is Paradise which we will give for an inheritance to those of our servants who are pious!

[65] We do not descend[2] save at the bidding

---

[1] Generally identified with Enoch.

[2] Amongst various conjectures the one most usually accepted

of thy Lord; His is what is before us, and what is behind us, and what is between those; for thy Lord is never forgetful,—the Lord of the heavens and the earth, and of what is between the two; then serve Him and persevere in His service. Dost thou know a namesake of His?

Man will say, 'What! when I have died shall I then come forth alive? Does not man then remember that we created him before when he was naught?'

And by thy Lord! we will surely gather them together, and the devils too; then we will surely bring them forward around hell, on their knees!

[70] Then we will drag off from every sect whichever of them has been most bold against the Merciful.

Then we know best which of them deserves most to be broiled therein.

There is not one of you who will not go down to it,—that is settled and decided by thy Lord[1].

Then we will save those who fear us; but we will leave the evildoers therein on their knees.

And when our signs are recited to them manifest, those who misbelieve say to those who believe, 'Which of the two parties is best placed and in the best company?'

[75] And how many generations before them

---

by the Mohammedan commentators is, that these are the words of the angel Gabriel, in answer to Mohammed's complaint of long intervals elapsing between the periods of revelation.

[1] This is interpreted by some to mean that all souls, good and bad, must pass through hell, but that the good will not be harmed. Others think it merely refers to the passage of the bridge of el Aarâf.

have we destroyed who were better off in property and appearance?

Say, 'Whosoever is in error, let the Merciful extend to him length of days!—until they see what they are threatened with, whether it be the torment or whether it be the Hour, then they shall know who is worse placed and weakest in forces!'

And those who are guided God will increase in guidance.

And enduring good works are best with thy Lord for a reward, and best for restoration.

[80] Hast thou seen him who disbelieves in our signs, and says, 'I shall surely be given wealth and children[1]?'

Has he become acquainted with the unseen, or has he taken a compact with the Merciful? Not so! We will write down what he says, and we will extend to him a length of torment, and we will make him inherit what he says, and he shall come to us alone. They take other gods besides God to be their glory. [85] Not so! They[2] shall deny their worship and shall be opponents of theirs!

Dost thou not see that we have sent the devils against the misbelievers, to drive them on to sin? but, be not thou hasty with them. Verily, we will number them a number (of days),—the day when we will gather the pious to the Merciful as ambassadors, and we will drive the sinners to hell like

[1] 'Hâsîy ibn Wâil, being indebted to '*H*abbâb, refused to pay him unless he renounced Mohammed. This '*H*abbâb said he would never do alive or dead, or when raised again at the last day. El 'Hâsîy told him to call for his money on the last day, as he should have wealth and children then.

[2] That is, the false gods.

(herds) to water! [90] They shall not possess intercession, save he who has taken a compact with the Merciful.

They say, 'The Merciful has taken to Himself a son:'—ye have brought a monstrous thing! The heavens well-nigh burst asunder thereat, and the earth is riven, and the mountains fall down broken, that they attribute to the Merciful a son! but it becomes not the Merciful to take to Himself a son! there is none in the heavens or the earth but comes to the Merciful as a servant; He counts them and numbers them by number, [95] and they are all coming to Him on the resurrection day singly.

Verily, those who believe and act aright, to them the Merciful will give love.

We have only made it easy for thy tongue that thou mayest thereby give glad tidings to the pious, and warn thereby a contentious people.

How many a generation before them have we destroyed? Canst thou find any one of them, or hear a whisper of them?

The Chapter of *T*. H.

(XX. Mecca.)

In the name of the merciful and compassionate God.

T. H. We have not sent down this Qur'ân to thee that thou shouldst be wretched; only as a reminder to him who fears—descending from Him who created the earth and the high heavens, the Merciful settled on the throne! [5] His are what is in the heavens, and what is in the earth, and what is between the two, and what is beneath the ground! And if thou art public in thy speech—yet, verily, he knows the secret, and more hidden still.

God, there is no god but He! His are the excellent names.

Has the story of Moses come to thee? When he saw the fire and said to his family, 'Tarry ye; verily, I perceive a fire! [10] Haply I may bring you therefrom a brand, or may find guidance by the fire[1].' And when he came to it he was called to, 'O Moses! verily, I am thy Lord, so take off thy sandals; verily, thou art in the holy valley *T*uvâ, and I have chosen thee. So listen to what is inspired thee; verily, I am God, there is no god but Me! then serve Me, and be steadfast in prayer to remember Me.

[15] 'Verily, the hour is coming, I almost make it appear[2], that every soul may be recompensed for its efforts.

'Let not then him who believes not therein and follows his lusts ever turn thee away therefrom, and thou be ruined.

'What is that in thy right hand, O Moses?'

Said he, 'It is my staff on which I lean, and

---

[1] The Arabs used to light fires to guide travellers to shelter and entertainment. These fires, 'the fire of hospitality,' 'the fire of war,' &c. are constantly referred to in the ancient Arabic poetry. No less than thirteen fires are enumerated by them.

[2] This may be also rendered, 'I almost conceal it (from myself);' i'*h*fâ'un having, like many words in Arabic, two meanings directly opposite to each other. This probably arose from words being adopted into the Qurâi*s* idiom from other dialects.

wherewith I beat down leaves for my flocks, and for which I have other uses.'

[20] Said He, 'Throw it down, O Moses!' and he threw it down, and behold! it was a snake that moved about.

Said He, 'Take hold of it and fear not; we will restore it to its first state.

'But press thy hand to thy side, it shall come forth white without harm,—another sign! to show thee of our great signs!

[25] 'Go unto Pharaoh, verily, he is outrageous!'

Said he, 'My Lord! expand for me my breast; and make what I am bidden easy to me; and loose the knot from my tongue[1], that they may understand my speech; [30] and make for me a minister[2] from my people,—Aaron my brother; gird up my loins through him[3], and join him with me in the affair; that we may celebrate Thy praises much and remember Thee much.

[35] 'Verily, Thou dost ever behold us!'

He said, 'Thou art granted thy request, O Moses! and we have already shown favours unto thee at another time. When we inspired thy mother with what we inspired her, "Hurl him into the ark, and hurl him into the sea; and the sea shall cast him on the shore, and an enemy of mine and of his shall take him;"—for on thee have I cast my

---

[1] The Muslim legend is that Moses burnt his tongue with a live coal when a child. This incident is related at length, together with other Mohammedan legends connected with Moses and the Exodus, in my 'Desert of the Exodus,' Appendix C. p. 533. Transl.

[2] Literally, vizîr, 'vizier,' 'one who bears the burden' of office.

[3] I.e. 'strengthen me.' The idiom is still in common use amongst the desert Arabs.

love, [40] that thou mayest be formed under my eye. When thy sister walked on and said, "Shall I guide you to one who will take charge of him?" And we restored thee to thy mother, that her eye might be cheered and that she should not grieve. And thou didst slay a person and we saved thee from the trouble, and we tried thee with various trials. And thou didst tarry for years amongst the people of Midian; then thou didst come (hither) at (our) decree, O Moses! And I have chosen thee for myself. Go, thou and thy brother, with my signs, and be not remiss in remembering me. [45] Go ye both to Pharaoh; verily, he is outrageous! and speak to him a gentle speech, haply he may be mindful or may fear.'

They two said, 'Our Lord! verily, we fear that he may trespass against us, or that he may be outrageous.'

He said, 'Fear not; verily, I am with you twain. I hear and see!

'So come ye to him and say, "Verily, we are the apostles of thy Lord; send then the children of Israel with us; and do not torment them. We have brought thee a sign from thy Lord, and peace be upon him who follows the guidance!

[50] '"Verily, we are inspired that the torment will surely come upon him who calls us liars and turns his back."'

Said he, 'And who is your Lord, O Moses?'

He said, 'Our Lord is He who gave everything its creation, then guided it.'

Said he, 'And what of the former generations?'

He said, 'The knowledge of them is with my Lord in a book; my Lord misleads not, nor forgets!

[55] Who made for you the earth a bed; and has traced for you paths therein; and has sent down from the sky water,—and we have brought forth thereby divers sorts of different vegetables. Eat and pasture your cattle therefrom; verily, in that are signs to those endued with intelligence. From it have we created you and into it will we send you back, and from it will we bring you forth another time.'

We did show him our signs, all of them, but he called them lies and did refuse.

Said he, 'Hast thou come to us, to turn us out of our land with thy magic, O Moses?
[60] Then we will bring you magic like it; and we will make between us and thee an appointment; we will not break it, nor do thou either;—a fair place.'

Said he, 'Let your appointment be for the day of adornment[1], and let the people assemble in the forenoon[2].'

But Pharaoh turned his back, and collected his tricks, and then he came.

Said Moses to them, 'Woe to you! do not forge against God a lie; lest He destroy you by torment; for disappointed has ever been he who has forged.'

[65] And they argued their matter among themselves; and secretly talked it over.

Said they, 'These twain are certainly two magicians, who wish to turn you out of your land by their magic, and to remove your most exemplary doctrine[3]. Collect therefore your tricks, and then

---

[1] I. e. the festival.

[2] In order that they might all see.

[3] Or, 'your most eminent men,' as some commentators interpret it, i. e. the children of Israel.

form a row; for he is prosperous to-day who has the upper hand.'

Said they, 'O Moses! either thou must throw, or we must be the first to throw.'

He said, 'Nay, throw ye!' and lo! their ropes and their staves appeared to move along. [70] And Moses felt a secret fear within his soul.

Said we, 'Fear not! thou shalt have the upper hand. Throw down what is in thy right hand; and it shall devour what they have made. Verily, what they have made is but a magician's trick; and no magician shall prosper wherever he comes.'

And the magicians were cast down in adoration; said they, 'We believe in the Lord of Aaron and of Moses!'

Said he[1], 'Do ye believe in Him before I give you leave? Verily, he is your master who taught you magic! Therefore will I surely cut off your hands and feet on alternate sides, and I will surely crucify you on the trunks of palm trees; and ye shall surely know which of us is keenest at torment and more lasting.'

[75] Said they, 'We will never prefer thee to what has come to us of manifest signs, and to Him who originated us. Decide then what thou canst decide; thou canst only decide in the life of this world! Verily, we believe in our Lord, that He may pardon us our sins, and the magic thou hast forced us to use; and God is better and more lasting!'

Verily, he who comes to his Lord a sinner,—verily, for him is hell; he shall not die therein, and shall not live.

---

[1] Pharaoh.

But he who comes to Him a believer who has done aright—these, for them are the highest ranks, —gardens of Eden beneath which rivers flow, to dwell therein for aye; for that is the reward of him who keeps pure.

And we inspired Moses, 'Journey by night with my servants, and strike out for them a dry road in the sea. [80] Fear not pursuit, nor be afraid!' Then Pharaoh followed them with his armies, and there overwhelmed them of the sea that which overwhelmed them. And Pharaoh and his people went astray and were not guided.

O children of Israel! We have saved you from your enemy; and we made an appointment with you on the right side of the mount; and we sent down upon you the manna and the quails. 'Eat of the good things we have provided you with, and do not exceed therein, lest my wrath light upon you; for whomsoever my wrath lights upon he falls!

'Yet am I forgiving unto him who repents and believes and does right, and then is guided.

[85] 'But what has hastened thee on away from thy people, O Moses?'

He said, 'They were here upon my track and I hastened on to Thee, my Lord! that thou mightest be pleased.'

Said He, 'Verily, we have tried thy people, since thou didst leave, and es Sâmarîy[1] has led them astray.'

And Moses returned to his people, wrathful, grieving!

[1] I.e. the Samaritan; some take it to mean a proper name, in order to avoid the anachronism.

Said he, 'O my people! did not your Lord promise you a good promise? Has the time seemed too long for you, or do you desire that wrath should light on you from your Lord, that ye have broken your promise to me?'

[90] They said, 'We have not broken our promise to thee of our own accord. But we were made to carry loads of the ornaments of the people, and we hurled them down, and so did es Sâmarîy cast; and he brought forth for the people a corporeal calf which lowed.' And they said, 'This is your god and the god of Moses, but he has forgotten!' What! do they not see that it does not return them any speech, and cannot control for them harm or profit? Aaron too told them before, 'O my people! ye are only being tried thereby; and, verily, your Lord is the Merciful, so follow me and obey my bidding.'

They said, 'We will not cease to pay devotion to it until Moses come back to us.'

Said he, 'O Aaron! what prevented thee, when thou didst see them go astray, from following me? Hast thou then rebelled against my bidding?'

[95] Said he, 'O son of my mother! seize me not by my beard, or my head! Verily, I feared lest thou shouldst say, "Thou hast made a division amongst the children of Israel, and hast not observed my word."'

Said he, 'What was thy design, O Sâmarîy?' Said he, 'I beheld what they beheld not, and I grasped a handful from the footprint of the messenger[1] and cast it; for thus my soul induced me.'

[1] A handful of dust from the footprint of the angel Gabriel's

Said he, 'Then get thee gone; verily, it shall be thine in life to say, "Touch me not[1]!" and, verily, for thee there is a threat which thou shalt surely never alter. But look at thy god to which thou wert just now devout; we will surely burn it, and then we will scatter it in scattered pieces in the sea.

'Your God is only God who,—there is no god but He,—He embraceth everything in His knowledge.'

Thus do we narrate to thee the history of what has gone before, and we have brought thee a reminder from us.

[100] Whoso turns therefrom, verily, he shall bear on the resurrection day a burden:—for them to bear for aye, and evil for them on the resurrection day will it be to bear.

On the day when the trumpet shall be blown, and we will gather the sinners in that day blue-eyed[2].

They shall whisper to each other, 'Ye have only tarried ten days.' We know best what they say, when the most exemplary of them in his way shall say, 'Ye have only tarried a day.'

[105] They will ask thee about the mountains;

---

horse, which, being cast into the calf, caused it to become animated and to low.

[1] The idea conveyed seems to be that he should be regarded as a leper, and obliged to warn people from coming near him. The reference is no doubt to the light in which the Samaritans (see Part II, p. 40, note 1) were regarded by the Jews.

[2] Because 'blue eyes' were especially detested by the Arabs as being characteristic of their greatest enemies, the Greeks. So they speak of an enemy as 'black-livered,' 'red-whiskered,' and 'blue-eyed.' The word in the text may also mean 'blear-eyed,' or 'blind.'

say, 'My Lord will scatter them in scattered pieces, and He will leave them a level plain, thou wilt see therein no crookedness or inequality.'

On that day they shall follow the caller in whom is no crookedness[1]; and the voices shall be hushed before the Merciful, and thou shalt hear naught but a shuffling.

On that day shall no intercession be of any avail, save from such as the Merciful permits, and who is acceptable to Him in speech.

He knows what is before them and what is behind them, but they do not comprehend knowledge of Him.

[110] Faces shall be humbled before the Living, the Self-subsistent; and he who bears injustice is ever lost.

But he who does righteous acts and is a believer, he shall fear neither wrong nor diminution.

Thus have we sent it down an Arabic Qur'ân; and we have turned about in it the threat,—haply they may fear, or it may cause them to remember.

Exalted then be God, the king, the truth! Hasten not the Qur'ân before its inspiration is decided for thee; but say, 'O Lord! increase me in knowledge[2].'

We did make a covenant with Adam of yore, but he forgot it, and we found no firm purpose in him.

[115] And when we said to the angels, 'Adore

---

[1] That is, the angel who is to summon them to judgment, and from whom none can escape, or who marches straight on.

[2] Cf. Part II, p. 16, note 2.

Adam,' they adored, save Iblîs, who refused. And we said, 'O Adam! verily, this is a foe to thee and to thy wife; never then let him drive you twain forth from the garden or thou wilt be wretched. Verily, thou hast not to be hungry there, nor naked! and, verily, thou shalt not thirst therein, nor feel the noonday heat!'

But the devil whispered to him. Said he, 'O Adam! shall I guide thee to the tree of immortality, and a kingdom that shall not wane?'

And they eat therefrom, and their shame became apparent to them; and they began to stitch upon themselves some leaves of the garden; and Adam rebelled against his Lord, and went astray.

[120] Then his Lord chose him, and relented towards him, and guided him. Said he, 'Go down, ye twain, therefrom altogether, some of you foes to the other. And if there should come to you from me a guidance; then whoso follows my guidance shall neither err nor be wretched. But he who turns away from my reminder, verily, for him shall be a straitened livelihood; and we will gather him on the resurrection day blind!'

[125] He shall say, 'My Lord! wherefore hast Thou gathered me blind when I used to see?' He shall say, 'Our signs came to thee, and thou didst forget them; thus to-day art thou forgotten!'

Thus do we recompense him who is extravagant and believes not in the signs of his Lord; and the torment of the hereafter is keener and more lasting!

Does it not occur to them[1] how many generations

[1] The Meccans.

we have destroyed before them?—they walk in their very dwelling-places; verily, in that are signs to those endued with intelligence.

And had it not been for thy Lord's word already passed (the punishment) would have been inevitable and (at) an appointed time.

[130] Bear patiently then what they say, and celebrate the praises of thy Lord before the rising of the sun, and before its setting, and at times in the night celebrate them; and at the ends of the day; haply thou mayest please (Him).

And do not strain after what we have provided a few [1] of them with—the flourish of the life of this world, to try them by; but the provision of thy Lord is better and more lasting.

Bid thy people prayer, and persevere in it; we do not ask thee to provide. We will provide, and the issue shall be to piety.

They say, 'Unless he bring us a sign from his Lord—What! has there not come to them the manifest sign of what was in the pages of yore?'

But had we destroyed them with torment before it, they would have said, 'Unless Thou hadst sent to us an apostle, that we might follow Thy signs before we were abased and put to shame.'

[135] Say, 'Each one has to wait, so wait ye! but in the end ye shall know who are the fellows of the level way, and who are guided!'

---

[1] Literally, 'pairs.'

The Chapter of the Prophets.

(XXI. Mecca.)

In the name of the merciful and compassionate God.

Their reckoning draws nigh to men, yet in heedlessness they turn aside.

No reminder comes to them from their Lord of late, but they listen while they mock, and their hearts make sport thereof! And those who do wrong discourse secretly (saying), 'Is this man aught but a mortal like yourselves? will ye accede to magic, while ye can see?'

Say, 'My Lord knows what is said in the heavens and the earth, He hears and knows!'

[5] 'Nay!' they say, '— a jumble of dreams; nay! he has forged it; nay! he is a poet; but let him bring us a sign as those of yore were sent.'

No city before them which we destroyed believed—how will they believe? Nor did we send before them any but men whom we inspired? Ask ye the people of the Scriptures if ye do not know. Nor did we make them bodies not to eat food, nor were they immortal. Yet we made our promise to them good, and we saved them and whom we pleased; but we destroyed those who committed excesses.

[10] We have sent down to you a book in which is a reminder for you; have ye then no sense?

How many a city which had done wrong have we broken up, and raised up after it another people! And when they perceived our violence they ran away from it. 'Run not away, but return to what ye delighted in, and to your dwellings! haply ye will be questioned.' Said they, 'O woe is us! verily, we were wrong-doers.'

[15] And that ceased not to be their cry until we made them mown down,—smouldering out!

We did not create the heaven and the earth and what is between the two in play. Had we wished to take to a sport, we would have taken to one from before ourselves; had we been bent on doing so. Nay, we hurl the truth against falsehood and it crashes into it, and lo! it vanishes, but woe to you for what ye attribute (to God)!

His are whosoever are in the heavens and the earth, and those who are with Him are not too big with pride for His service, nor do they weary. [20] They celebrate His praises by night and day without intermission. Or have they taken gods from the earth who can raise up (the dead)?

Were there in both (heaven and earth) gods beside God, both would surely have been corrupted. Celebrated then be the praise of God, the Lord of the throne, above what they ascribe!

He shall not be questioned concerning what He does, but they shall be questioned.

Have they taken gods beside Him? Say, 'Bring your proofs. This is the reminder of those who are with me, and of those who were before me.' Nay, most of them know not the truth, and they do turn aside.

[25] We have not sent any prophet before thee, but we inspired him that, 'There is no god but Me, so serve ye Me.'

And they say, 'The Merciful has taken a son[1];

[1] Or, child, since the passage refers both to the Christian

celebrated be His praise!'—Nay, honoured servants; they do not speak until He speaks; but at His bidding do they act. He knows what is before them, and what is behind them, and they shall not intercede except for him whom He is pleased with; and they shrink through fear.

[30] And whoso of them should say, 'Verily, I am god instead of Him,' such a one we recompense with hell; thus do we recompense the wrong-doers.

Do not those who misbelieve see that the heavens and the earth were both solid, and we burst them asunder; and we made from water every living thing—will they then not believe?

And we placed on the earth firm mountains lest it should move with them, and He made therein open roads for paths, haply they may be guided! and we made the heaven a guarded roof; yet from our signs they turn aside!

He it is who created the night and the day, and the sun and the moon, each floating in a sky.

[35] We never made for any mortal before thee immortality; what, if thou shouldst die, will they live on for aye?

Every soul shall taste of death! we will test them with evil and with good, as a trial; and unto us shall they return!

And when those who misbelieve see thee[1], they only take thee for a jest, 'Is this he who mentions your gods?' Yet they at the mention of the Merciful do disbelieve.

---

doctrine and to the Arab notion that the angels are daughters of God.

[1] Mohammed.

Man is created out of haste. I will show you my signs; but do not hurry Me.

And they say, 'When will this threat (come to pass), if ye tell the truth?'

[40] Did those who misbelieve but know when the fire shall not be warded off from their faces nor from their backs, and they shall not be helped! Nay, it shall come on them suddenly, and shall dumbfounder them, and they shall not be able to repel it, nor shall they be respited.

Prophets before thee have been mocked at, but that whereat they jested encompassed those who mocked.

Say, 'Who shall guard you by night and by day from the Merciful?' Nay, but they from the mention of their Lord do turn aside.

Have they gods to defend them against us? These cannot help themselves, nor shall they be abetted against us.

[45] Nay, but we have granted enjoyment to these men and to their fathers whilst life was prolonged. Do they not see that we come to the land and shorten its borders? Shall they then prevail?

Say, 'I only warn you by inspiration;' but the deaf hear not the call when they are warned. But if a blast of the torment of thy Lord touches them, they will surely say, 'O, woe is us! verily, we were wrong-doers!'

We will place just balances upon the resurrection day, and no soul shall be wronged at all, even though it be the weight of a grain of mustard seed, we will bring it; for we are good enough at reckoning up.

We did give to Moses and Aaron the Discrimination, and a light and a reminder to those who fear; [50] who are afraid of their Lord in secret; and who at the Hour do shrink.

This is a blessed reminder which we have sent down, will ye then deny it?

And we gave Abraham a right direction before; for about him we knew. When he said to his father and to his people, 'What are these images to which ye pay devotion?' Said they, 'We found our fathers serving them.' [55] Said he, 'Both you and your fathers have been in obvious error.' They said, 'Dost thou come to us with the truth, or art thou but of those who play?'

He said, 'Nay, but your Lord is Lord of the heavens and the earth, which He originated; and I am of those who testify to this; and, by God! I will plot against your idols after ye have turned and shown me your backs!'

So he brake them all in pieces, except a large one they had; that haply they might refer it to that.

[60] Said they, 'Who has done this with our gods? verily, he is of the wrong-doers!' They said, 'We heard a youth mention them who is called Abraham.'

Said they, 'Then bring him before the eyes of men; haply they will bear witness.'

Said they, 'Was it thou who did this to our gods, O Abraham?' Said he, 'Nay, it was this largest of them; but ask them, if they can speak.'

[65] Then they came to themselves and said, 'Verily, ye are the wrong-doers.' Then they turned

upside down again[1]: 'Thou knewest that these cannot speak.'

Said he, 'Will ye then serve, beside God, what cannot profit you at all, nor harm you? fie upon you, and what ye serve beside God! have ye then no sense?'

Said they, 'Burn him, and help your gods, if ye are going to do so!'

We said, 'O fire! be thou cool and a safety for Abraham!'

[70] They desired to plot against him, but we made them the losers.

And we brought him and Lot safely to the land which we have blessed for the world, and we bestowed upon him Isaac and Jacob as a fresh gift, and each of them we made righteous persons; and we made them high priests[2] to guide (men) by our bidding, and we inspired them to do good works, and to be steadfast in prayer, and to give alms; and they did serve us.

And Lot, to him we gave judgment and knowledge, and we brought him safely out of the city which had done vile acts; verily, they were a people who wrought abominations! [75] And we made him enter into our mercy; verily, he was of the righteous!

And Noah, when he cried aforetime, and we answered him and saved him and his people from the mighty trouble, and we helped him against the people who said our signs were lies; verily,

[1] Literally, 'they turned upside down upon their heads,' the metaphor implying that they suddenly changed their opinion and relapsed into belief in their idols.

[2] See Part I, p. 17, note 1.

they were a bad people, so we drowned them all together.

And David and Solomon, when they gave judgment concerning the field, when some people's sheep had strayed therein at night; and we testified to their judgment [1]; and this we gave Solomon to understand. To each of them we gave judgment and knowledge; and to David we subjected the mountains to celebrate our praises, and the birds too,— it was we who did it [2].

[80] And we taught him the art of making coats of mail for you, to shield you from each other's violence; are ye then grateful?

And to Solomon (we subjected) the wind blowing stormily, to run on at his bidding to the land [3] which we have blessed,—for all things did we know,—and some devils to dive for him, and to do other works beside that; and we kept guard over them.

And Job, when he cried to his Lord, 'As for me, harm has touched me, but Thou art the most merciful of the merciful ones.' And we answered

---

[1] This case, say the commentators, being brought before David and Solomon, David said that the owner of the field should take the sheep in compensation for the damage; but Solomon, who was only eleven years old at the time, gave judgment that the owner of the field should enjoy the produce of the sheep—that is, their milk, wool, and lambs—until the shepherd had restored the field to its former state of cultivation, and this judgment was approved by David.

[2] This legend, adopted from the Talmud, arises from a too literal interpretation of Psalm cxlviii.

[3] The legend of Solomon, his seal inscribed with the holy name by which he could control all the powers of nature, his carpet or throne that used to be transported with him on the wind wherever he pleased, his power over the *g*inns, and his knowledge of the language of birds and beasts are commonplaces in Arabic writings.

him, and removed from him the distress that was upon him; and we gave his family, and the like of them with them, as a mercy from us, and a remembrance to those who serve us.

[85] And Ishmael, and Idrîs, and Dhu 'l Kifl[1], all of these were of the patient: and we made them enter into our mercy; verily, they were among the righteous.

And Dhu 'nnûn[2], when he went away in wrath and thought that we had no power over him; and he cried out in the darkness, 'There is no god but Thou, celebrated be Thy praise! Verily, I was of the evildoers!' And we answered him, and saved him from the trouble. Thus do we save believers!

And Zachariah, when he cried unto his Lord, 'O Lord! leave me not alone; for thou art the best of heirs[3].' [90] And we answered him, and bestowed upon him John; and we made his wife right for him; verily, these vied in good works, and called on us with longing and dread, and were humble before us.

And she who guarded her private parts, and we breathed into her of our Spirit, and we made her and her son a sign unto the worlds. Verily, this your nation[4] is one nation; and I am your Lord, so serve me.

---

[1] That is, Elias, or, as some say, Joshua, and some say Zachariah, so called because he had a portion from God Most High, and guaranteed his people, or because he had double the work of the prophets of his time and their reward; the word Kifl being used in the various senses of 'portion,' 'sponsorship,' and 'double.'—Bâi*dh*âvî.

[2] Literally, 'he of the fish,' that is, Jonah.

[3] See Part II, p. 27.

[4] The word 'ummatun' is here used in the sense rather of

But they cut up their affair amongst themselves; they all shall return to us; and he who acts aright, and he who is a believer, there is no denial of his efforts, for, verily, we will write them down for him.

[95] There is a ban upon a city which we have destroyed that they shall not return, until Yâ*g*û*g* and Mâ*g*û*g* are let out [1], and they from every hummock [2] shall glide forth.

And the true promise draws nigh, and lo! they are staring—the eyes of those who misbelieve! O, woe is us! we were heedless of this, nay, we were wrong-doers!

Verily, ye, and what ye serve beside God, shall be the pebbles of hell [3], to it shall ye go down!

Had these been God's they would not have gone down thereto: but all shall dwell therein for aye;
[100] for them therein is groaning, but they therein shall not be heard.

Verily, those for whom the good (reward) from us was fore-ordained, they from it shall be kept far away; they shall not hear the slightest sound thereof, and they in what their souls desire shall dwell for aye. The greatest terror shall not grieve them; and the angels shall meet them, (saying), 'This is your day which ye were promised!'

'religion,' regarding the various nations and generations as each professing and representing a particular faith, and means that the religion preached to the Meccans was the same as that preached to their followers by the various prophets who are mentioned in this chapter.

[1] See Part II, p. 25.

[2] 'Hadab, some read *g*adath, 'grave.'

[3] See Part I, p. 4, l. 1.

The day when we will roll up the heavens as es-Sigill rolls up the books[1]; as we produced it at its first creation will we bring it back again—a promise binding upon us; verily, we are going to do it. And already have we written in the Psalms [105] after the reminder that 'the earth shall my righteous servants inherit[2].'

Verily, in this is preaching for a people who serve me!

We have only sent thee as a mercy to the worlds.

Say, 'I am only inspired that your God is one God; are ye then resigned?' But if they turn their backs say, 'I have proclaimed (war) against all alike, but I know not if what ye are threatened with be near or far!'

[110] Verily, He knows what is spoken openly, and He knows what ye hide.

I know not, haply it is a trial for you and a provision for a season.

Say, 'My Lord! judge thou with truth! and our Lord is the Merciful whom we ask for aid against what they ascribe!'

---

[1] Es-Sigill is the name of the angel who has charge of the book on which each human being's fate is written, which book he rolls up at a person's death. The word, however, may mean a scroll or register, and the passage may be rendered, 'like the rolling up of a scroll for writings.'

[2] Psalm xxxvii. 29.

The Chapter of the Pilgrimage.

(XXII. Mecca.)

In the name of the merciful and compassionate God.

O ye folk! fear your Lord. Verily, the earthquake of the Hour is a mighty thing.

On the day ye shall see it, every suckling woman shall be scared away from that to which she gave suck; and every pregnant woman shall lay down her load; and thou shalt see men drunken, though they be not drunken: but the torment of God is severe.

And amongst men is one who wrangles about God without knowledge, and follows every rebellious devil; against whom it is written down that whoso takes him for a patron, verily, he will lead him astray, and will guide him towards the torment of the blaze!

[5] O ye folk! if ye are in doubt about the raising (of the dead),—verily, we created you from earth, then from a clot, then from congealed blood, then from a morsel, shaped or shapeless, that we may explain to you. And we make what we please rest in the womb until an appointed time; then we bring you forth babes; then let you reach your full age; and of you are some who die; and of you are some who are kept back till the most decrepit age, till he knows no longer aught of knowledge. And ye see the earth parched, and when we send down water on it, it stirs and swells, and brings forth herbs of every beauteous kind.

That is because God, He is the truth, and because

He quickens the dead, and because He is mighty over all; and because the Hour is coming, there is no doubt therein, and because God raises up those who are in the tombs.

And amongst men is one who wrangles about God without knowledge or guidance or an illuminating book; twisting his neck from the way of God; for him is disgrace in this world, and we will make him taste, upon the resurrection day, the torment of burning.

[10] That is for what thy hands have done before, and for that God is not unjust unto His servants.

And amongst men is one who serves God (wavering) on a brink; and if there befall him good, he is comforted; but if there befall him a trial, he turns round again, and loses this world and the next—that is an obvious loss. He calls, besides God, on what can neither harm him nor profit him;—that is a wide error.

He calls on him whose harm is nigher than his profit,—a bad lord and a bad comrade.

Verily, God makes those who believe and do aright enter into gardens beneath which rivers flow; verily, God does what He will.

[15] He who thinks that God will never help him in this world or the next—let him stretch a cord to the roof[1] and put an end to himself; and let him cut it and see if his stratagem will remove what he is enraged at.

Thus have we sent down manifest signs; for, verily, God guides whom He will.

Verily, those who believe, and those who are

[1] The word may also be rendered 'sky.'

Jews, and the Sabæans, and the Christians, and the Magians, and those who join other gods with God, verily, God will decide between them on the resurrection day; verily, God is witness over all.

Do they not see that God, whosoever is in the heavens adores Him, and whosoever is in the earth, and the sun, and the moon, and the stars, and the mountains, and the beasts, and many among men, though many a one deserves the torments?

Whomsoever God abases there is none to honour him; verily, God does what He pleases.

[20] These are two disputants[1] who dispute about their Lord, but those who misbelieve, for them are cut out garments of fire, there shall be poured over their heads boiling water, wherewith what is in their bellies shall be dissolved and their skins too, and for them are maces of iron. Whenever they desire to come forth therefrom through pain, they are sent back into it: 'And taste ye the torment of the burning!'

Verily, God will make those who believe and do right enter into gardens beneath which rivers flow; they shall be bedecked therein with bracelets of gold and with pearls, and their garments therein shall be of silk, and they shall be guided to the goodly speech, and they shall be guided to the laudable way.

[25] Verily, those who misbelieve and who turn men away from God's path and the Sacred Mosque, which we have made for all men alike, the dweller therein, and the stranger, and he who desires therein profanation with injustice, we will make him taste grievous woe.

---

[1] Namely, the believers and the misbelievers.

And when we established for Abraham the place of the House, (saying), 'Associate naught with me, but cleanse my House for those who make the circuits, for those who stand to pray, for those who bow, and for those too who adore.

'And proclaim amongst men the Pilgrimage; let them come to you on foot and on every slim camel, from every deep pass, that they may witness advantages for them, and may mention the name of God for the stated days[1] over what God has provided them with of brute beasts, then eat thereof and feed the badly off, the poor.

[30] 'Then let them finish the neglect of their persons[2], and let them pay their vows and make the circuit round the old House.

'That do. And whoso magnifies the sacred things of God it is better for him with his Lord.

'Cattle are lawful for you, except what is recited to you; and avoid the abomination of idols, and avoid speaking falsely, being 'Hanîfs to God, not associating aught with Him; for he who associates aught with God, it is as though he had fallen from heaven, and the birds snatch him up, or the wind blows him away into a far distant place.

'That—and he who makes grand the symbols[3] of God, they come from piety of heart.

---

[1] The first ten days of Dhu 'l 'Higgeh, or the tenth day of that month, when the sacrifices were offered in the vale of Minâ, and the three following days.

[2] Such as not shaving their heads and other parts of their bodies, or cutting their beards and nails, which are forbidden the pilgrim from the moment he has put on the I'hrâm, or pilgrim garb, until the offering of the sacrifice at Minâ.

[3] This means by presenting fine and comely offerings.

'Therein have ye advantages for an appointed time, then the place for sacrificing them is at the old House.'

[35] To every nation have we appointed rites, to mention the name of God over what He has provided them with of brute beasts; and your God is one God, to Him then be resigned, and give glad tidings to the lowly, whose hearts when God is mentioned are afraid, and to those who are patient of what befalls them, and to those who are steadfast in prayer and of what we have given them expend in alms.

The bulky (camels) we have made for you one of the symbols of God, therein have ye good; so mention the name of God over them as they stand in a row[1], and when they fall down (dead) eat of them, and feed the easily contented and him who begs.

Thus have we subjected them to you; haply, ye may give thanks!

Their meat will never reach to God, nor yet their blood, but the piety from you will reach to Him.

Thus hath He subjected them to you that ye may magnify God for guiding you: and give thou glad tidings to those who do good.

Verily, God will defend those who believe; verily, God loves not any misbelieving traitor.

[40] Permission is given to those who fight because they have been wronged,—and, verily, God to help them has the might,—who have been driven forth from their homes undeservedly, only for that they said, 'Our Lord is God;' and were it not for God's repelling some men with others, cloisters and churches and synagogues and mosques, wherein God's name is

[1] Waiting to be sacrificed.

mentioned much, would be destroyed. But God will surely help him who helps Him; verily, God is powerful, mighty.

Who, if we stablish them in the earth, are steadfast in prayer, and give alms, and bid what is right, and forbid what is wrong; and God's is the future of affairs.

But if they call thee liar, the people of Noah called him liar before them, as did 'Âd and Thamûd, and the people of Abraham, and the people of Lot, and the fellows of Midian; and Moses was called a liar too: but I let the misbelievers range at large, and then I seized on them, and how great was the change!

And how many a city have we destroyed while it yet did wrong, and it was turned over on its roofs, and (how many) a deserted well and lofty palace!

[45] Have they not travelled on through the land? and have they not hearts to understand with, or ears to hear with? for it is not their eyes which are blind, but blind are the hearts which are within their breasts.

They will bid thee hasten on the torment, but God will never fail in his promise; for, verily, a day with thy Lord is as a thousand years of what ye number.

And to how many a city have I given full range while it yet did wrong! then I seized on it, and unto me was the return.

Say, 'O ye folk! I am naught but a plain warner to you, but those who believe and do right, for them is forgiveness and a generous provision; [50] but those who strive to discredit our signs, they are the fellows of hell!'

We have not sent before thee any apostle or prophet, but that when he wished, Satan threw not something into his wish[1]; but God annuls what Satan throws; then does God confirm his signs, and God is knowing, wise—to make what Satan throws a trial unto those in whose hearts is sickness, and those whose hearts are hard; and, verily, the wrong-doers are in a wide schism—and that those who have been given 'the knowledge' may know that it is the truth from thy Lord, and may believe therein, and that their hearts may be lowly; for, verily, God surely will guide those who believe into a right way.

But those who misbelieve will not cease to be in doubt thereof until the Hour comes on them suddenly, or there comes on them the torment of the barren day[2].

[55] The kingdom on that day shall be God's, He shall judge between them; and those who believe

---

[1] Some say that the word tamannâ means 'reading,' and the passage should then be translated, 'but that when he read Satan threw something into his reading;' the occasion on which the verse was produced being that when Mohammed was reciting the words of the Qur'ân, Chapter LIII, verses 19, 20, 'Have ye considered Allât and Al 'Huzzâ and Manât the other third?' Satan put it into his mouth to add, 'they are the two high-soaring cranes, and, verily, their intercession may be hoped for;' at this praise of their favourite idols the Qurâis were much pleased, and at the end of the recitation joined the prophet and his followers in adoration. Mohammed, being informed by the angel Gabriel of the reason for their doing so, was much concerned until this verse was revealed for his consolation. The objectionable passage was of course annulled, and the verse made to read as it now stands.

[2] Either 'the day of resurrection,' as giving birth to no day after it, or, 'a day of battle and defeat,' that makes mothers childless, such as the infidels experienced at Bedr.

and do aright shall be in gardens of pleasure, but those who misbelieve and say our signs are lies, these—for them is shameful woe.

And those who flee in God's way, and then are slain or die, God will provide them with a goodly provision; for, verily, God is the best of providers.

He shall surely make them enter by an entrance that they like; for, verily, God is knowing, clement.

That (is so). Whoever punishes with the like of what he has been injured with, and shall then be outraged again, God shall surely help him; verily, God pardons, forgives.

[60] That for that God joins on the night to the day, and joins on the day to the night, and that God is hearing, seeing; that is for that God is the truth, and for that what ye call on beside Him is falsehood, and that God is the high, the great.

Hast thou not seen that God sends down from the sky water, and on the morrow the earth is green? verily, God is kind and well aware.

His is what is in the heavens and what is in the earth; and, verily, God is rich and to be praised.

Hast thou not seen that God has subjected for you what is in the earth, and the ship that runs on in the sea at His bidding, and He holds back the sky from falling on the earth save at His bidding[1]? verily, God to men is gracious, merciful.

[65] He it is who quickens you, then makes you

---

[1] As it will do at the last day. The words of the text might also be rendered 'withholds the rain,' though the commentators do not seem to notice this sense.

die, then will He quicken you again—verily, man is indeed ungrateful.

For every nation have we made rites which they observe; let them not then dispute about the matter, but call upon thy Lord; verily, thou art surely in a right guidance!

But if they wrangle with thee, say, 'God best knows what ye do.'

God shall judge between them on the resurrection day concerning that whereon they disagreed.

Didst thou not know that God knows what is in the heavens and the earth? verily, that is in a book; verily, that for God is easy.

[70] And they serve beside God what He has sent down no power for, and what they have no knowledge of; but the wrong-doers shall have none to help them.

When our signs are read to them manifest, thou mayest recognise in the faces of those who misbelieve disdain; they well-nigh rush at those who recite to them our signs. Say, 'Shall I inform you of something worse than that for you, the Fire which God has promised to those who misbelieve? an evil journey shall it be!'

O ye folk! a parable is struck out for you, so listen to it. Verily, those on whom ye call beside God could never create a fly if they all united together to do it, and if the fly should despoil them of aught they could not snatch it away from it—weak is both the seeker and the sought.

They do not value God at His true value; verily, God is powerful, mighty.

God chooses apostles of the angels and of men; verily, God hears and sees. [75] He knows what is before them and what is behind them; and unto God affairs return.

O ye who believe! bow down and adore, and serve your Lord, and do well, haply ye may prosper; and fight strenuously for God, as is His due. He has elected you, and has not put upon you any hindrance by your religion,—the faith of your father Abraham. He has named you Muslims before and in this (book), that the Apostle may be a witness against you, and that ye may be witnesses against men.

Be ye then steadfast in prayer, and give alms, and hold fast by God; He is your sovereign, and an excellent sovereign, and an excellent help!

The Chapter of Believers.

(XXIII. Mecca.)

In the name of the merciful and compassionate God.

Prosperous are the believers who in their prayers are humble, and who from vain talk turn aside, and who in almsgiving are active. [5] And who guard their private parts—except for their wives or what their right hands possess for then, verily, they are not to be blamed;—but whoso craves aught beyond that, they are the transgressors—and who observe their trusts and covenants, and who guard well their prayers: [10] these are the heirs who shall inherit Paradise; they shall dwell therein for aye!

We have created man from an extract of clay; then we made him a clot in a sure depository; then we created the clot congealed blood, and we created the congealed blood a morsel; then we created the morsel bone, and we clothed the bone with flesh; then we produced it another creation; and blessed be God, the best of creators[1]!

[15] Then shall ye after that surely die; then shall ye on the day of resurrection be raised.

And we have created above you seven roads[2]; nor are we heedless of the creation.

And we send down from the heaven water by measure, and we make it rest in the earth; but, verily, we are able to take it away; and we produce for you thereby gardens of palms and grapes wherein ye have many fruits, and whence ye eat.

[20] And a tree growing out of Mount Sinai which produces oil, and a condiment for those who eat.

And, verily, ye have a lesson in the cattle; we give you to drink of what is in their bellies; and ye have therein many advantages, and of them ye eat, and on them and on ships ye are borne!

We sent Noah unto his people, and he said, 'O my people! worship God, ye have no god but Him; do ye then not fear?'

Said the chiefs of those who misbelieved among his people, 'This is nothing but a mortal like yourselves who wishes to have preference over you, and had God pleased He would have sent angels; we have not heard of this amongst our fathers of yore:
[25] he is nothing but a man possessed; let him bide then for a season.'

Said he, 'Help me, for they call me liar!'

And we inspired him, 'Make the ark under

---

[1] See Part I, p. 126, note 2.

[2] That is, 'seven heavens.'

our eyes and inspiration; and when the oven boils over, conduct into it of every kind two, with thy family, except him of them against whom the word has passed; and do not address me for those who do wrong, verily, they are to be drowned!

'But when thou art settled, thou and those with thee in the ark, say, "Praise belongs to God, who saved us from the unjust people!"

[30] 'And say, "My Lord! make me to alight in a blessed alighting-place, for Thou art the best of those who cause men to alight!"' Verily, in that is a sign, and, verily, we were trying them.

Then we raised up after them another generation; and we sent amongst them a prophet of themselves (saying), 'Serve God, ye have no god but He; will ye then not fear?'

Said the chiefs of his people who misbelieved, and called the meeting of the last day a lie, and to whom we gave enjoyment in the life of this world, 'This is only a mortal like yourselves, who eats of what ye eat, [35] and drinks of what ye drink; and if ye obey a mortal like yourselves, verily, ye will then be surely losers! Does he promise you that when ye are dead, and have become dust and bones, that then ye will be brought forth?

'Away, away with what ye are threatened,—there is only our life in the world! We die and we live, and we shall not be raised! [40] He is only a man who forges against God a lie. And we believe not in him!'

Said he, 'My Lord! help me, for they call me liar!' He said, 'Within a little they will surely awake repenting!'

And the noise seized them deservedly; and we

made them as rubbish borne by a torrent; so, away with the unjust people!

Then we raised up after them other generations.

[45] No nation can anticipate its appointed time, nor keep it back.

Then we sent our apostles one after another. Whenever its apostle came to any nation they called him a liar; and we made some to follow others; and we made them legends; away then with a people who do not believe!

Then we sent Moses and his brother Aaron with our signs, and with plain authority to Pharaoh and his chiefs, but they were too big with pride, and were a haughty people.

And they said, 'Shall we believe two mortals like ourselves, when their people are servants of ours?'

[50] So they called them liars, and were of those who perished.

And we gave Moses the Book, that haply they might be guided.

And we made the son of Mary and his mother a sign; and we lodged them both on a high place, furnished with security and a spring.

O ye apostles! eat of the good things and do right; verily, what ye do I know!

And, verily, this nation[1] of yours is one nation, and I am your Lord; so fear me.

[55] And they have become divided as to their affair amongst themselves into sects[2], each party

[1] Or, 'religion.'

[2] Literally, 'into Scriptures,' i.e. into sects, each appealing to a particular book.

rejoicing in what they have themselves. So leave them in their flood (of error) for a time.

Do they reckon that that of which we grant them such an extent, of wealth and children, we hasten to them as good things—nay, but they do not perceive!

Verily, those who shrink with terror at their Lord, [60] and those who in the signs of their Lord believe, and those who with their Lord join none, and those who give what they do give while their hearts are afraid that they unto their Lord will return,—these hasten to good things and are first to gain the same. But we will not oblige a soul beyond its capacity; for with us is a book that utters the truth, and they shall not be wronged.

[65] Nay, their hearts are in a flood (of error) at this, and they have works beside this which they do[1]. Until we catch the affluent ones amongst them with the torment; then lo! they cry for aid.

Cry not for aid to-day! verily, against us ye will not be helped. My signs were recited to you, but upon your heels did ye turn back, big with pride at it[2], in vain discourse by night.

[70] Is it that they did not ponder over the words, whether that has come to them which came not to their fathers of yore? Or did they not know their apostle, that they thus deny him? Or do they say, 'He is possessed by a *g*inn?' Nay, he came to them with the truth, and most of them are averse from the truth.

But if the truth were to follow their lusts, the

---

[1] I.e. their works are far different to the good works just described.

[2] At their possession of the Kaabah. The Qurâi*s* are meant.

heavens and the earth would be corrupted with all who in them are!—Nay, we brought them their reminder, but they from their reminder turn aside.

Or dost thou ask them for a tribute? but the tribute of thy Lord is better, for He is the best of those who provide.

[75] And, verily, thou dost call them to a right way; but, verily, those who believe not in the hereafter from the way do veer.

But if we had mercy on them, and removed the distress[1] they have, they would persist in their rebellion, blindly wandering on!

And we caught them with the torment[2], but they did not abase themselves before their Lord, nor did they humble themselves; until we opened for them a door with grievous torment, then lo! they are in despair.

[80] He it is who produced for you hearing, and sight, and minds,—little is it that ye thank. And He it is who created you in the earth, and unto Him shall ye be gathered. And He it is who gives you life and death: and His is the alternation of the night and the day; have ye then no sense?

Nay, but they said like that which those of yore did say.

They said, 'What! when we have become earth and bones, are we then going to be raised? [85] We have been promised this, and our fathers too, before;—this is naught but old folks' tales!'

Say, 'Whose is the earth and those who are therein, if ye but know?'

---

[1] The famine which the Meccans suffered; and which was attributed to Mohammed's denunciations.

[2] Their defeat at Bedr.

They will say, 'God's.' Say, 'Do ye not then mind?'

Say, 'Who is Lord of the seven heavens, and Lord of the mighty throne?'

They will say, 'God.' Say, 'Do ye not then fear?'

[90] Say, 'In whose hand is the dominion of everything; He succours but is not succoured,—if ye did but know?'

They will say, 'God's.' Say, 'Then how can ye be so infatuated?'

Nay, we have brought them the truth, but, verily, they are liars!

God never took a son, nor was there ever any god with Him;—then each god would have gone off with what he had created, and some would have exalted themselves over others,—celebrated be His praises above what they attribute (to Him)!

He who knows the unseen and the visible, exalted be He above what they join with Him!

[95] Say, 'My Lord! if Thou shouldst show me what they are threatened,—my Lord! then place me not amongst the unjust people.'

Repel evil by what is better[1]. We know best what they attribute (to thee). And say, 'My Lord! I seek refuge in Thee from the incitings of the devils; [100] and I seek refuge in Thee from their presence!'

Until when death comes to any one of them he says, 'My Lord! send ye me back[2], haply I may do right in that which I have left!'

---

[1] I. e. by doing good for evil, provided that the cause of Islâm suffers nothing from it.

[2] I. e. back to life. The plural is used 'by way of respect,' say the commentators.

Not so!—a mere word he speaks!—but behind them is a bar until the day they shall be raised.

And when the trumpet shall be blown, and there shall be no relation between them on that day, nor shall they beg of each other then!

[105] And he whose scales are heavy,—they are the prosperous. But he whose scales are light,—these are they who lose themselves, in hell to dwell for aye! The fire shall scorch their faces, and they shall curl their lips therein! 'Were not my signs recited to you? and ye said that they were lies!' They say, 'Our Lord! our misery overcame us, and we were a people who did err! Our Lord! take us out therefrom, and if we return[1], then shall we be unjust.'

[110] He will say, 'Go ye away into it and speak not to me!'

Verily, there was a sect of my servants who said, Our Lord! we believe, so pardon us, and have mercy upon us, for Thou art the best of the merciful ones.'

And ye took them for a jest until ye forgat my reminder and did laugh thereat. Verily, I have recompensed them this day for their patience; verily, they are happy now.

He will say, 'How long a number of years did ye tarry on earth?' [115] They will say, 'We tarried a day or part of a day, but ask the Numberers[2].'

He will say, 'Ye have only tarried a little, were ye but to know it. Did ye then reckon that we created you for sport, and that to us ye would not return?' But exalted be God, the true; there is no god but He, the Lord of the noble throne! and

[1] To our evil ways.

[2] That is, the recording angels.

whoso calls upon another god with God has no proof of it, but, verily, his account is with his Lord; verily, the misbelievers shall not prosper. And say, 'Lord, pardon and be merciful, for Thou art the best of the merciful ones!'

THE CHAPTER OF LIGHT.

(XXIV. Medînah.)

IN the name of the merciful and compassionate God.

A chapter which we have sent down and determined, and have sent down therein manifest signs; haply ye may be mindful.

The whore and the whoremonger. Scourge each of them with a hundred stripes, and do not let pity for them take hold of you in God's religion, if ye believe in God and the last day; and let a party of the believers witness their torment. And the whoremonger shall marry none but a whore or an idolatress; and the whore shall none marry but an adulterer or an idolater; God has prohibited this to the believers; but those who cast (imputations) on chaste women and then do not bring four witnesses, scourge them with eighty stripes, and do not receive any testimony of theirs ever, for these are the workers of abomination. [5] Except such as repent after that and act aright, for, verily, God is forgiving and compassionate.

And those who cast (imputation) on their wives and have no witnesses except themselves, then the testimony of one of them shall be to testify four times that, by God, he is of those who speak the truth; and the fifth testimony shall be that the curse of God shall be on him if he be of those who lie. And it shall avert the punishment from her if she bears testimony four times that, by God, he is of those who lie; and the fifth that the wrath of God shall be on her if he be of those who speak the truth.

[10] And were it not for God's grace upon you and His mercy, and that God is relenting, wise . . .[1]

Verily, those who bring forward the lie, a band of you,—reckon it not as an evil for you, nay, it is good for you; every man of them shall have what he has earned of sin; and he of them who managed to aggravate it, for him is mighty woe[2].

Why did not, when ye heard it, the believing men and believing women think good in themselves, and say, 'This is an obvious lie?' Why did they not bring four witnesses to it? but since they did not bring the witnesses, then they in God's eyes are

[1] He would punish you.

[2] This passage and what follows refers to the scandal about Mohammed's favourite wife Ayesha, who, having been accidentally left behind when the prophet and his followers were starting at night on an expedition, in the sixth year of the Hi*g*rah, was brought on to the camp in the morning by Zafwân ibn de Mu'ha*ll*al: this gave rise to rumours derogatory to Ayesha's character, which these verses are intended to refute. Ayesha never forgave those who credited the reports against her innocence, and 'Ali, who had spoken in a disparaging manner of her on the occasion, so seriously incurred her displeasure that she contrived to bring about the ruin of his family, and the murder of his two sons Hasan and Husein; the principal parties concerned in the actual spread of the calumny were punished with the fourscore stripes above ordained, with the exception of the ringlèader, Abdallah ibn Ubbâi, who was too important a person to be so treated.

the liars. And but for God's grace upon you, and His mercy in this world and the next, there would have touched you, for that which ye spread abroad, mighty woe. When ye reported it with your tongues, and spake with your mouths what ye had no knowledge of, and reckoned it a light thing, while in God's eyes it was grave.

[15] And why did ye not say when ye heard it, 'It is not for us to speak of this? Celebrated be His praises, this is a mighty calumny!'

God admonishes you that ye return not to the like of it ever, if ye be believers; and God manifests to you the signs, for God is knowing, wise.

Verily, those who love that scandal should go abroad amongst those who believe, for them is grievous woe in this world and the next; for God knows, but ye do not know.

[20] And but for God's grace upon you, and His mercy, and that God is kind and compassionate . . . !

O ye who believe! follow not the footsteps of Satan, for he who follows the footsteps of Satan, verily, he bids you sin and do wrong; and but for God's grace upon you and His mercy, not one of you would be ever pure; but God purifies whom He will, for God both hears and knows. And let not those amongst you who have plenty and ample means swear that they will not give aught to their kinsman and the poor[1] and those who have fled their homes in God's way, but let them pardon and pass it over. Do ye not like God to forgive you? and God is forgiving, compassionate.

[1] Abu bekr had sworn not to do anything more for a relation of his, named Mis/a'h, who had taken part in spreading the reports against Ayesha.

Verily, those who cast imputations on chaste women who are negligent but believing shall be cursed in this world and the next; and for them is mighty woe. The day when their tongues and hands and feet shall bear witness against them of what they did, on [25] that day God will pay them their just due; and they shall know that God, He is the plain truth.

The vile women to the vile men, and the vile men to the vile women; and the good women to the good men, and the good men to the good women: these are clear of what they say to them — forgiveness and a noble provision!

O ye who believe! enter not into houses which are not your own houses, until ye have asked leave and saluted the people thereof, that is better for you; haply ye may be mindful. And if ye find no one therein, then do not enter them until permission is given you, and if it be said to you, 'Go back!' then go back, it is purer for you; for God of what ye do doth know. It is no crime against you that ye enter uninhabited houses,—a convenience for you;—and God knows what ye show and what ye hide.

[30] Say to the believers that they cast down their looks and guard their private parts; that is purer for them; verily, God is well aware of what they do.

And say to the believing women that they cast down their looks and guard their private parts, and display not their ornaments, except those which are outside; and let them pull their kerchiefs over their bosoms and not display their ornaments save to their husbands and fathers, or the fathers of their husbands, or their sons, or the sons of their husbands, or their brothers, or their brothers' sons, or their sisters' sons, or their women, or what their right hands possess, or their male attendants who are incapable[1], or to children who do not note women's nakedness; and that they beat not with their feet that their hidden ornaments may be known[2];—but turn ye all repentant to God, O ye believers! haply ye may prosper.

And marry the single amongst you, and the righteous among your servants and your handmaidens. If they be poor, God will enrich them of His grace, for God both comprehends and knows. And let those who cannot find a match, until God enriches them of His grace, keep chaste.

And such of those whom your right hands possess as crave a writing[3], write it for them, if ye know any good in them, and give them of the wealth of God which He has given you. And do not compel your slave girls to prostitution, if they desire to keep continent, in order to crave the goods of the life of this world; but he who does compel them, then, verily, God after they are compelled is forgiving, compassionate[4].

Now have we sent down to you manifest signs, and the like of those who have passed away before you[5], and as an admonition to those who fear.

[1] Or, according to some, of deficient intellect.

[2] I. e. they are not to tinkle their bangles or ankle-rings.

[3] I. e. a document allowing them to redeem themselves on payment of a certain sum.

[4] Abdallah ibn Ubbâi, mentioned in Part II, p. 74, note 2, had six slave girls whom he compelled to live by prostitution. One of them complained to Mohammed, whence this passage.

[5] I. e. like the stories of Joseph, Part I, p. 221, and the Virgin

[35] God is the light of the heavens and the earth; His light is as a niche in which is a lamp, and the lamp is in a glass, the glass is as though it were a glittering star; it is lit from a blessed tree, an olive neither of the east nor of the west, the oil of which would well-nigh give light though no fire touched it,—light upon light!—God guides to His light whom He pleases; and God strikes out parables for men, and God all things doth know.

In the houses God has permitted to be reared and His name to be mentioned therein—His praises are celebrated therein mornings and evenings.

Men whom neither merchandize nor selling divert from the remembrance of God and steadfastness in prayer and giving alms, who fear a day when hearts and eyes shall be upset;—that God may recompense them for the best that they have done, and give them increase of His grace; for God provides whom He pleases without count.

But those who misbelieve, their works are like the mirage in a plain, the thirsty counts it water till when he comes to it he finds nothing, but he finds that God is with him; and He will pay him his account, for God is quick to take account.

[40] Or like darkness on a deep sea, there covers it a wave above which is a wave, above which is a cloud,—darknesses one above the other,—when one puts out his hand he can scarcely see it; for he to whom God has given no light, he has no light.

Mary, Part II, p. 29, both of whom, like Ayesha, were accused of incontinence, and miraculously proved innocent.

Hast thou not seen that God,—all who are in the heavens and the earth celebrate His praises, and the birds too spreading out their wings; each one knows its prayer and its praise, and God knows what they do?

Hast thou not seen that God drives the clouds, and then re-unites them, and then accumulates them, and thou mayest see the rain coming forth from their midst; and He sends down from the sky mountains[1] with hail therein, and He makes it fall on whom He pleases, and He turns it from whom He pleases; the flashing of His lightning well-nigh goes off with their sight?

God interchanges the night and the day; verily, in that is a lesson to those endowed with sight.

And God created every beast from water, and of them is one that walks upon its belly, and of them one that walks upon two feet, and of them one that walks upon four. God creates what He pleases; verily, God is mighty over all!

[45] Now have we sent down manifest signs, and God guides whom He pleases unto the right way.

They will say, 'We believe in God and in the Apostle, and we obey.' Then a sect of them turned their backs after that, and they are not believers.

And when they are called to God and His Apostle to judge between them, lo! a sect of them do turn aside. But had the right been on their side they would have come to him submissively enough.

Is there a sickness in their hearts, or do they doubt, or do they fear lest God and His Apostle

[1] I. e. masses of cloud as large as mountains.

should deal unfairly by them?—Nay, it is they who are unjust.

[50] The speech of the believers, when they are called to God and His Apostle to judge between them, is only to say, 'We hear and we obey;' and these it is who are the prosperous, for whoso obeys God and His Apostle and dreads God and fears Him, these it is who are the happy.

They swear by God with their most strenuous oath that hadst Thou ordered them they would surely go forth. Say, 'Do not swear—reasonable obedience[1]; verily, God knows what ye do.'

Say, 'Obey God and obey the Apostle; but if ye turn your backs he has only his burden to bear, and ye have only your burden to bear. But if ye obey him, ye are guided; but the Apostle has only his plain message to deliver.'

God promises those of you who believe and do right that He will give them the succession in the earth as He gave the succession to those before them, and He will establish for them their religion which He has chosen for them, and to give them, after their fear, safety in exchange;—they shall worship me, they shall not associate aught with me: but whoso disbelieves after that, those it is who are the sinners.

[55] And be steadfast in prayer and give alms and obey the Apostle, haply ye may obtain mercy.

Do not reckon that those who misbelieve can

---

[1] The construction of the original is vague, and the commentators themselves make but little of it. The most approved rendering, however, seems to be either that obedience is the reasonable course to pursue, and not the mere swearing to obey.

frustrate (God) in the earth, for their resort is the Fire, and an ill journey shall it be.

O ye who believe! let those whom your right hands possess, and those amongst you who have not reached puberty, ask leave of you three times: before the prayer of dawn, and when ye put off your clothes at noon, and after the evening prayer; —three times of privacy for you[1]: there is no crime on either you or them after these while ye are continually going one about the other. Thus does God explain to you His signs, for God is knowing, wise.

And when your children reach puberty let them ask leave as those before them asked leave. Thus does God explain to you His signs, for God is knowing, wise.

And those women who have stopped (child-bearing), who do not hope for a match, it is no crime on them that they put off their clothes so as not to display their ornaments; but that they abstain is better for them, for God both hears and knows.

[60] There is no hindrance to the blind, and no hindrance to the lame, and no hindrance to the sick, and none upon yourselves that you eat from your houses, or the houses of your fathers, or the houses of your mothers, or the houses of your brothers, or the houses of your sisters, or the houses of your paternal uncles, or the houses of your paternal aunts, or the houses of your maternal uncles,

[1] I.e. at the times when persons are undressed, namely, to rise in the morning, to sleep at noon, and to retire for the night, their attendants and children must not come in without first asking permission.

or the houses of your maternal aunts, or what ye possess the keys of, or of your friend, there is no crime on you that ye eat all together or separately[1].

And when ye enter houses then greet each other with a salutation from God, blessed and good. Thus does God explain to you His signs, haply ye may understand.

Only those are believers who believe in God and His Apostle, and when they are with Him upon public business go not away until they have asked his leave; verily, those who ask thy leave they it is who believe in God and His Apostle.

But when they ask thy leave for any of their own concerns, then give leave to whomsoever thou wilt of them, and ask pardon for them of God; verily, God is forgiving and merciful.

Make not the calling of the Apostle amongst yourselves like your calling one to the other[2]; God knows those of you who withdraw themselves covertly. And let those who disobey his order beware lest there befall them some trial or there befall them grievous woe. Ay, God's is what is in the heavens and the earth, He knows what ye are at; and the day ye shall be sent back to Him then He will inform you of what ye have done, for God all things doth know.

[1] The Arabs in Mohammed's time were superstitiously scrupulous about eating in any one's house but their own.

[2] That is, do not address the prophet without some respectful title.

The Chapter of the Discrimination [1].

(XXV. Mecca.)

In the name of the merciful and compassionate God.

Blessed be He who sent down the Discrimination to His servant that he might be unto the world a warner; whose is the kingdom of the heavens and the earth, and who has not taken to Himself a son, and who has no partner in His kingdom, and created everything, and then decreed it determinately! And they take beside Him gods who create not aught, but are themselves created, and cannot control for themselves harm or profit, and cannot control death, or life, or resurrection.

[5] And those who misbelieve say, 'This is nothing but a lie which he has forged, and another people hath helped him at it;' but they have wrought an injustice and a falsehood.

And they say, 'Old folks' tales, which he has got written down while they are dictated to him morning and evening.'

Say, 'He sent it down who knows the secret in the heavens and the earth; verily, He is ever forgiving, merciful!'

And they say, 'What ails this prophet that he eats food and walks in the markets?—unless there be sent down to him an angel and be a warner with him . . . . Or there be thrown to him a treasury

---

[1] In Arabic Al Furqân, which is one of the names of the Qur'ân.

or he have a garden to eat therefrom . . . . !' and the unjust say, 'Ye only follow an infatuated man.'

[10] See how they strike out for thee parables, and err, and cannot find a way.

Blessed be He who, if He please, can make for thee better than that, gardens beneath which rivers flow, and can make for thee castles!

Nay, but they call the Hour a lie; but we have prepared for those who call the Hour a lie a blaze: when it seizes them from a far-off place they shall hear its raging and roaring; and when they are thrown into a narrow place thereof, fastened together, they shall call there for destruction.

[15] Call not to-day for one destruction, but call for many destructions!

Say, 'Is that better or the garden of eternity which was promised to those who fear—which is ever for them a recompense and a retreat?' They shall have therein what they please, to dwell therein for aye: that is of thy Lord a promise to be demanded.

And the day He shall gather them and what they served beside God, and He shall say, 'Was it ye who led my servants here astray, or did they err from the way?'

They shall say, 'Celebrated be Thy praise, it was not befitting for us to take any patrons but Thee; but Thou didst give them and their fathers enjoyment until they forgot the Reminder and were a lost people!'

[20] And now have they proved you liars for what ye say, and they[1] cannot ward off or help.

[1] Another reading of the text is, 'ye cannot.'

And he of you who does wrong we will make him taste great torment.

We have not sent before thee any messengers but that they ate food and walked in the markets; but we have made some of you a trial to others: will ye be patient? thy Lord doth ever look.

And those who do not hope to meet us say, 'Unless the angels be sent down to us, or we see our Lord....!' They are too big with pride in their souls and they have exceeded with a great excess!

The day they shall see the angels,—no glad tidings on that day for the sinners, and they shall say, 'It is rigorously forbidden[1]!'

[25] And we will go on to the works which they have done, and make them like motes in a sunbeam scattered! The fellows of Paradise on that day shall be in a better abiding-place and a better noonday rest.

The day the heavens shall be cleft asunder with the clouds, and the angels shall be sent down descending.

The true kingdom on that day shall belong to the Merciful, and it shall be a hard day for the misbelievers.

And the day when the unjust shall bite his hands[2] and say, 'O, would that I had taken a way with the Apostle[3]! [30] O, woe is me! would that I had

[1] The ancient Arabs used this formula when they met an enemy during a sacred month, and the person addressed would then abstain from hostilities. The sinners in this passage are supposed to use it to the angels, but without effect. Some commentators take it to mean that the 'glad tidings' are 'rigorously forbidden,' and that the angels are the speakers.

[2] See Chapter III, verse 115.

[3] That is, followed him.

not taken such a one for a friend now, for he did lead me astray from the Reminder after it had come to me, for Satan leaves man in the lurch!'

The Apostle said, 'O my Lord! verily, my people have taken this Qur'ân to be obsolete!'

Thus have we made for every prophet an enemy from among the sinners; but thy Lord is good guide and helper enough.

Those who misbelieve said, 'Unless the Qur'ân be sent down to him all at once[1].... !'—thus—that we may stablish thy heart therewith, did we reveal it piecemeal[2]. [35] Nor shall they come to thee with a parable without our bringing thee the truth and the best interpretation.

They who shall be gathered upon their faces to hell,—these are in the worst place, and err most from the path.

And we did give to Moses the Book, and place with him his brother Aaron as a minister; and we said, 'Go ye to the people who say our signs are lies, for we will destroy them with utter destruction.'

And the people of Noah, when they said the apostles were liars, we drowned them, and we made them a sign for men; and we prepared for the unjust a grievous woe.

[40] And 'Âd and Thamûd and the people of ar Rass[3], and many generations between them.

---

[1] Like the Pentateuch and Gospels, which were revealed all at once, according to the Mohammedan tradition.

[2] Or it may be rendered, 'slowly and distinctly;' the whole revelation of the Qur'ân extends over a period of twenty-three years.

[3] The commentators do not know where to place ar Rass; some say it was a city in Yamâmah, others that it was a well near Midian, and others again that it was in 'Ha*dh*ramaut.

For each one have we struck out parables, and each one have we ruined with utter ruin.

Why, they[1] have come past the cities which were rained on with an evil rain; have they not seen them?—nay, they do not hope to be raised up again.

And when they saw thee they only took thee for a jest, 'Is this he whom God has sent as an apostle? he well-nigh leads us astray from our gods, had we not been patient about them.' But they shall know, when they see the torment, who errs most from the path. [45] Dost thou consider him who takes his lusts for his god? wilt thou then be in charge over him? or dost thou reckon that most of them will hear or understand? they are only like the cattle, nay, they err more from the way.

Hast thou not looked to thy Lord how He prolongs the shadow? but had He willed He would have made it stationary; then we make the sun a guide thereto, then we contract it towards us with an easy contraction.

And He it is who made the night for a garment; and sleep for repose, and made the day for men to rise up again. [50] And He it is who sent the winds with glad tidings before His mercy; and we send down from the heavens pure water, to quicken therewith the dead country, and to give it for drink to what we have created,—the cattle and many folk.

We have turned it[2] in various ways amongst them that they may remember; though most men

---

[1] That is, the idolatrous Meccans; see Part I, p. 249, note 2.

[2] That is, either the Qur'ân, cf. Part II, p. 5, line 25; or the words may be rendered, 'We distribute it' (the rain), &c.

refuse aught but to misbelieve. But, had we pleased, we would have sent in every city a warner. So obey not the unbelievers and fight strenuously with them in many a strenuous fight.

[55] He it is who has let loose the two seas, this one sweet and fresh, that one bitter and pungent, and has made between them a rigorous prohibition.

And He it is who has created man from water, and has made for him blood relationship and marriage relationship; for thy Lord is mighty.

Yet they worship beside God what can neither profit them nor harm them; but he who misbelieves in his Lord backs up (the devil).

We have only sent thee to give glad tidings and to warn. Say, 'I ask you not for it a hire unless one please to take unto his Lord a way[1].' [60] And rely thou upon the Living One who dies not; and celebrate His praise, for He knows well enough about the thoughts of His servants. He who created the heavens and the earth, and what is between them, in six days, and then made for the throne; the Merciful One, ask concerning Him of One who is aware.

And when it is said, 'Adore ye the Merciful!' they say, 'What is the Merciful? shall we adore what thou dost order us?' and it only increases their aversion.

Blessed be He who placed in the heavens zodiacal signs, and placed therein the lamp and an illuminating moon!

And He it is who made the night and the day

---

[1] That is, that if a man chose to expend anything for the cause of God he can do so.

alternating for him who desires to remember or who wishes to be thankful.

And the servants of the Merciful are those who walk upon the earth lowly, and when the ignorant address them, say, 'Peace!' [65] And those who pass the night adoring their Lord and standing[1]; and those who say, 'O our Lord! turn from us the torment of hell; verily, its torments are persistent; verily, they are evil as an abode and a station.'

And those who when they spend are neither extravagant nor miserly, but who ever take their stand between the two; and who call not upon another god with God; and kill not the soul which God has prohibited save deservedly[2]; and do not commit fornication: for he who does that shall meet with a penalty; doubled for him shall be the torment on the resurrection day, and he shall be therein for aye despised. [70] Save he who turns again and believes and does a righteous work; for, as to those, God will change their evil deeds to good, for God is ever forgiving, merciful.

And he who turns again and does right, verily, he turns again to God repentant.

And those who do not testify falsely; and when they pass by frivolous discourse, pass by it honourably; and those who when they are reminded of the signs of their Lord do not fall down thereat deaf and blind; and those who say, 'Our Lord! grant us from our wives and seed that which may cheer our eyes, and make us models to the pious!'

[75] These shall be rewarded with a high place[3] for that they were patient: and they shall meet

[1] For prayer. [2] See Part I, p. 135, note 1. [3] In Paradise.

therein with salutation and peace,—to dwell therein for aye; a good abode and station shall it be!

Say, 'My Lord cares not for you though you should not call (on Him); and ye have called (the Apostle) a liar, but it shall be (a punishment) which ye cannot shake off.'

The Chapter of the Poets.

(XXVI. Mecca.)

In the name of the merciful and compassionate God.

T. S. M. Those are the signs of the perspicuous Book; haply thou art vexing thyself to death that they will not be believers!

If we please we will send down upon them from the heaven a sign, and their necks shall be humbled thereto. But there comes not to them any recent Reminder from the Merciful One that they do not turn away from. [5] They have called (thee) liar! but there shall come to them a message of that at which they mocked.

Have they not looked to the earth, how we caused to grow therein of every noble kind? verily, in that is a sign; but most of them will never be believers! but, verily, thy Lord He is mighty and merciful.

And when thy Lord called Moses (saying), 'Come to the unjust people, [10] to the people of Pharaoh, will they not fear?' Said he, 'My Lord! verily, I fear that they will call me liar; and my breast is straitened, and my tongue is not fluent; send then unto Aaron[1], for they have a crime against me, and I fear that they may kill me[2].' Said He, 'Not so; but go with our signs, verily, we are with you listening.

[15] 'And go to Pharaoh and say, "Verily, we are the apostles of the Lord of the worlds (to tell thee to) send with us the children of Israel."'

And he said, 'Did we not bring thee up amongst us as a child? and thou didst dwell amongst us for years of thy life; and thou didst do thy deed which thou hast done, and thou art of the ungrateful!'

Said he, 'I did commit this, and I was of those who erred.

[20] 'And I fled from you when I feared you, and my Lord granted me judgment, and made me one of His messengers; and this is the favour thou hast obliged me with, that thou hast enslaved the children of Israel!'

Said Pharaoh, 'Who is the Lord of the worlds?' Said he, 'The Lord of the heavens and the earth and what is between the two, if ye are but sure.'

Said he to those about him, 'Do ye not listen?'
[25] Said he, 'Your Lord and the Lord of your fathers of yore!'

Said he, 'Verily, your apostle who is sent to you is surely mad!'

Said he, 'The Lord of the east and of the west, and of what is between the two, if ye had but sense!'

Said he, 'If thou dost take a god besides Me I will surely make thee one of the imprisoned!'

Said he, 'What, if I come to thee with something obvious?'

---

[1] That he may be my minister.

[2] The slaying of the Egyptian.

[30] Said he, 'Bring it, if thou art of those who
tell the truth!'

And he threw down his rod, and, behold, it was an
obvious serpent! and he plucked out his hand, and,
behold, it was white to the spectators!

He[1] said to the chiefs around him, 'Verily, this is
a knowing sorcerer, he desires to turn you out of
your land! what is it then ye bid?'

[35] They said, 'Give him and his brother some
hope, and send into the cities to collect and bring
to thee every knowing sorcerer.'

And the sorcerers assembled at the appointed
time on a stated day, and it was said to the people,
'Are ye assembled? haply we may follow the sor-
cerers if we gain the upper hand.'

[40] And when the sorcerers came they said to
Pharaoh, 'Shall we, verily, have a hire if we gain
the upper hand?' Said he, 'Yes; and, verily, ye shall
then be of those who are nigh (my throne).' And
Moses said to them, 'Throw down what ye have to
throw down.' So they threw down their ropes and
their rods and said, 'By Pharaoh's might, verily, we
it is who shall gain the upper hand!'

And Moses threw down his rod, and, lo, it
swallowed up what they falsely devised!

[45] And the sorcerers threw themselves down,
adoring. Said they, 'We believe in the Lord of
the worlds, the Lord of Moses and Aaron!' Said
he, 'Do ye believe in Him ere I give you leave?
Verily, he is your chief who has taught you sorcery,
but soon ye shall know. I will surely cut off your
hands and your feet from opposite sides, and I will
crucify you all together!'

[1] Pharaoh.

[50] They said, 'No harm; verily, unto our Lord do we return! verily, we hope that our Lord will forgive us our sins, for we are the first of believers!'

And we inspired Moses, 'Journey by night with my servants; verily, ye are pursued.'

And Pharaoh sent into the cities to collect; 'Verily, these are a small company. [55] And, verily, they are enraged with us; but we are a multitude, wary!

'Turn them out of gardens and springs, and treasuries, and a noble station!'—thus,—and we made the children of Israel to inherit them.

[60] And they followed them at dawn; and when the two hosts saw each other, Moses' companions said, 'Verily, we are overtaken!' Said he, 'Not so; verily, with me is my Lord, He will guide me.'

And we inspired Moses, 'Strike with thy rod the sea;' and it was cleft asunder, and each part was like a mighty mountain. And then we brought the others. [65] And we saved Moses and those with him all together; then we drowned the others; and that is a sign: but most of them will never be believers! And, verily, thy Lord He is mighty, merciful.

And recite to them the story of Abraham; [70] when he said to his father and his people, 'What do ye serve?' They said, 'We serve idols, and we are still devoted to them. He said, 'Can they hear you when ye call, or profit you, or harm?'

They said, 'No; but we found our fathers doing thus.' [75] He said, 'Have ye considered what ye have been serving, ye and your fathers before you? Verily, they are foes to me, save only the Lord of the worlds, who created me and guides me, and who gives me food and drink. [80] And when I am sick He heals me; He who will kill me, and then bring me to life; and who I hope will forgive me my sins on the day of judgment! Lord, grant me judgment, and let me reach the righteous; and give me a tongue of good report amongst posterity; [85] and make me of the heirs of the paradise of pleasure; and pardon my father, verily, he is of those who err; and disgrace me not on the day when they are raised up again; the day when wealth shall profit not, nor sons, but only he who comes to God with a sound heart. [90] And paradise shall be brought near to the pious; and hell shall be brought forth to those who go astray, and it shall be said to them, "Where is what ye used to worship beside God? can they help you, or get help themselves?" And they shall fall headlong into it, they and those who have gone astray, [95] and the hosts of Iblîs all together!

'They shall say, while they quarrel therein, "By God! we were surely in an obvious error, when we made you equal to the Lord of the worlds! but it was only sinners who led us astray. [100] But we have no intercessors and no warm friend; but had we a turn we would be of the believers."'—Verily, in that is a sign, but most of them will never be believers; and, verily, thy Lord He is mighty and merciful.

[105] The people of Noah said the apostles were liars, when their brother Noah said to them, 'Will ye not fear? verily, I am a faithful apostle to you; then fear God and obey me. I do not ask you for it any hire; my hire is only with the Lord of the worlds. [110] So fear God and obey me.' They

said, 'Shall we believe in thee, when the reprobates follow thee?' He said, 'I did not know what they were doing; their account is only with my Lord, if ye but perceive. And I am not one to drive awav the believers, [115] I am only a plain warner.'

They said, 'Verily, if thou desist not, O Noah! thou shalt surely be of those who are stoned!' Said he, 'My Lord! verily, my people call me liar; open between me and between them an opening, and save me and those of the believers who are with me!'

So we saved him and those with him in the laden ark, [120] then we drowned the rest; verily, in that is a sign, but most of them will never be believers; and, verily, thy Lord He is mighty and merciful.

And 'Âd called the apostles liars; when their brother Hûd said to them, 'Will ye not fear? [125] Verily, I am to you a faithful apostle; then fear God and obey me. I do not ask you for it any hire; my hire is only with the Lord of the worlds. Do ye build on every height a landmark in sport, and take to works that haply ye may be immortal?

[130] 'And when ye assault ye assault like tyrants; but fear God and obey me; and fear Him who hath given you an extent of cattle and sons, and gardens and springs. [135] Verily, I fear for you the torment of a mighty day!'

They said, 'It is the same to us if thou admonish or art not of those who do admonish; this is nothing but old folks' fictions, for we shall not be tormented!'

And they called him liar! but we destroyed them. Verily, in that is a sign, but most of them will never be believers. [140] And, verily, thy Lord is mighty, merciful.

Thamûd called the apostles liars; when their brother Zâli'h said to them, 'Do ye not fear? verily, I am to you a faithful apostle; so fear God and obey me. [145] I do not ask you for it any hire; my hire is only with the Lord of the worlds. Shall ye be left here in safety with gardens and springs, and corn-fields and palms, the spathes whereof are fine? and ye hew out of the mountains houses skilfully. [150] But fear God and obey me; and obey not the bidding of the extravagant, who do evil in the earth and do not act aright!'

They said, 'Thou art only of the infatuated; thou art but mortal like ourselves; so bring us a sign, if thou be of those who speak the truth!'

[155] He said, 'This she-camel shall have her drink and you your drink on a certain day; but touch her not with evil, or there will seize you the torment of a mighty day!'

But they hamstrung her, and on the morrow they repented; and the torment seized them; verily, in that is a sign; but most of them will never be believers: but verily, thy Lord He is mighty, merciful.

[160] The people of Lot called the apostles liars; when their brother Lot said to them, 'Do ye not fear? verily, I am to you a faithful apostle; then fear God and obey me. I do not ask you for it any hire; my hire is only with the Lord of the worlds. [165] Do ye approach males of all the world and leave what God your Lord has created for you of your wives? nay, but ye are people who transgress!'

They said, 'Surely, if thou dost not desist, O Lot! thou shalt be of those who are expelled!'

Said he, 'Verily, I am of those who hate your deed; my Lord! save me and my people from what they do.'

[170] And we saved him and his people all together, except an old woman amongst those who lingered. Then we destroyed the others; and we rained down upon them a rain; and evil was the rain of those who were warned. Verily, in that is a sign; but most of them will never be believers. [175] And, verily, thy Lord He is mighty, merciful, compassionate.

The fellows of the Grove[1] called the apostles liars; Sho'hâib said to them, 'Will ye not fear? verily, I am to you a faithful apostle, then fear God and obey me. [180] I do not ask you for it any hire; my hire is only with the Lord of the worlds. Give good measure, and be not of those who diminish; and weigh with a fair balance, and do not cheat men of their goods; and waste not the land, despoiling it; and fear Him who created you and the races of yore!' [185] Said they, 'Thou art only of the infatuated; and thou art only a mortal like ourselves; and, verily, we think that thou art surely of the liars; so make a portion of the heaven to fall down upon us, if thou art of those who tell the truth!'

Said he, 'My Lord knows best what ye do!' but they called him liar, and the torment of the day of the shadow seized them; for it was the torment of a mighty day: [190] verily, in that is a sign; but

[1] See Part I, p. 249, note 3.

most of them will never be believers; but, verily, thy Lord He is mighty, merciful!

And, verily, it[1] is a revelation from the Lord of the worlds; the Faithful Spirit came down with it[2] upon thy heart, that thou shouldst be of those who warn;—[195] in plain Arabic language, and, verily, it is (foretold) in the scriptures of yore! Have they not a sign, that the learned men of the children of Israel recognise it[3]? Had we sent it down to any barbarian, and he had read it to them, they would not have believed therein. [200] Thus have we made for it[4] a way into the hearts of the sinners; they will not believe therein until they see the grievous woe! and it shall come to them suddenly while they do not perceive! They will say, 'Shall we be respited?—What! do they wish to hasten on our torment?'

[205] What thinkest thou? if we let them enjoy themselves for years, and then there come to them what they are threatened, that will not avail them which they had to enjoy! But we do not destroy any city without its having warners as a reminder, for we are never unjust.

[210] The devils did not descend therewith; it is not fit work for them; nor are they able to do it. Verily, they are deposed from listening[5]; call not then with God upon other gods, or thou wilt be of the tormented; but warn thy clansmen who are near of kin. [215] And lower[6] thy wing to those of the believers who follow thee; but if they rebel against thee, say, 'Verily, I am clear of what ye

[1] The Qur'ân.
[2] The angel Gabriel.
[3] The Qur'ân.
[4] Infidelity.
[5] See Part I, p. 50.
[6] See Part I, p. 250, note 2.

do,' and rely thou upon the mighty, merciful One, who sees thee when thou dost stand up, and thy posturing amongst those who adore[1]. [220] Verily, He both hears and knows!

Shall I inform you upon whom the devils descend? they descend upon every sinful liar, and impart what they have heard[2]; but most of them are liars.

And the poets do those follow who go astray! [225] Dost thou not see that they wander distraught in every vale? and that they say that which they do not do? save those who believe, and do right, and remember God much, and defend themselves after they are wronged; but those who do wrong shall know with what a turn they shall be turned[3].

The Chapter of the Ant.

(XXVII. Mecca.)

In the name of the merciful and compassionate God.

T.S. Those are the signs of the Qur'ân and the perspicuous Book; a guidance and glad tidings to the believers, who are steadfast at prayer, and give alms, and of the hereafter are sure; verily, those who believe not in the hereafter we have made seemly for them their works, and they shall wander

---

[1] Or, it may be thy going to and fro amongst believers, as Mohammed is reported to have done one night, to see what they were about, and he found the whole settlement 'buzzing like a hornet's nest with the sound of the recitation of the Qur'ân and of their prayers.'

[2] That is, by listening at the door of heaven; see Part I, p. 50, note 2.

[3] That is, in what condition they shall be brought before God.

blindly on! [5] These are they who shall have an evil torment, and they in the hereafter shall be those who most lose! Verily, thou dost meet with this Qur'ân from the wise, the knowing One!

When Moses said to his people, 'Verily, I perceive a fire, I will bring you therefrom news; or I will bring you a burning brand; haply ye may be warmed.' But when he came to it he was called to, 'Blessed be He who is in the fire, and he who is about it! and celebrated be the praises of God, the Lord of the worlds! O Moses! verily, I am God, the mighty, wise; [10] throw down thy staff!' and when he saw it quivering, as though it were a snake, he turned back fleeing, and did not return. 'O Moses! fear not; verily, as for me—apostles fear not with me; save only those who have done wrong and then substitute good for evil; for, verily, I am forgiving, merciful! but put thy hand in thy bosom, it shall come forth white without hurt;—one of nine signs to Pharaoh and his people; verily, they are a people who act abominably.'

And when our signs came to them visibly, they said, 'This is obvious sorcery!' and they gainsaid them—though their souls made sure of them—unjustly, haughtily; but, behold what was the end of the evildoers!

[15] And we gave David and Solomon knowledge; and they both said, 'Praise belongs to God, who hath preferred us over many of His servants who believe!'

And Solomon was David's heir; and said, 'O ye folk! we have been taught the speech of birds, and we have been given everything; verily, this is an obvious grace!'

And assembled for Solomon were his hosts of the *g*inns, and men, and birds, and they were marshalled; until they came upon the valley of the ants. Said an ant, 'O ye ants! go into your dwellings, that Solomon and his hosts crush you not while they do not perceive.'

And he smiled, laughing at her speech, and said, 'O Lord! excite me to be thankful for Thy favour, wherewith Thou hast favoured me and my parents, and to do righteousness which may please Thee; and make me enter into Thy mercy amongst Thy righteous servants!'

[20] And he reviewed the birds, and said, 'How is it I see not the hoopoe? is he then amongst the absent? I will surely torment him with a severe torment; or I will surely slaughter him; or he shall bring me obvious authority.'

And he tarried not long, and said, 'I have compassed what ye compassed not; for I bring you from Sebâ[1] a sure information: verily, I found a woman ruling over them, and she was given all things, and she had a mighty throne; and I found her and her people adoring the sun instead of God, for Satan had made seemly to them their works, and turned them from the path, so that they are not guided. [25] Will they not adore God who brings forth the secrets in the heavens, and knows what they hide and what they manifest?—God, there is no god but He, the Lord of the mighty throne!'

Said he, 'We will see whether thou hast told the truth, or whether thou art of those who lie. Go with this my letter and throw it before them,

[1] The Sheba of the Bible, in the south of the Arabian peninsula.

then turn back away from them, and see what they return.'

Said she, 'O ye chiefs! verily, a noble letter has been thrown before me. [30] It is from Solomon, and, verily, it is, "In the name of the merciful and compassionate God. Do not rise up against me, but come to me resigned!"' She said, 'O ye chiefs! pronounce sentence for me in my affair. I never decide an affair until ye testify for me.'

They said, 'We are endowed with strength, and endowed with keen violence; but the bidding is thine, see then what it is that thou wilt bid.'

She said, 'Verily, kings when they enter a city despoil it, and make the mighty ones of its people the meanest; thus it is they do! [35] So, verily, I am going to send to them a gift, and will wait to see with what the messengers return.'

And when he came to Solomon, he said, 'Do ye proffer me wealth, when what God has given me is better than what He has given you? nay, ye in your gifts rejoice! return to them, for we will surely come to them with hosts which they cannot confront; and we will surely drive them out therefrom mean and made small!'

Said he, 'O ye chiefs! which of you will bring me her throne before they come to me resigned?'

Said a demon of the *g*inns, 'I will bring thee it before thou canst rise up from thy place, for I therein am strong and faithful.'

[40] He who had the knowledge of the Book[1] said, 'I will bring it to thee before thy glance can

[1] The commentators are uncertain as to whether this was 'Âzaf, Solomon's prime minister, or whether it was the prophet '*Hidh*r. or the angel Gabriel, or, indeed, Solomon himself.

turn.' And when he saw it settled down beside him, he said, 'This is of my Lord's grace, that He may try me whether I am grateful or ungrateful, and he who is grateful is only grateful for his own soul, and he who is ungrateful,—verily, my Lord is rich and generous.'

Said he, 'Disguise for her her throne; let us see whether she is guided, or whether she is of those who are not guided.' And when she came it was said, 'Was thy throne like this?' She said, 'It might be it;' and we were given knowledge before her, but we were resigned [1].

But that which she served beside God turned her away; verily, she was of the unbelieving people. And it was said to her, 'Enter the court;' and when she saw it, she reckoned it to be an abyss of water, and she uncovered her legs. Said he, 'Verily, it is a court paved with glass!' [45] Said she, 'My Lord! verily, I have wronged myself, but I am resigned with Solomon to God the Lord of the worlds!'

And we sent unto Thamûd their brother Zâli'h, 'Serve God;' but behold, they were two parties who contended!

Said he, 'O my people! why do ye hasten on evil acts before good deeds? why do ye not ask forgiveness of God? haply ye may obtain mercy.' They said, 'We have taken an augury concerning thee and those who are with thee.' Said he, 'Your augury is in God's hands; nay, but ye are a people who are tried!'

---

[1] Commentators differ as to whether the last words are to be taken as the conclusion of the Queen of Sheba's speech, or as Solomon's comment upon it.

And there were in the city nine persons who despoiled the land and did not right. [50] Said they, 'Swear to each other by God, we will surely fall on him by night and on his people; then we will surely say unto his next of kin, "We witnessed not the destruction of his people, and we do surely tell the truth!"' And they plotted a plot, and we plotted a plot, but they did not perceive. Behold, how was the end of their plot, that we destroyed them and their people all together!

Thus are their houses overturned, for that they were unjust; verily, in that is a sign to people who do know!

But we saved those who believed and who did fear.

[55] And Lot when he said to his people, 'Do ye approach an abominable sin while ye can see? do ye indeed approach men lustfully rather than women? nay! ye are a people who are ignorant.' But the answer of his people was only to say, 'Drive out Lot's family from your city! verily, they are a folk who would keep pure.'

But we saved him and his family except his wife, her we destined to be of those who lingered; and we rained down upon them rain, and evil was the rain of those who were warned.

[60] Say, 'Praise belongs to God; and peace be upon His servants whom He has chosen! Is God best, or what they associate with Him?' He who created the heavens and the earth; and sends down upon you from the heaven water; and we cause to grow therewith gardens fraught with beauty; ye could not cause the trees thereof to grow! Is there a god with God? nay, but they are a people

who make peers with Him! He who made the earth, settled, and placed amongst it rivers; and placed upon it firm mountains; and placed between the two seas a barrier; is there a god with God? nay, but most of them know not! He who answers the distressed when he calls upon Him and removes the evil; and makes you successors in the earth; is there a god with God? little is it that ye are mindful. He who guides you in the darkness, of the land and of the sea; and who sends winds as glad tidings before His mercy; is there a god with God? exalted be God above what they associate with Him! [65] He who began the creation and then will make it return again; and who provides you from the heaven and the earth; is there a god with God? so bring your proofs if ye do speak the truth!

Say, 'None in the heavens or the earth know the unseen save only God; but they perceive not when they shall be raised!'—nay, but their knowledge attains to somewhat of the hereafter; nay, but they are in doubt concerning it! nay, but they are blind!

And those who disbelieved said, 'What! when we have become dust and our fathers too, shall we indeed be brought forth? [70] We were promised this, we and our fathers before us, this is nothing but old folks' tales!'

Say, 'Journey on through the land and see how was the end of the sinners! and grieve not for them, and be not straitened at what they plot.'

They say, 'When shall this threat be if ye do tell the truth?' Say, 'It may be that there is pressing close behind you a part of what ye would hasten on!' [75] But, verily, thy Lord is full of grace to men, but most of them will not be thankful; and, verily, thy Lord knows what their breasts conceal and what they manifest; and there is no secret thing in the heaven or the earth, save that it is in the perspicuous Book!

Verily, this Qur'ân relates to the people of Israel most of that whereon they do dispute; and, verily, it is a guidance and a mercy to the believers.
[80] Verily, thy Lord decides between them by His judgment, for He is mighty, knowing. Rely thou then upon God, verily, thou art standing on obvious truth. Verily, thou canst not make the dead to hear, and thou canst not make the deaf to hear the call when they turn their backs on thee; nor art thou a guide to the blind, out of their error: thou canst only make to hear such as believe in our signs, and such as are resigned.

And when the sentence falls upon them we will bring forth a beast out of the earth that shall speak to them, (and say) that, 'Men of our signs would not be sure.'

[85] And the day when we will gather from every nation a troop of those who said our signs were lies; and they shall be marshalled; until they come, and He will say, 'Did ye say my signs were lies, when ye had compassed no knowledge thereof? or what is it that ye were doing?' and the sentence shall fall upon them for that they did wrong, and they shall not have speech.

Did they not see that we have made the night for them to rest in, and the day to see by? verily, in that are signs to people who believe.

And the day when the trumpet shall be blown and all who are in the heavens and the earth shall be startled, save whom God pleases! and all shall come abjectly to Him. [90] And thou shalt see the mountains, which thou dost deem solid, pass away like the passing of the clouds;—the work of God who orders all things; verily, He is well aware of what ye do!

He who brings a good deed shall have better than it; and from the alarm of that day they shall be safe: but those who bring an evil deed shall be thrown down upon their faces in the fire. Shall ye be rewarded save for what ye have done?

I am bidden to serve the Lord of this country who has made it sacred, and whose are all things; and I am bidden to be of those who are resigned, and to recite the Qur'ân; and he who is guided he is only guided for himself; and he who errs,— say, 'I am only of those who warn!'

[95] And say, 'Praise be to God, He will show you His signs, and ye shall recognise them; for thy Lord is not heedless of what ye do!'

The Chapter of the Story.

(XXVIII. Mecca.)

In the name of the merciful and compassionate God.

T. S. M. Those are the signs of the perspicuous Book; we recite to thee from the history of Moses and Pharaoh in truth unto a people who believe.

Verily, Pharaoh was lofty in the land and made the people thereof sects; one party of them he weakened, slaughtering their sons and letting their women live. Verily, he was of the despoilers.

And we wished to be gracious to those who were weakened in the earth, and to make them models, and to make them the heirs;
[5] and to establish for them in the earth; and to show Pharaoh and Hâmân[1] and their hosts what they had to beware of from them.

And we inspired the mother of Moses, 'Suckle him; and when thou art afraid for him then throw him into the river, and fear not and grieve not; verily, we are going to restore him to thee, and to make him of the apostles!'

And Pharaoh's family picked him up that he might be for them a foe and a grief; verily, Pharaoh and Hâmân and their hosts were sinners.

And Pharaoh's wife said, 'He is a cheering of the eye to me, and to thee. Kill him not; it may be that he will profit us, or that we may take him for a son;' for they did not perceive.

And the heart of Moses' mother was void on the morrow[2]; she well-nigh disclosed him, had it not been that we bound up her heart that she might be of the believers.

[10] And she said to his sister, 'Follow him up.' And she looked after him from afar, and they did not perceive. And we made unlawful for him the wet-nurses[3]. And she said, 'Shall I guide you to

[1] Hâmân, according to the Qur'ân, is made out to be the prime minister of Pharaoh.

[2] Either devoid of patience, according to some, or of anxiety, according to others, or it may be to everything but the thought of Moses.

[3] That is, Moses was made to refuse the breast of the Egyptian woman before his sister came to offer her services, and point out a nurse who would rear him.

the people of a house who will take care of him for you, and who will be sincere respecting him?'

So we restored him to his mother that her eye might be cheered, and that she might not grieve, and that she might know that the promise of God is true, though most of them know not.

And when he reached puberty, and was settled, we gave him judgment and knowledge; for thus do we reward those who do well. And he entered into the city at the time the people thereof were heedless, and he found therein two men fighting; the one of his sect and the other of his foes. And he who was of his sect asked his aid against him who was of his foes; and Moses smote him with his fist and finished him. Said he, 'This is of the work of Satan, verily, he is a misleading obvious foe.'

[15] Said he, 'My Lord! verily, I have wronged my soul, but forgive me.' So He forgave him; for He is forgiving and merciful.

Said he, 'My Lord! for that Thou hast been gracious to me, I will surely not back up the sinners.'

And on the morrow he was afraid in the city, expectant. And behold, he whom he had helped the day before cried (again) to him for aid. Said Moses to him, 'Verily, thou art obviously quarrelsome.' And when he wished to assault him who was the enemy to them both, he said, 'O Moses! dost thou desire to kill me as thou didst kill a person yesterday? thou dost only desire to be a tyrant in the earth; and thou dost not desire to be of those who do right!' And a man came from the remote parts of the city running, said he, 'O Moses!' verily, the chiefs are deliberating concerning thee to kill thee; go then forth; verily, I am to you a sincere adviser!'

[20] So he went forth therefrom, afraid and expectant. Said he, 'Lord, save me from the unjust people!'

And when he turned his face in the direction of Midian, he said, 'It may be that my Lord will guide me to a level path!' And when he went down to the water of Midian he found thereat a nation of people watering their flocks.

And he found beside them two women keeping back their flocks. Said he, 'What is your design?' They said, 'We cannot water our flocks until the herdsmen have finished; for our father is a very old man.' So he watered for them; then he turned back towards the shade and said, 'My Lord! verily, I stand in need of what Thou sendest down to me of good.'

[25] And one of the two came to him walking modestly; said she, 'Verily; my father calls thee, to reward thee with hire for having watered our flocks for us.' And when he came to him and related to him the story, said he, 'Fear not, thou art safe from the unjust people.' Said one of them, 'O my sire! hire him; verily, the best of those whom thou canst hire is the strong and faithful.'

Said he, 'Verily, I desire to marry thee to one of these daughters of mine, on condition that thou dost serve me for hire eight years; and if thou shalt fulfil ten it is of thyself; for I do not wish to make it wretched for thee; thou wilt find me, if it please God, of the righteous!'

Said he, 'That is between you and me; whichever of the two terms I fulfil, let there be no enmity against me, for God over what we say keeps guard.'

And when Moses had fulfilled the appointed time, and was journeying with his people, he perceived from the side of the mountain a fire; said he to his people, 'Tarry ye here; verily, I have perceived a fire, haply I may bring you good news therefrom, or a brand of fire that haply ye may be warmed [1].'

[30] And when he came to it he was called to, from the right side of the wady, in the blessed valley, out of the tree, 'O Moses! verily, I am God the Lord of the worlds; so throw down thy rod;' and when he saw it quivering as though it were a snake, he turned away and fled and did not return. 'O Moses! approach and fear not, verily, thou art amongst the safe. Thrust thy hand into thy bosom, it shall come out white, without hurt; and then fold again thy wing, that thou dost now stretch out through dread; for those are two signs from thy Lord to Pharaoh and his chiefs; verily, they are a people who work abomination!'

Said he, 'My Lord! verily, I have killed a person amongst them, and I fear that they will kill me: and my brother Aaron, he is more eloquent of tongue than I; send him then with me as a support, to verify me; verily, I fear that they will call me liar!'

[35] Said He, 'We will strengthen thine arm with thy brother; and we will make for you both authority, and they shall not reach you in our signs; ye two and those who follow you shall gain the upper hand.'

And when Moses came to them with our manifest signs, they said, 'This is only sorcery devised;

[1] See Part II, p. 35, note 1.

and we have not heard of this amongst our fathers
of yore.'

Moses said, 'My Lord knows best who comes
with guidance from Him, and whose shall be the
issue of the abode. Verily, the unjust shall not
prosper!'

And Pharaoh said, 'O ye chiefs! I do not know
any god for you except me; then set fire, O Hâmân!
to some clay and make for me a tower, haply I may
mount up to the God of Moses; for, verily, I think
he is of those who lie!'

And he grew big with pride, he and his armies
in the land, without right; and they thought that
they to us should not return. [40] And we over-
took him and his army, and we flung them into the
sea; behold, then, how was the end of the unjust

But we made them models calling to the fire;
and on the resurrection day they shall not be
helped; and we followed them up in this world with
a curse; and on the resurrection day they shall
be abhorred!

And we gave Moses the Book, after that we had
destroyed the former generations, as an insight to
men and a guidance and a mercy; haply they may
be mindful!

Thou wast not upon the western side when we
decided for Moses, but afar off; nor wast thou of
the witnesses. [45] But we raised up (other) genera-
tions, and life was prolonged for them; and thou
wast not staying amidst the people of Midian, re-
citing to them our signs; but we were sending
our apostles.

Nor wast thou by the side of the mountain when
we called; but it is a mercy from thy Lord, that

thou mayest warn a people to whom no warner has come before thee; haply they may be mindful! And lest there should befall them a mishap for what their hands have sent before, and they should say, 'Our Lord! why didst thou not send to us an apostle? for we would have followed thy signs and been of the believers.'

And when the truth comes to them from us they say, 'We are given the like of what Moses was given.' Did they not disbelieve in what Moses was given before?—they say, 'Two works of sorcery[1] back up each other;' and they say, 'Verily, we do disbelieve in all.'

Say, 'Bring, then, a book from God which shall be a better guide than both, and I will follow it, if ye do tell the truth!'

[50] And if they cannot answer thee, then know that they follow their own lusts; and who is more in error than he who follows his own lust without guidance from God? verily, God guides not an unjust people!

And we caused the word to reach them, haply they may be mindful!

Those to whom we gave the Book before it, they believe therein; and when it is recited to them they say, 'We believe in it as truth from our Lord; verily, we were resigned before it came!' These shall be given their hire twice over, for that they were patient, and repelled evil with good, and of what we have bestowed upon them give alms.

[55] And when they hear vain talk, they turn away from it and say, 'We have our works, and ye

[1] That is, the Pentateuch and Qur'ân.

have your works. Peace be upon you! we do not seek the ignorant!'

Verily, thou canst not guide whom thou dost like, but God guides whom He pleases; for He knows best who are to be guided.

And they say, 'If we follow the guidance we shall be snatched away from the land.' Have we not established for them a safe sanctuary, to which are imported the fruits of everything as a provision from us? but most of them do not know.

How many a city have we destroyed that exulted in its means of subsistence? These are their dwellings, never dwelt in after them, except a little; for we were the heirs.

But thy Lord would never destroy cities until He sent to the metropolis thereof an apostle, to recite to them our signs; nor would we destroy cities unless their people were unjust. [60] Whatever thing ye may be given, it is a provision for this world's life and the adornment thereof; but what is with God is better and more enduring; have ye then no sense?

Is He to whom we have promised a goodly promise, which he shall meet with, like him to whom we have given the enjoyment of the life of this world, and who upon the resurrection day shall be of the arraigned?

And on the day when He will call them and will say, 'Where are those associates which ye did pretend?' And those against whom the sentence is due shall say, 'Our Lord! these are those whom we have seduced; we seduced them as we were seduced ourselves: but we clear ourselves to thee;—they did not worship us!'

And it will be said, 'Call upon your partners;' and they will call upon them, but they will not answer them, and they shall see the torment; would that they had been guided.

[65] And the day when He shall call them and shall say, 'What was it ye answered the apostles?' and the history shall be blindly confusing to them on that day, and they shall not ask each other.

But, as for him who turns again and believes and does right, it may be that he will be among the prosperous. For thy Lord creates what He pleases and chooses; they have not the choice! Celebrated be the praise of God! and exalted be He above what they associate with Him!

Thy Lord knows what they conceal in their breasts and what they manifest.

[70] He is God, there is no god but He; to Him belongs praise, in the first and the last; and His is the judgment; and unto Him shall ye return!

Have ye considered, if God were to make for you the night endless until the resurrection day, who is the god, but God, to bring you light? can ye not then hear?

Say, 'Have ye considered, if God were to make for you the day endless until the day of judgment, who is the god, except God, to bring you the night to rest therein? can ye not then see?' But of His mercy He has made for you the night and the day, that ye may rest therein, and crave of His grace, haply ye may give thanks.

And the day when He shall call them and shall say, 'Where are my partners whom ye did pretend?'
[75] And we will pluck from every nation a witness; and we will say, 'Bring your proof and know that

the truth is God's;' and that which they had devised shall stray away from them.

Verily, Korah[1] was of the people of Moses, and he was outrageous against them; and we gave him treasuries of which the keys would bear down a band of men endowed with strength. When his people said to him, 'Exult not; verily, God loves not those who exult! but crave, through what God has given thee, the future abode; and forget not thy portion in this world, and do good, as God has done good to thee; and seek not evil doing in the earth; verily, God loves not the evildoers!'

Said he, 'I have only been given it for knowledge which I have!' did he not know that God had destroyed before him many generations of those who were stronger than he, and had amassed more? But the sinners need not to be asked concerning their crimes.

And he went out amongst the people in his ornaments; those who desired the life of this world said, 'O would that we had the like of what Korah has been given! verily, he is endowed with mighty fortune!'

[80] But those who had been given knowledge said, 'Woe to you! the reward of God is better for him who believes and does right; but none shall meet with it except the patient. And we clave the earth with him and with his house; and he had no troop to help him against God, nor was he of those who were helped!'

And on the morrow those who had yearned for

---

[1] In Arabic Qârûn. The legend based upon Talmudic tradition of Korah's immense wealth appears to be also confused with that of Crœsus.

his place the day before said, 'Ah, ah! God extends provision to whom He pleases of His servants, or He doles it out; had not God been gracious to us, the earth would have cleft open with us! Ah, ah! the unbelievers shall not prosper!'

That is the future abode; we make it for those who do not wish to be haughty in the earth, nor to do evil, and the end is for the pious.

He who brings a good deed shall have better than it; and he who brings an evil deed—those who do evil deeds shall only be rewarded for that which they have done. [85] Verily, He who hath ordained the Qur'ân for thee will restore thee to thy returning place. Say, 'My Lord knows best who brings guidance, and who is in obvious error; nor couldst thou hope that the Book would be thrown to thee, save as a mercy from thy Lord! be not then a backer up of those who misbelieve; and let them not turn thee from the signs of God, after they have been sent down to thee; but call unto thy Lord and be not of the idolaters; and call not with God upon any other god; there is no god but He! everything is perishable, except His face; His is the judgment, and unto Him shall ye return!

The Chapter of the Spider.

(XXIX. Mecca.)

In the name of the merciful and compassionate God.

A. L. M. Do men then reckon that they will be left alone to say, 'We believe,' and not be tried?

we did try those who were before them, and God will surely know those who are truthful, and He will surely know the liars. Do those who do evil reckon that they can outstrip us? evil is it that they judge.

He who hopes for the meeting of God,—verily, God's appointed time will come; and He both hears and knows! [5] And he who fights strenuously, fights strenuously only for his own soul; verily, God is independent of the worlds.

Those who believe and do right, we will surely cover for them their offences; and we will surely reward them with better than that which they have done.

And we have enjoined on man kindness to his parents; and if they strive with thee that thou mayest join with me, what thou hast no knowledge of, then obey them not; to me is your return, and I will inform you of that which ye have done.

But those who believe and do right, we will make them enter amongst the righteous.

And there are those among men who say, 'We believe in God!' but when they are hurt in God's cause, they deem the trials of men like the torment of God; but if help come from thy Lord they will say, 'Verily, we were with you!' does not God know best what is in the breasts of the worlds? [10] God will surely know those who believe, and will surely know the hypocrites.

And those who misbelieved said to those who believed, 'Follow our path, we will bear your sins;' but they could not bear their sins at all; verily, they are liars! But they shall surely bear their own burdens, and burdens with their burdens; and they shall surely be asked upon the resurrection day concerning what they did devise.

And we sent Noah to his people, and he dwelt among them for a thousand years save fifty years; and the deluge overtook them while they were unjust: but we saved him and the fellows of the ark, and we made it a sign unto the worlds.

And Abraham when he said to his people, 'Serve God and fear Him, that is better for you if ye did but know. [15] Ye only serve beside God idols and do create a lie; verily, those whom ye serve beside God cannot control for themselves provision; then crave provision with God, and serve Him, and give thanks to Him; unto Him shall ye return! And if ye say it is a lie, nations before you called (the apostles) liars too; but an apostle has only his plain message to preach!'

Have they not seen how God produces the creation, and then turns it back? verily, that to God is easy.

Say, 'Journey ye on in the land, and behold how the creation appeared; then God produces another production: verily, God is mighty over all!'

[20] He torments whom He will, and has mercy on whom He will; and unto Him shall ye be returned.

Nor can ye make Him helpless in the earth, nor in the heavens; nor have ye beside God a patron or a helper.

And those who disbelieve in God's signs and in meeting with Him, these shall despair of my mercy; and these, for them is grievous woe.

But the answer of his people was only to say, 'Kill him or burn him!' But God saved him from the fire; verily, in that are signs unto a people who believe.

He said, 'Verily, ye take beside God idols, through mutual friendship in the life of this world; then on the day of judgment ye shall deny each other, and shall curse each other, and your resort shall be the fire, and ye shall have none to help.'

[25] And Lot believed him. And (Abraham) said, 'Verily, I flee unto my Lord! Verily, He is mighty, wise! and we granted him Isaac and Jacob; and we placed in his seed prophecy and the Book; and we gave him his hire in this world; and, verily, he in the next shall be among the righteous.'

And Lot when he said to his people, 'Verily, ye approach an abomination which no one in all the world ever anticipated you in! What! do ye approach men? and stop folks on the highway? and approach in your assembly sin?' but the answer of his people was only to say, 'Bring us God's torment, if thou art of those who speak the truth!'

Said he, 'My Lord! help me against a people who do evil!'

[30] And when our messengers came to Abraham with the glad tidings, they said, 'We are about to destroy the people of this city. Verily, the people thereof are wrong-doers.'

Said he, 'Verily, in it is Lot;' they said, 'We know best who is therein; we shall of a surety save him and his people, except his wife, who is of those who linger.' And when our messengers came to Lot, he was vexed for them, and his arm was straitened for them; and they said, 'Fear not, neither grieve; we are about to save thee and thy people, except thy wife, who is of those who linger. Verily, we are about to send down upon the people of this city a horror from heaven, for that they have sinned; and we have left therefrom a manifest sign unto a people who have sense.'

[35] And unto Midian we sent their brother Sho'hâib, and he said, 'My people, serve God, and hope for the last day; and waste not the land, despoiling it.'

But they called him liar; and the convulsion seized them, and on the morrow they lay in their dwellings prone.

And 'Âd and Thamûd—but it is plain to you from their habitations; for Satan made seemly to them their works, and turned them from the way, sagacious though they were!

And Korah and Pharaoh and Hâmân—Moses did come to them with manifest signs, but they were too big with pride in the earth, although they could not outstrip us!

And each of them we seized in his sin; and of them were some against whom we sent a sand-storm; and of them were some whom the noise seized; and of them were some with whom we cleaved the earth open; and of them were some we drowned: God would not have wronged them, but it was themselves they wronged.

[40] The likeness of those who take, beside God, patrons is as the likeness of a spider, that takes to himself a house; and, verily, the weakest of houses is a spider's house, if they did but know!

Verily, God knows whatever thing they call upon beside Him; for He is the mighty, wise.

These are parables which we have struck out

for men; but none will understand them, save those who know.

God created the heavens and the earth in truth; verily, in this is a sign unto believers.

Recite what has been revealed to thee of the Book; and be steadfast in prayer; verily, prayer forbids sin and wrong; and surely the mention of God is greater; for God knows what ye do.
[45] And do not wrangle with the people of the
Book, except for what is better; save with those who have been unjust amongst them and who say, 'We believe in what is sent down to us, and what has been sent down to you; our God and your God is one, and we are unto Him resigned.'

Thus did we send down to thee the Book; and every one to whom we have given the Book believes therein. But these will not believe therein; though none gainsay our signs except the misbelievers.

Thou couldst not recite before this any book, nor write it with thy right hand, for in that case those who deem it vain would have doubted. Nay, but it is evident signs in the breasts of those who are endued with knowledge, and none but the unjust would gainsay our signs!

They say, 'Unless there be sent down upon him signs from his Lord —;' say, 'Verily, signs are with God, and, verily, I am an obvious warner!'

[50] Is it not enough for them that we have sent
down to thee the Book which thou dost recite to them? verily, in that is a mercy and a reminder to a people who believe.

Say, 'God is witness enough between me and you; He knows what is in the heavens and what is in the earth; and those who believe in falsehood and misbelieve in God, they shall be the losers.' They will wish thee to hasten on the torment; but were it not for a stated and appointed time, the torment would have come upon them suddenly, while yet they did not perceive.

They will wish thee to hurry on the torment, but, verily, hell encompasses the misbelievers!

[55] On the day when the torment shall cover them from above them and from beneath their feet, and He shall say, 'Taste that which ye have done!'

O my servants who believe! verily, my land is spacious enough[1]; me therefore do ye worship.

Every soul must taste of death, then unto us shall ye return; and those who believe and act aright, we will surely inform them of upper chambers in Paradise, beneath which rivers flow; to dwell therein for aye—pleasant is the hire of those who work! those who are patient and rely upon their Lord!

[60] How many a beast cannot carry its own provision! God provides for it and for you; He both hears and knows!

And if thou shouldst ask them, 'Who created the heavens and the earth, and subjected the sun and the moon?' they will surely say, 'God!' how then can they lie?

God extends provision to whomsoever He will of His servants, or doles it out to him; verily, God all things doth know.

And if thou shouldst ask them, 'Who sends down from the heavens water and quickens therewith the

[1] I. e. if you are pressed in Mecca, there are plenty of places where you can take shelter, as Mohammed himself and a few of his followers did at Medînah.

earth in its death?' they will surely say, 'God!' say, 'And praise be to God!' nay, most of them have no sense.

This life of the world is nothing but a sport and a play; but, verily, the abode of the next world, that is life,—if they did but know!

[65] And when they ride in the ship they call upon God, making their religion seem sincere to Him; but when He saves them to the shore, behold, they associate others with Him; that they may disbelieve in our signs; and that they may have some enjoyment: but soon they shall know.

Have they not seen that we have made a safe sanctuary whilst people are being snatched away around them? is it then in falsehood that they will believe, and for the favours of God be ungrateful?

But who is more unjust than he who devises against God a lie, or calls the truth a lie when it comes to him? Is there not in hell a resort for the misbelievers? but those who fight strenuously for us we will surely guide them into our way, for, verily, God is with those who do well.

The Chapter of the Greeks[1].

(XXX. Mecca.)

In the name of the merciful and compassionate God.

The Greeks are overcome in the nighest parts of the land; but after being overcome they shall

[1] In Arabic Rûm, by which is meant the Byzantine or eastern Roman empire.

overcome[1] in a few years; to God belongs the order before and after; and on that day the believers shall rejoice in the help of God;—God helps whom He will, and He is mighty, merciful.
[5]—God's promise!—God breaks not His promise, but most men do not know!

They know the outside of this world's life, but of the hereafter they are heedless. Have they not reflected in themselves, that God created not the heavens and the earth, and what is between the two except in truth, and for a stated and appointed time? but, verily, many men in the meeting of their Lord do disbelieve.

Have they not journeyed on in the land and seen how was the end of those before them who were stronger than they, and who turned up the ground and cultivated it more than they do cultivate it? and there came to them their apostles with manifest signs; for God would never wrong them: it was themselves they wronged!

Then evil was the end of those who did evil, in that they said the signs of God were lies and mocked thereat.

---

[1] About the beginning of the sixth year before the Higrah the Persians conquered Syria, and made themselves masters also of Palestine, and took Jerusalem. The Greeks were so distressed by their defeat that there appeared little likelihood of their being able to retrieve their fortune, and in the following year the Persians proceeded to lay siege to Constantinople itself. In the year 625 A.D., however, the fourth year before the Higrah, the Greeks gained a signal victory over the Persians, and not only drove them out of the borders of the Byzantine empire, but carried the war into Persian territory, and despoiled the city of Medayen. It is the defeat which is alluded to in this passage, and the subsequent victory that is prophesied, the date of the chapter being ascribed to the period when the Persians took Jerusalem.

[10] God produces a creation, then He makes it go back again, then unto Him shall ye return.

And on the day when the Hour shall rise, the sinners shall be confused; and they shall not have amongst their partners intercessors; and their partners shall they deny.

And on the day when the Hour shall rise, on that day shall they be scattered apart; and as for those who believe and do right, they in the garden shall be joyful; [15] and as for those who misbelieved and said our signs and the meeting of the hereafter were lies, they shall be in the torment arraigned.

Celebrated be the praises of God, when ye are in the evening and when ye are in the morning! for to Him belongs praise in the heavens and the earth! and at the evening, and when ye are at noon.

He brings forth the living from the dead, and brings forth the dead from the living; and He quickens the earth after its death, and thus shall ye too be brought forth.

And of His signs is this, that He hath created you from dust; then, behold, ye are mortals who are spread abroad.

[20] And of His signs is this, that He hath created for you of yourselves wives with whom ye may cohabit; He has made between you affection and pity. Verily, in that are signs unto a people who reflect.

And of His signs is the creation of the heavens and the earth, and the diversity of your tongues and colours; verily, in that are signs unto the worlds[1].

---

[1] Or, according to another reading, 'unto those who know;' cf. Part II, p. 122, line 2.

And of His signs is your sleep by night and by day; and your craving after His grace. Verily, in that are signs unto a people who do hear.

And of His signs is this, that He shows you lightning for fear and hope; and sends down from the sky water, and quickens therewith the earth after its death; verily, in that are signs unto a people who have sense.

And of His signs is this, that the heavens and the earth stand by His order; then when He calls you from the earth, lo! ye shall come forth. [25] His are those who are in the heavens and the earth, and all to Him are devoted. And He it is who produces a creation and then makes it to go back again; for it is very easy to Him; and His are the loftiest similitudes in the heavens and the earth; and He is the mighty, wise!

He has struck out for you a parable from yourselves; have ye of what your right hand possess partners in what we have bestowed upon you, so that ye share alike therein? do ye fear them as ye fear each other?—Thus do we detail the signs unto a people who have sense[1].

Nay, when those who are unjust follow their lusts without knowledge,—and who shall guide him whom God has led astray? and they shall have none to help.

Set thy face steadfast towards the religion as an

[1] I. e. as they, the Meccans, do not consider their slaves their equals, still less does God hold the false gods they associate with Him to be His equals, it being always remembered that these partners or false gods were not spoken of in the Qur'ân, as non-existent, but as supernatural beings, to whom divinity has been wrongly ascribed.

'Hanîf, according to the constitution whereon God has constituted men; there is no altering the creation of God, that is the standard religion, though most men do not know.

[30] Turn repentant towards Him; and fear Him, and be steadfast in prayer; and be not of the idolaters.

Of those who have divided their religion and become sects, every party in what they have, rejoice.

And when distress touches men they call upon their Lord, repentant towards Him; then when He has made them taste mercy from Himself, behold! a party of them associate others with their Lord, that they may disbelieve in what we have brought them;—but enjoy yourselves; for hereafter ye shall know!

Or have we sent down to them authority which speaks of what they do associate with Him?

[35] And when we have made men taste of mercy, they rejoice therein; and if there befall them evil for what their hands have sent before, behold! they are in despair.

Have they not seen that God extends provision to whom He pleases, or doles it out? verily, in that are signs unto a people who believe.

Then give to the kinsman his due, and to the poor and to the wayfarer; that is better for those who desire the face of God, and these it is who are prosperous.

And what ye put out to usury that it may increase with the wealth of men, it shall not increase with God; but what ye put out in alms, desiring the face of God—these it is who shall gain double.

It is God who created you and then provided for

you; and then will make you die, and then will quicken you again; is there any of your partners who can do aught of that? Celebrated be His praises, and exalted be He above what they associate with Him!

[40] Trouble hath appeared in the land and the sea, for what men's hands have gained! to make them taste a part of that which they have done,—haply they may return!

Say, 'Journey on in the land, and behold what was the end of those before you,—most of them were idolaters!'

Set thy face steadfast to the standard religion, before there come a day from God which there is no averting; on that day shall they be parted into two bands.

He who misbelieves, upon him is his misbelief; but whoso does right, for themselves they are spreading couches[1]:

That He may reward those who believe and do right of His grace; verily, He loves not the misbelievers!

[45] And of His signs is this, that He sends forth the winds with glad tidings, to make you taste of His mercy, and to make the ships go on at His bidding, and that ye may crave of His grace, and haply ye may give thanks.

We have sent before thee apostles unto their people, and they came to them with manifest signs: and we took vengeance upon those who sinned, but due from us it was to help the believers.

God it is who sends forth the winds to stir up

[1] In Paradise.

clouds; then He spreads them forth over the sky as he pleases; and He breaks them up and ye see the rain come forth from amongst them; and when He causes it to fall upon whom He pleases of His servants, behold they hail it with joy, although before it was sent down upon them they were before then confused!

Look then to the vestiges of God's mercy, how He quickens the earth after its death; verily, that is the quickener of the dead, and He is mighty over all!

[50] But if we should send a wind and they should see it yellow[1], they would after that become misbelievers.

But, verily, thou canst not make the dead to hear, nor canst thou make the deaf to hear the call, when they turn their backs and flee; nor hast thou to guide the blind out of their error; thou canst only make those to hear who believe in our signs and who are resigned.

God it is who created you of weakness, then made for you after weakness strength; then made for you after strength, weakness and grey hairs: He creates what He pleases, for He is the knowing, the powerful!

And on the day when the Hour shall rise, the sinners shall swear [55] that they have not tarried save an hour; thus were they wont to lie!

But those who are given knowledge and faith will say, 'We have tarried according to the Book of God, until the day of resurrection;' and this is the day of resurrection, but ye—ye do not know.

And on that day their excuse shall profit not

[1] I.e. see the young corn parched.

those who did wrong; nor shall they be asked to please God again.

We have struck out to men in this Qur'ân every kind of parable; but if thou shouldst bring them a sign[1] then those who misbelieve will surely say, 'Ye are but followers of vanity; thus does God set a stamp upon the hearts of those who do not know.'

[60] Be thou patient then; verily, God's promise is true! and let them not flurry thee who are not sure.

The Chapter of Loqmân[2].

(XXXI. Mecca.)

In the name of the merciful and compassionate God.

A. L. M. These are the signs of the wise Book, a guidance and a mercy to those who do well, who are steadfast in prayer and give alms and who of the hereafter are sure; these are in guidance from their Lord, and these are the prosperous.

[5] And amongst men is one[3] who buys sportive legends, to lead astray from God's path, without knowledge, and to make a jest of it; these, for

---

[1] I. e. a verse.

[2] This sage is generally identified with the Aesop of the Greeks. The legends current in the East concerning him accord exactly with those of the Greek fabulist.

[3] An Na*dh*r ibn al 'Hareth had purchased in Persia some of the old legends of Rustam and Isfendiâr, which were afterwards embodied in the Shâh-nâmeh of Firdausî. These he read to the Qurâi*s* as being more wonderful than the Qur'ân.

them is shameful woe! And when our signs are recited to him, he turns his back, too big with pride, as though he heard them not,—as if in his two ears were dulness. But give to him glad tidings of grievous woe!

Verily, those who believe and do right, for them are gardens of pleasure, to dwell therein for aye;—God's promise in truth, and He is mighty, wise.

He created the heavens without pillars that ye can see, and He threw upon the earth firm mountains lest it should move with you; and He dispersed thereon every sort of beast; and we send down from the heavens water, and we caused to grow therein of every noble kind.

[10] This is God's creation; show me what others beside Him have created;—nay, the unjust are in obvious error!

We did give unto Loqmân wisdom, saying, 'Thank God; for he who thanks God is only thankful for his own soul; and he who is ungrateful—verily, God is independent, worthy of praise!'

And when Loqmân said to his son while admonishing him, 'O my boy! associate none with God, for, verily, such association is a mighty wrong.'—

For we have commended his parents to man; his mother bore him with weakness upon weakness; and his weaning is in two years;—'Be thankful to me and to thy parents; for unto me shall your journey be. But if they strive with thee that thou shouldst associate with me that which thou hast no knowledge of, then obey them not. But associate with them in the world with kindness, and follow the way of him who turns repentant unto me; then unto me is your return, and I will inform you of that which ye have done!—

[15] 'O my son! verily, if there were the weight of a grain of mustard seed and it were (hidden) in the rock, or in the heaven, or in the earth, God would bring it (to light). Verily, God is subtle, well aware!

'O my son! be steadfast in prayer, and bid what is reasonable and forbid what is wrong; be patient of what befalls thee, verily, that is one of the determined affairs.

'And twist not thy cheek proudly, nor walk in the land haughtily; verily, God loves not every arrogant boaster: but be moderate in thy walk, and lower thy voice; verily, the most disagreeable of voices is the voice of asses!'

Have ye not seen that God has subjected to you what is in the heavens and what is in the earth, and has poured down upon you His favours, outwardly and inwardly? but amongst men are those who wrangle about God, without knowledge, and without guidance, and without an illuminating book!

[20] And when it is said to them, 'Follow what God has sent down;' they say, 'Nay! we will follow what we found our fathers agreed upon;'—what! though Satan calls them to the torment of the blaze?

But he who resigns his face unto God, and does good, he has grasped the firm handle; unto God is the issue of affairs. But he who misbelieves, let not his misbelief grieve thee; to us is their return, and we will inform them of what they do;—for, verily, God knows the nature of men's breasts!

We will let them enjoy themselves a little; then we will force them to rigorous woe!

And if thou shouldst ask them who created the heavens and the earth, they will surely say, 'God.' Say, 'Praise be to God!' but most of them do not know.

[25] God's is what is in the heavens and what is in the earth; verily, God, He is the independent, worthy of praise.

And were the trees that are in the earth pens, and the sea (ink) with seven more seas to swell its tide, the words of God would not be spent; verily, God is mighty, wise!

Your creation and your rising again are but as that of one soul; verily, God both hears and sees!

Dost thou not see that God joins on the night to the day, and joins on the day to the night, and has subjected the sun and the moon,—each of them runs on unto an appointed time? and that God of what ye do is well aware?

That is because God, He is true, and because what ye call on beside Him is falsehood, and because God, He is the high, the great!

[30] Dost thou not see that the ship rides on in the sea by the favour of God, that He may show you of His signs? verily, in that are signs to every grateful person.

And when a wave like shadows covers them, they call on God, being sincere in their religion; and when He saves them to the shore, then amongst them are some who halt between two opinions. But none gainsays our signs save every perfidious misbeliever.

O ye folk! fear your Lord and dread the day when the father shall not atone for his son, nor shall the child atone aught for its parent.

Verily, the promise of God is true! Say, 'Let not the life of this world beguile you; and let not the beguiler beguile you concerning God.'

Verily, God, with Him is the knowledge of the Hour; and He sends down the rain; and He knows what is in the wombs; and no soul knows what it is that it shall earn to-morrow; and no soul knows in what land it shall die; verily, God is knowing, well aware!

The Chapter of Adoration.

(XXXII. Mecca.)

In the name of the merciful and compassionate God.

A. L. M. The revelation of the Book, there is no doubt therein, from the Lord of the worlds.

Do they say, 'He has forged it?' Nay! it is the truth from thy Lord, that thou mayest warn a people, to whom no warner has come before thee, haply they may be guided.

God it is who created the heavens and the earth and what is between the two in six days; then He made for the throne! ye have no patron beside Him and no intercessor; are ye not then mindful?

He governs the affair from the heaven unto the earth; then shall it ascend to him in a day, the measure of which is as a thousand years of what ye number.

[5] That is He who knows the unseen and the visible; the mighty, the merciful, who has made the best of the creation of everything, and produced the

creation of man from clay; then He made his stock from an extract of despicable water; then He fashioned him and breathed into him of His spirit, and made for you hearing and eyesight and hearts;—little is it that ye give thanks!

And they say, 'When we are lost in the earth, shall we then become a new creation?' [10] Nay! in the meeting of their Lord they disbelieve.

Say, 'The angel of death shall take you away, he who is given charge of you; then unto your Lord shall ye be returned.'

And couldst thou see when the sinners hang down their heads before their Lord, 'O Lord! we have seen and we have heard; send us back then and we will do right. Verily, we are sure!'

Had we pleased we would have given to everything its guidance; but the sentence was due from me;—I will surely fill hell with the *g*inns and with men all together: 'So taste ye, for that ye forgat the meeting of this day of yours,—verily, we have forgotten you! and taste ye the torment of eternity for that which ye have done!'

[15] They only believe in our signs who when they are reminded of them fall down adoring and celebrate the praises of their Lord, and are not too big with pride. As their sides forsake their beds, they call upon their Lord with fear and hope; and of what we have bestowed upon them do they give alms. No soul knows what is reserved for them of cheerfulness for eye, as a reward for that which they have done! Is he who is a believer like him who is a sinner? they shall not be held equal.

As for those who believe and do right, for them

are the gardens of resort, an entertainment for that which they have done!

[20] But as for those who commit abomination their resort is the Fire. Every time that they desire to go forth therefrom, we will send them back therein, and it will be said to them, 'Taste ye the torment of the fire which ye did call a lie!' and we will surely make them taste of the torment of the nearer torment beside the greater torment [1],—haply they may yet return.

Who is more unjust than he who is reminded of the signs of his Lord, and then turns away from them? Verily, we will take vengeance on the sinners!

And we did give Moses the Book; be not then in doubt concerning the meeting with him [2]; and we made it a guidance to the children of Israel.

And we made amongst them high priests who guided by our bidding, since they were patient and were sure of our signs.

[25] Verily, thy Lord, he shall decide between them on the resurrection day concerning that whereon they do dispute.

Is it not conspicuous to them how many generations we have destroyed before them? they walk

---

[1] I.e. the torment of this world as well as that of the next.

[2] This may refer to the alleged meeting of Mohammed and Moses in heaven during the 'night journey;' or it may be translated, 'the reception of it,' i.e. the Qur'ân, the expression in Chapter XXVII, 6, being derived from the same root in Arabic, which means 'to meet.' The native commentators are divided in opinion as to these two interpretations. It is quite possible, however, that it may mean, 'be not in doubt as to a meeting with Him,' and be a mere reiteration of the sentiment so often expressed, that Muslims are to be certain of a meeting with their Lord.

over their dwellings! verily, in that are signs: do they not then hear?

Have they not seen that we drive the water to the sterile land, and bring forth thereby corn from which their cattle and themselves do eat? do they not then see?

And they say, 'When shall this decision come if ye do tell the truth?' Say, 'On the day of the decision their faith shall not profit those who misbelieved, nor shall they be respited;' [30] turn then from them and wait; verily, they are waiting too!

The Chapter of the Confederates[1].

(XXXIII. Medînah.)

In the name of the merciful and compassionate God.

O thou prophet! fear God and obey not the misbelievers and hypocrites; verily, God is ever knowing, wise!

But follow what thou art inspired with from thy Lord; verily, God of what you do is ever well aware. And rely upon God, for God is guardian enough.

God has not made for any man two hearts in his inside; nor has He made your wives,—whom you back away from,—your real mothers[2]; nor has He

---

[1] When this sûrah was written Medînah was besieged by a confederation of the Jewish tribes with the Arabs of Mecca, Ne*g*d and Tehâmah, at the instigation of the Jewish tribe of Na*dh*îr, whom Mohammed had expelled from Mecca the year before. The event took place in the fifth year of the Hi*g*rah.

[2] The Arabs were in the habit of divorcing their wives on certain occasions with the words, 'Thy back is to me as my

made your adopted sons your real sons. That is what ye speak with your mouths; but God speaks the truth and He guides to the path!

[5] Call them by their fathers' names; that is more just in God's sight; but if ye know not their fathers, then they are your brothers in religion and your clients. There is no crime against you for what mistakes ye make therein; but what your hearts do purposely—but God is ever forgiving and merciful.

The prophet is nearer of kin to the believers than themselves, and his wives are their mothers. And blood relations are nearer in kin to each other by the Book of God than the believers and those who fled[1]; only your doing kindness to your kindred, that is traced in the Book.

And when we took of the prophets their compact[2], from thee and from Noah, and Abraham, and Moses, and Jesus the son of Mary, and took of them a rigid compact, that He might ask the truth-tellers of their truth. But He has prepared for those who misbelieve a grievous woe.

O ye who believe! remember God's favours towards you when hosts came to you and we sent against them a wind and hosts[3] that ye could not see;—and God knew what ye were doing.

mother's back,' after which they considered it as unnatural to approach them as though they were their real mothers. This practice Mohammed here forbids. They used also to consider their adopted children in the same light as real children of their body; in forbidding this practice also, Mohammed legalised his marriage with Zâinab, the divorced wife of his freedman Zâid, who was also his adopted son.

[1] The Muhâgerîn.

[2] See Part I, p. 57, note 1.

[3] Of angels.

[10] When they came upon you from above you and from below[1] you, and when your eyesights were distracted and your hearts came up into your throats, and ye suspected God with certain suspicions.

There were the believers tried and were made to quake with a severe quaking.

And when the hypocrites and those in whose hearts was sickness said, 'God and His Apostle have only promised us deceitfully.' And when a party of them said, 'O people of Yathreb[2]; there is no place for you (here)[3], return then (to the city).' And a part of them asked leave of the prophet (to return), saying, 'Verily, our houses are defenceless;' but they were not defenceless, they only wished for flight.

But had they been entered upon from its environs and then been asked to show treason they would have done so; but they would only have tarried there a little while[4].

---

[1] On the approach of the confederate army, to the number of 12,000, Mohammed, by the advice of Selmân the Persian, ordered a deep trench to be dug round Medînah, and himself went out to defend it with 3,000 men. The two forces remained for nearly a month in their respective camps without coming to an actual conflict: until one night a piercing east wind blew so violently, and made such disorder in the camp of the besiegers, that a panic seized upon them, and they retired precipitately. Some of them had been encamped on the heights to the east of the town, the others in the lower part of the valley.

[2] The ancient name of the city; it was only called 'El Medînah, 'the city,' after it had become famous by giving shelter to Mohammed.

[3] In the trenches.

[4] I. e. if the confederates had effected an entry, these half-hearted persons would have listened to their proposals, and have deserted the prophet.

[15] They had covenanted with God before, that they would not turn their backs; and God's covenant shall be enquired of.

Say, 'Flight shall avail you naught; if ye fly from death or slaughter, even then ye shall be granted enjoyment only for a little!'

Say, 'Who is it that can save you from God, if He wish you evil, or wish you mercy?' but they will not find beside God a patron or a helper.

Say, 'God knows the hinderers amongst you, and those who say to their brethren, "Come along unto us," and show but little valour;—covetous towards you[1].' When fear comes thou wilt see them looking towards thee, their eyes rolling like one fainting with death; but when the fear has passed away they will assail you with sharp tongues, covetous of the best[2]. These have never believed, and God will make vain their works, for that is easy with God.

[20] They reckoned that the confederates would never go away; and if the confederates should come they would fain be in the desert with the Arabs, asking for news of you! and if they were amongst you they would fight but little.

Ye had in the Apostle of God a good example for him who hopes for God and the last day, and who remembers God much.

And when the believers saw the confederates they said, 'This is what God and His Apostle promised us; God and His Apostle are true!' and it only increased them in faith and resignation.

Amongst the believers are men who have been

---

[1] I. e. chary of helping you, but greedy of the spoils.

[2] I. e. the best share of the spoils.

true to their covenant with God, and there are some who have fulfilled their vow[1], and some who wait and have not changed[2] with fickleness.

That God might reward the truthful for their truth, and punish the hypocrites if He please, or turn again towards them;—verily, God is forgiving, merciful!

[25] And God drove back the misbelievers in their rage; they gat no advantage;—God was enough for the believers in the fight, for God is strong, mighty!

And He drove down those of the people of the Book who had helped them[3] from their fortresses[4] and hurled dread into their hearts; a part ye slew and ye took captive a part: and He gave you their land, and their dwellings, and their property for an inheritance, and a land ye had not trodden, for God is ever mighty over all.

O thou prophet! say to thy wives, 'If ye be desirous of the life of this world and its adornments, come, I will give you them to enjoy and I will let you range handsomely at large! But if ye be desirous of God and His Apostle and of the abode of the hereafter, verily, God has prepared for those of you who do good a mighty hire[5]!'

---

[1] I. e. their vow to fight till they obtained martyrdom.

[2] I. e. changed their mind.

[3] I. e. who had helped the confederates.

[4] The Qurâi*th*ah Jews, whom Mohammed attacked after the siege of Medînah had been raised, and punished for their treachery in having joined the confederates although in league with him at the time.

[5] Mohammed being annoyed by the demands made by his wives for costly dresses and the like, offered them the choice of divorce or of being content with their usual mode of living. They chose the latter.

[30] O ye women of the prophet! whosoever of you commits manifest fornication, doubled shall be her torment twice; and that is easy unto God!

But that one of you who is devoted to God and His Apostle and does right we will give her her hire twice over, and we have prepared for her a noble provision.

O ye women of the prophet! ye are not like any other women; if ye fear God then be not too complaisant in speech, or he in whose heart is sickness will lust after you; but speak a reasonable speech.

And stay still in your houses and show not yourselves with the ostentation of the ignorance of yore; and be steadfast in prayer, and give alms, and obey God and His Apostle;—God only wishes to take away from you[1] the horror as people of His House and to purify you thoroughly.

And remember what is recited in your houses of the signs of God and of wisdom; verily, God is subtle and aware!

[35] Verily, men resigned and women resigned[2], and believing men and believing women, and devout men and devout women, and truthful men and truthful women, and patient men and patient women, and humble men and humble women, and almsgiving men and almsgiving women, and fasting men and fasting women, and men who guard their private parts and women who guard their private parts, and

---

[1] Here the pronoun is changed from feminine to masculine, and the passage is appealed to by the Shiahs as showing the intimate relations that existed between Mohammed and 'Alî, for they say that by 'his household' are particularly meant Fa/imah and 'Alî, In the next paragraph the feminine is again used.

[2] I. e. Muslims; see Part I, p. 15, note 1.

men who remember God much, and women who remember Him,—God has prepared for them forgiveness and a mighty hire.

It is not for a believing man or for a believing woman, when God and His Apostle have decided an affair, to have the choice in that affair; and whoso rebels against God and His Apostle has erred with an obvious error.

And when thou didst say to him God had shown favour to and thou hadst shown favour to, 'Keep thy wife to thyself and fear God;' and thou didst conceal in thy soul what God was about to display; and didst fear men, though God is more deserving that thou shouldst fear Him; and when Zâid had fulfilled his desire of her[1] we did wed thee to her that there should be no hindrance to the believers in the matter of the wives of their adopted sons when they have fulfilled their desire of them: and so God's bidding to be done[2].

There is no hindrance to the prophet about what God has ordained for him;—(such was) the course of God with those who have passed away before,—and God's bidding is a decreed decree! Those who

---

[1] I. e. divorced her.

[2] Zâid was Mohammed's freedman and adopted son. Mohammed had seen and admired Zâid's wife Zâinab, and her husband at once offered to divorce her: this Mohammed dissuaded him from until the transaction was sanctioned by the verse. The relations of the Arabs to their adopted children were, as has been remarked before, p. 138, note 2, very strict; and Mohammed's marriage with Zâinab occasioned much scandal among his contemporaries. This passage and those at the commencement of the chapter abrogate all these inconvenient restrictions. Zâid and Abu Laheb, Sûrah CXI, are the only two persons of Mohammed's acquaintance who are mentioned in the Qur'ân by name.

preach God's messages and fear Him and fear not any one except God,—but God is good enough at reckoning up.

[40] Mohammed is not the father of any of your men, but the Apostle of God, and the Seal of the Prophets; for God all things doth know!

O ye who believe! remember God with frequent remembrance, and celebrate His praises morning and evening.

He it is who prays[1] for you and His angels too, to bring you forth out of the darkness into the light, for He is merciful to the believers.

Their salutation on the day they meet Him shall be 'Peace!' and He has prepared for them a noble hire.

O thou prophet! verily, we have sent thee as a witness and a herald of glad tidings and a warner, [45] and to call (men) unto God by His permission, and as an illuminating lamp.

Give glad tidings then to the believers, that for them is great grace from God. And follow not the unbelievers and the hypocrites; but let alone their ill-treatment[2], and rely upon God, for God is guardian enough.

O ye who believe! when ye wed believing women, and then divorce them before ye have touched them,

---

[1] The same word is used as is rendered 'pray' in all the other passages in the Qur'ân, though the commentators interpret it here as meaning 'bless.' So, too, in the formula which is always used after Mohammed's name, zalla 'llâhu 'alâihi wa sallam, 'may God bless and preserve him!' is literally, 'may God pray for him and salute him!'

[2] Either, 'do not ill-treat them,' or, 'take no notice of their ill-treating thee.'

ye have no term that ye need observe; so make them some provision, and let them go handsomely at large.

O thou prophet! verily, we make lawful for thee thy wives to whom thou hast given their hire[1], and what thy right hand possesses[2] out of the booty that God has granted thee, and the daughters of thy paternal uncle and the daughters of thy paternal aunts, and the daughters of thy maternal uncle and the daughters of thy maternal aunts, provided they have fled with thee, and any believing woman if she give herself to the prophet, if the prophet desire to marry her;—a special privilege this for thee, above the other believers.

[50] We knew what we ordained for them concerning their wives and what their right hands possess, that there should be no hindrance to thee; and God is forgiving, merciful.

Put off[3] whomsoever thou wilt of them and take to thyself whomsoever thou wilt, or whomsoever thou cravest of those whom thou hast deposed[4], and it shall be no crime against thee. That is nigher to cheering their eyes and that they should not grieve, and should be satisfied with what thou dost bring them all; but God knows best what is in their hearts; and God is knowing, clement.

It is not lawful to thee to take women after (this), nor to change them for (other) wives, even though their beauty please thee; except what thy right hand possesses, for God is ever watchful over all.

---

[1] I. e. dowry. [2] Slave girls.

[3] I. e. from her turn of conjugal rights.

[4] I. e. divorced.

O ye who believe! do not enter the houses of the prophet, unless leave be given you, for a meal,—not watching till it is cooked! But when ye are invited, then enter; and when ye have fed, disperse, not engaging in familiar discourse. Verily, that would annoy the prophet and he would be ashamed for your sake [1], but God is not ashamed of the truth [2].

And when ye ask them [3] for an article, ask them from behind a curtain [4]; that is purer for your hearts and for theirs. It is not right for you to annoy the prophet of God, nor to wed his wives after him ever; verily, that is with God a serious thing.

If ye display a thing or conceal it, verily, God all things doth know.

[55] There is no crime against them [5] (if they

---

[1] He would be reluctantly obliged to ask you to leave.

[2] The tent of an Arab chief is looked upon as a place of general entertainment, and is always besieged by visitors. The advent of a stranger, or indeed any occasion that demands the preparation of food or any form of entertainment, is the signal for every adult male of the encampment to sit round it, and wait for an invitation to partake of the meal. This becomes a very serious tax upon the sheikh, as the laws of Arab hospitality imperatively require every person present to be inivited to join in the repast. The translator has often witnessed scenes—especially among the Arabs of Edom and Moab—which gave a very living significance to these words of the Qur'ân. Mohammed's exceptionally prominent position exposed him in a peculiar manner to these irruptions of unbidden guests. Another saying bearing upon the point is traditionally ascribed to him, zur *gh*ibban tazdâd 'hubban, 'visit seldom and you will get more love.'

[3] The prophet's wives.

[4] The women to the present day always remain behind a curtain which screens off their part of the tent from the rest, but freely converse with their husband and his guests, and hand over the dishes and any other articles that may be required by the company.

[5] The prophet's wives.

speak unveiled) to their fathers, or their sons, or their brothers, or their brothers' sons, or their sisters' sons, or their women, or what their right hands possess; but let them fear God,—verily, God is witness over all.

Verily, God and His angels pray for the prophet. O ye who believe! pray for him and salute him with a salutation[1]!

Verily, those who annoy God and His Apostle, God will curse them in this world and the next, and prepare for them shameful woe!

And those who annoy the believers for what they have not earned, such have to bear (the guilt of) calumny and obvious sin.

O thou prophet! tell thy wives and thy daughters, and the women of the believers, to let down over them their outer wrappers; that is nearer for them to be known and that they should not be annoyed; but God is forgiving, merciful.

[60] Surely if the hypocrites and those in whose hearts is a sickness and the insurrectionists in Medînah do not desist, we will surely incite thee against them. Then they shall not dwell near thee therein save for a little while. Cursed wherever they are found,—taken and slain with slaughter!

God's course with those who have passed away before: and thou shalt never find in God's course any alteration.

The folk will ask thee about the Hour; say, 'The knowledge thereof is only with God, and what is to make thee perceive that the Hour is haply nigh?'

---

[1] See p. 145, note 1.

Verily, God has cursed the misbelievers and has prepared for them a blaze!

[65] To dwell therein for ever and for aye; they shall not find a patron or a helper!

On the day when their faces shall writhe in the fire they shall say, 'O, would that we had obeyed God and obeyed the Apostle!'

And they shall say, 'Our Lord! verily, we obeyed our chiefs and our great men and they led us astray from the path! Our Lord! give them double torment and curse them with a great curse!'

O ye who believe! be not like those who annoyed Moses; but God cleared him of what they said, and he was regarded in the sight of God [1].

[70] O ye who believe! fear God and speak a straightforward speech. He will correct for you your works, and pardon you your sins; for he who obeys God and His Apostle has attained a mighty happiness.

Verily, we offered the trust [2] to the heavens and the earth and the mountains, but they refused to bear it, and shrank from it; but man bore it: verily, he is ever unjust and ignorant. That God may torment the hypocritical men and hypocritical women, and the idolaters and idolatresses; and that God may turn relenting towards the believing men and believing women; verily, God is ever forgiving, merciful.

---

[1] The occasion of the revelation of this verse is said to have been that Mohammed being accused of unfairly dividing certain spoils, said, 'God, have mercy on my brother Moses; he was wronged more than this, and bore it patiently.'

[2] That is, 'the faith.'

The Chapter of Sebâ[1].

(XXXIV. Mecca.)

In the name of the merciful and compassionate God.

Praise belongs to God, whose is whatsoever is in the heavens and whatsoever is in the earth; His is the praise in the next world, and He is the wise and well aware!

He knows what goes into the earth, and what comes forth therefrom, and what comes down from the sky, and what ascends thereto; for He is the merciful, forgiving.

Those who misbelieve say, 'The Hour shall not come to us;' say, 'Yea, by my Lord it shall surely come to you! by Him who knows the unseen! nor shall there escape from it the weight of an atom, in the heavens or in the earth, or even less than that, or greater, save in the perspicuous Book;' and that He may reward those who believe and do right; these,—for them is forgiveness and a noble provision.

[5] But those who strive concerning our signs to frustrate them; these,—for them is the torment of a grievous plague.

And those to whom knowledge has been given see that what is sent down to thee from thy Lord is the truth, and guides unto the way of the mighty, the praiseworthy.

And those who misbelieve say, 'Shall we guide

[1] A city of Yemen was also called Mârab; it was about three days' journey from Sanâ'h. The bursting of the dyke of Mârab and the destruction of the city by a flood are historical facts, and happened in about the first or second century of our era.

you to a man who will inform you that when ye are torn all to pieces, then ye shall be a new creation? he has forged against God a lie, or there is a *g*inn in him;'—nay, those who believe not in the hereafter are in the torment and in the remote error!

Have they not looked at what is before them and what is behind them of the heaven and the earth? if we pleased we would cleave the earth open with them, or we would make to fall upon them a portion of the heaven; verily, in that is a sign to every repentant servant.

[10] And we did give David grace from us, 'O ye mountains! echo (God's praises) with him, and ye birds!' and we softened for him iron: Make thou coats of mail and adapt the rings thereof, and do right; verily, I at what ye do do look.' And to Solomon the wind; its morning journey was a month, and its evening journey was a month; and we made to flow for him a fountain of molten brass; and of the *g*inns some to work before him by the permission of his Lord; and whoso swerves amongst them from our bidding we will give him to taste the torment and the blaze; and they made for him what he pleased of chambers, and images, and dishes like troughs, and firm pots; —work, O ye family of David! thankfully; few is it of my servants who are thankful.

And when we decreed for him death, naught guided them to his death save a reptile of the earth that ate his staff; and when he fell down it was made manifest to the *g*inns that, had they but known the unseen, they need not have tarried in the shameful torment[1].

[1] The Mohammedan legend is that Solomon had employed the

Sebâ had in their dwellings a sign; two gardens, on the right hand and on the left, 'Eat from the provision of your Lord; and give thanks to Him! a good country and a forgiving Lord!' [15] but they turned away, and we sent against them the flood of the dyke; and we changed for them their two gardens into two gardens that grew bitter fruit and tamarisk, and some few lote trees [1].

This did we reward them with, for that they misbelieved; and do we so reward any but misbelievers?

And we made between them and the cities which we had blessed (other) cities which were evident; and we measured out the journey: 'Journey ye thereto nights and days in safety!' And they said, 'Our Lord! make a greater distance between our journeys;' and they wronged themselves, and we made them legends; and we tore them all to pieces; verily, in that are signs to every patient, grateful person. And Iblîs verified his suspicion concerning them,

---

ginns to construct the temple of Jerusalem for him, and perceiving that he must die before it was completed, he prayed God to conceal his death from them lest they should relinquish the work when no longer compelled to keep to it by fear of his presence. This prayer was heard, and Solomon, who died while resting on his staff, remained in this position for a year without his death being suspected, until a worm having eaten away his staff it broke, and the corpse fell to the ground, thus revealing the fact of his death. The shameful torment which the ginns might have avoided is their forced labour in building the temple.

[1] The Rhamnus Nabeca of Forshâl, the Rhamnus Nabeca Spina Christi of Linnæus, its fruit, which is called Nebuk, is a small round berry, in taste something like the jargonelle pear, and is a great favourite with the Bedawîn. It grows freely in the Sinaitic peninsula.

and they followed him, save a party of the believers[1].

[20] Yet had he no authority over them, save that we might know who it was that believed in the hereafter from him who amongst them was in doubt; for thy Lord guards everything.

Say, 'Call on those whom ye pretend beside God;' they cannot control the weight of an atom in the heavens or in the earth; nor have they any partnership in either; nor has He amongst them any supporter; nor is intercession of any avail with Him, except for him whom He permits; so that when fright is removed from their hearts they say, 'What is it that your Lord says?' they say, 'The truth; for He is the high, the great.'

Say, 'Who provides from the heavens and the earth?' Say, 'God.' And, verily, we or ye are surely in guidance or in an obvious error.

Say, 'Ye shall not be asked about what we have sent, nor shall we be asked about what ye do.

[25] 'Our Lord shall assemble us together; then He shall open between us in truth, for He is the opener who knows.'

Say, 'Show me those whom ye have added to Him as partners; not so! nay, but He is God, the mighty, the wise!'

---

[1] A great trade used formerly to exist between Sebâ and Syria. The Mohammedan commentators suppose that the cessation of traffic, which naturally caused the gradual ruin of the intermediate towns, and the subsequent destruction of Sebâ or Mâreb itself by the flood, was a punishment for the covetous wish of the people of the city, that the distances which traders had to pass over were longer, so that they themselves might earn more money by providing them with camels and escorts.

We have only sent thee to men generally as a herald of glad tidings and a warner; but most men do not know.

And they say, 'When shall this promise be, if ye do speak the truth?' say, 'For you is the appointment of a day of which ye shall not keep back an hour, nor shall ye bring it on!'

[30] And those who misbelieve say, 'We will never believe in this Qur'ân or in what is before it;' but couldst thou see when the unjust are set before their Lord, they shall rebut each other in speech.

Those who were thought weak shall say to those who were big with pride, 'Had it not been for you we should have been believers.' Those who were big with pride shall say to those who were thought weak, 'Was it we who turned you away from the guidance after it came to you? nay, ye were sinners.'

And those who were thought weak shall say to those who were big with pride, 'Nay, but it was the plotting by night and day, when ye did bid us to disbelieve in God, and to make peers for Him!' and they shall display repentance when they see the torment; and we will put fetters on the necks of those who misbelieved. Shall they be rewarded except for that which they have done?

We have not sent to any city a warner but the opulent thereof said, 'We, in what ye are sent with, disbelieve.'

And they say, 'We have more wealth and children, and we shall not be tormented.'

[35] Say, 'Verily, my Lord extends provision to whom He pleases or doles it out, but most men do not know; but neither your wealth nor your children

is that which will bring you to a near approach to us, save him who believes and does right; these, for them is a double reward for what they have done, and they in upper rooms [1] shall be secure.'

And those who strive concerning our signs to frustrate them, these in the torment shall be arraigned. Verily, my Lord extends provision to whomsoever He will of His servants, or doles it out to him. And what ye expend in alms at all, He will repay it; for He is the best of providers.

And on the day He will gather them all together, then He will say to the angels, 'Are these those who used to worship you?'

[40] They shall say, 'Celebrated be thy praises! thou art our patron instead of them. Nay, they used to worship the *g*inns, most of them believe in them [2]. But to-day they cannot control for each other, either profit or harm;' and we will say to those who have done wrong, 'Taste ye the torment of the fire wherein ye did disbelieve!'

And when our signs are recited to them they say, 'This is only a man who wishes to turn you from what your fathers served;' and they say, 'This is only a lie forged,' and those who misbelieve will say of the truth when it comes to them, 'It is only obvious sorcery!'

But we have not brought them any book which they may study, and we have not sent to them before thee a warner.

Those before them said it was a lie, and these [3] have not reached a tithe of what we had given them.

[1] In Paradise.

[2] See Part I, p. 127, note 2.

[3] That is, the Meccans.

And they said my apostles were liars, and how great a change was then!

[45] Say, 'I only admonish you of one thing, that ye should stand up before God in twos or singly, and then that ye reflect that there is no ginn in your companion[1]. He is only a warner to you before the keen torment.'

Say, 'I do not ask you for it a hire; that is for yourselves; my hire is only from God, and He is witness over all.'

Say, 'Verily, my Lord hurls forth the truth; and He well knows the unseen.'

Say, 'The truth has come, and falsehood shall vanish and shall not come back.'

Say, 'If I err I only err against myself; and if I am guided it is all what my Lord inspires me; verily, He is the hearing, the nigh!'

[50] And couldst thou see when they are scared, and there shall be no escape, and they shall be taken from a place that is nigh. And they say, 'We believe in it.' But how can they partake of it from a distant place? They misbelieved before, and conjectured about the unseen from a distant place. And there shall be a barrier between them and that which they lust after; as we did with their fellow sectaries before; verily, they were in hesitating doubt.

---

[1] That he, Mohammed, is not possessed by a ginn.

The Chapter of the Angels[1].

(XXXV. Mecca.)

In the name of the merciful and compassionate God.

Praise belongs to God, the originator of the heavens and the earth; who makes the angels His messengers, endued with wings in pairs, or threes or fours; He adds to creation what He pleases; verily, God is mighty over all!

What God opens to men of His mercy there is none to withhold; and what He withholds, there is none can send it forth after Him; for He is the mighty, the wise.

O ye folk! remember the favours of God towards you; is there a creator beside God, who provides you from the heavens and from the earth? There is no god but He; how then can ye lie?

And if they call thee liar, apostles were called liars before thee, and unto God affairs return.

[5] O ye folk! verily, God's promise is true; then let not the life of this world beguile you, and let not the beguiler beguile you concerning God. Verily, the devil is to you a foe, so take him as a foe; he only calls his crew to be the fellows of the blaze.

Those who misbelieve, for them is keen torment.

But those who believe and do right, for them is forgiveness and a great hire.

What! is he whose evil act is made seemly for him, so that he looks upon it as good, ——?

[1] Also called 'of the Originator.'

Verily, God leads astray whom He pleases and guides whom He pleases; let not thy soul then be wasted in sighing for them; verily, God knows what they do!

[10] It is God who sends the winds, and they stir up a cloud, and we irrigate therewith a dead country, and we quicken therewith the earth after its death; so shall the resurrection be!

Whosoever desires honour—honour belongs wholely to God; to Him good words ascend, and a righteous deed He takes up; and those who plot evil deeds, for them is keen torment, and their plotting is in vain.

God created you from earth, then from a clot; then He made you pairs; and no female bears or is delivered, except by His knowledge; nor does he who is aged reach old age, or is aught diminished from his life, without it is in the Book; verily, that is easy unto God.

The two seas are not equal: one is sweet and fresh and pleasant to drink, and the other is salt and pungent; but from each do ye eat fresh flesh, and bring forth ornaments which ye wear; and thou mayest see the ships cleave through it, that ye may search after His grace, and haply ye may give thanks.

He turns the night into day, and He turns the day into night; and He subjects the sun and the moon, each of them runs on to an appointed goal; that is God, your Lord! His is the kingdom; but those ye call on beside Him possess not a straw[1].

[15] If you call upon them they cannot hear your

[1] Literally, the husk of a date stone.

call, and if they hear they cannot answer you; and on the resurrection day they will deny your associating them with God; but none can inform thee like the One who is aware.

O ye folk! ye are in need of God; but God, He is independent, praiseworthy.

If He please He will take you off, and will bring a fresh creation; for that is no hard matter unto God.

And no burdened soul shall bear the burden of another; and if a heavily laden one shall call for its load (to be carried) it shall not be carried for it at all, even though it be a kinsman!—thou canst only warn those who fear their Lord in the unseen and who are steadfast in prayer; and he who is pure is only pure for himself; and unto God the journey is.

[20] The blind is not equal with him who sees, nor the darkness with the night, nor the shade with the hot blast; nor are the living equal with the dead; verily, God causes whom He pleases to hear, and thou canst not make those who are in their graves hear; thou art but a warner!

Verily, we have sent thee in truth a herald of glad tidings and a warner; and there is no nation but its warner has passed away with it.

And if they called thee liar, those before thee called their apostles liars too, who came to them with manifest signs, and the Scriptures, and the illuminating Book.

Then I seized those who misbelieved, and what a change it was!

[25] Dost thou not see that God has sent down from the heaven water, and has brought forth therewith fruits varied in hue, and on the mountains

dykes[1], white and red, various in hue, and some intensely black, and men and beasts and cattle, various in hue? thus! none fear God but the wise among His servants; but, verily, God is mighty, forgiving.

Verily, those who recite the Book of God, and are steadfast in prayer, and give alms of what we have bestowed in secret and in public, hope for the merchandise that shall not come to naught; that He may pay them their hire, and give them increase of His grace; verily, He is forgiving, grateful.

What we have inspired thee with of the Book is true, verifying what was before it; verily, God of His servants is well aware and sees.

Then we gave the Book for an inheritance to those whom we chose of our servants, and of them are some who wrong themselves, and of them are some who take a middle course, and of them are some who vie in good works by the permission of their Lord; that is great grace.

[30] Gardens of Eden shall they enter, adorned therein with bracelets of gold and pearls; and their garments therein shall be silk; and they shall say, 'Praise belongs to God, who has removed from us our grief; verily, our Lord is forgiving, grateful! who has made us alight in an enduring abode of His grace, wherein no toil shall touch us, and there shall touch us no fatigue.'

But those who misbelieve, for them is the fire of

---

[1] The word is here used in its geological sense, and is applied to the various coloured streaks which are so plainly to be seen in the bare mountain sides of Arabia. The Arabs of the desert to this day call them by the same name as is here used in the Qur'ân.

hell; it shall not be decreed for them to die, nor shall aught of the torment be lightened from them; thus do we reward every misbeliever; and they shall shriek therein, 'O our Lord! bring us forth, and we will do right, not what we used to do!'—'Did we not let you grow old enough for every one who would be mindful to be mindful? and there came to you a warner!—[35] So taste it, for the unjust shall have none to help!' verily, God knows the unseen things of the heavens and of the earth; verily, He knows the nature of men's breasts, He it is who made you vicegerents in the earth, and he who misbelieves, his misbelief is against himself; but their misbelief shall only increase the misbelievers in hatred with their Lord; and their misbelief shall only increase the misbelievers in loss.

Say, 'Have ye considered your associates whom ye call on beside God?' show me what they created of the earth; have they a share in the heavens, or have we given them a book that they rest on a manifest sign? nay, the unjust promise each other naught but guile.

Verily, God holds back the heavens and the earth lest they should decline; and if they should decline there is none to hold them back after Him; verily, He is clement, forgiving.

[40] They swore by God with their most strenuous oath, verily, if there come to them a warner they would be more guided than any one of the nations; but when a warner comes to them, it only increases them in aversion, and in being big with pride in the earth, and in plotting evil; but the plotting of evil only entangles those who practise it; can they then expect aught but the course of those of yore? but

thou shalt not find any alteration in the course of God; and they shall not find any change in the course of God.

Have they not journeyed on in the land and seen what was the end of those before them who were stronger than they? but God, nothing can ever make Him helpless in the heavens or in the earth; verily, He is knowing, powerful.

Were God to catch men up for what they earn, He would not leave upon the back of it[1] a beast; but He respites them until an appointed time.
[45] When their appointed time comes, verily, God looks upon His servants.

The Chapter of Y. S.

(XXXVI. Mecca.)

In the name of the merciful and compassionate God.

Y.S. By the wise Qur'ân, verily, thou art of the apostles upon a right way. The revelation of the
mighty, the merciful! [5] That thou mayest warn
a people whose fathers were not warned, and who themselves are heedless.

Now is the sentence due against most of them, for they will not believe. Verily, we will place upon their necks fetters, and they shall reach up to their chins, and they shall have their heads forced back; and we will place before them a barrier, and behind them a barrier; and we will cover them and they shall not see; and it is all the same to them if thou

[1] The earth.

dost warn them or dost warn them not, they will not believe. [10] Thou canst only warn him who fol lows the reminder, and fears the Merciful in the unseen; but give him glad tidings of forgiveness and a noble hire.

Verily, we quicken the dead, and write down what they have done before, and what vestiges they leave behind; and everything have we counted in a plain model[1].

Strike out for them a parable: the fellows of the city when there came to it the apostles; when we sent those two and they called them both liars, and we strengthened them with a third; and they said, 'Verily, we are sent to you.'

They said, 'Ye are only mortals like ourselves, nor has the Merciful sent down aught; ye are naught but liars.'

[15] They said, 'Our Lord knows that we are sent to you, and we have only our plain message to preach.'

They said, 'Verily, we have augured concerning you, and if ye do not desist we will surely stone you, and there shall touch you from us a grievous woe.'

Said they, 'Your augury is with you; what! if ye are reminded—? Nay, ye are an extravagant people!'

And there came from the remote part of the city a man hastening up. Said he, 'O my people! follow the apostles; [20] follow those who do not ask you a hire, and who are guided. What ails me that I should not worship Him who originated me, and unto whom I must return? Shall I take gods

[1] The Umm al Kitâb. See Part I, p. 2, note 2.

beside Him? If the Merciful One desires harm for me, their intercession cannot avail me at all, nor can they rescue me. Verily, I should then be in obvious error; verily, I believe in your Lord, then listen ye to me!'

[25] It was said, 'Enter thou into Paradise!' said he, 'O, would that my people did but know! for that my Lord has forgiven me, and has made me of the honoured.'

And we did send down upon his people no hosts from heaven, nor yet what we were wont to send down; it was but a single noise, and lo! they were extinct[1].

Alas for the servants! there comes to them no apostle but they mock at him!

[30] Have they not seen how many generations we have destroyed before them? verily, they shall not return to them; but all of them shall surely altogether be arraigned.

And a sign for them is the dead earth which we have quickened and brought forth therefrom seed, and from it do they eat; and we made therein gardens and palms and grapes, and we have caused fountains to gush forth therein, [35] that they may eat from the fruit thereof, and of what their hands have made; will they not then give thanks?

Celebrated be the praises of Him who created

[1] The legend is that Jesus sent two of His disciples to the city of Antioch, none believing them but one 'Habîb en Na*gg*âr, that is, ''Habîb the carpenter,' and all three were thrown into prison. Simon Peter was subsequently sent to their rescue; a great many were converted, and the rest were destroyed by a shout from the angel Gabriel. The shrine of 'Habîb en Na*gg*âr at Antioch is still a favourite place of pilgrimage for Mohammedans.

all kinds, of what the earth brings forth, and of themselves, and what they know not of!

And a sign to them is the night, from which we strip off the day, and lo! they are in the dark; and the sun runs on to a place of rest for it[1]; that is the ordinance of the mighty, the wise.

And the moon, we have ordered for it stations, until it comes again to be like an old dry palm branch.

[40] Neither is it proper for it to catch up the moon, nor for the night to outstrip the day, but each one floats on in its sky.

And a sign for them is that we bear their seed in a laden ship[2], and we have created for them the like thereof whereon to ride; and if we please, we drown them, and there is none for them to appeal to; nor are they rescued, save by mercy from us, as a provision for a season.

[45] And when it is said to them, 'Fear what is before you and what is behind you, haply ye may obtain mercy[3];' and thou bringest them not any one of the signs of their Lord, but they turn away therefrom; and when it is said to them, 'Expend in alms of what God has bestowed upon you,' those who misbelieve say to those who believe, 'Shall we feed him whom, if God pleased, He would feed? ye are only in an obvious error.'

They say, 'When shall this promise come to pass, if ye do tell the truth?' They await but a single noise, that shall seize them as they are contending. [50] And they shall not be able to

[1] There is a various reading here, 'and has no place of rest.'

[2] Some take this to refer to Noah's ark.

[3] That is, the punishment of this world and the next.

make a bequest; nor to their people shall they return; but the trumpet shall be blown, and, behold, from their graves unto their Lord shall they slip out!

They shall say, 'O, woe is us! who has raised us up from our sleeping-place? this is what the Merciful promised, and the apostles told the truth!' It shall be but a single noise, and lo! they are all arraigned before us.

And on that day no soul shall be wronged at all, nor shall ye be rewarded for aught but that which ye have done.

[55] Verily, the fellows of Paradise upon that day shall be employed in enjoyment; they and their wives, in shade upon thrones, reclining; therein shall they have fruits, and they shall have what they may call for. 'Peace!'—a speech from the merciful Lord!

'Separate yourselves to-day, O ye sinners! [60]
Did I not covenant with you, O children of Adam! that ye should not serve Satan? verily, he is to you an open foe; but serve ye me, this is the right way. But he led astray a numerous race of you; what! had ye then no sense? this is hell, which ye were threatened; broil therein to-day, for that ye misbelieved!'

[65] On that day we will seal their mouths, and their hands shall speak to us, and their feet shall bear witness of what they earned. And if we please we could put out their eyes, and they would race along the road; and then how could they see? And if we pleased we would transform them in their places, and they should not be able to go on, nor yet to return. And him to whom we grant old age,

we bow him down in his form; have they then no sense?

We have not taught him[1] poetry, nor was it proper for him; it is but a reminder and a plain Qur'ân, [70] to warn him who is living; but the sentence is due against the misbelievers.

Have they not seen that we have created for them of what our hands have made for them, cattle, and they are owners thereof? and we have tamed them for them, and of them are some to ride, and of them are what they eat, and therein have they advantages and beverages; will they not then give thanks?

But they take, beside God, gods that haply they may be helped. [75] They cannot help them; yet are they a host ready for them[2].

But let not their speech grieve thee: verily, we know what they conceal and what they display.

Has not man seen that we have created him from a clot? and lo! he is an open opponent; and he strikes out for us a likeness; and forgets his creation; and says, 'Who shall quicken bones when they are rotten?' Say, 'He shall quicken them who produced them at first; for every creation does He know; [80] who has made for you fire out of a green tree, and lo! ye kindle therewith.'

Is not He who created the heavens and the earth able to create the like thereof? yea! He is the knowing Creator; His bidding is only, when He desires anything to say to it, 'BE,' and it is. Then celebrated be the praises of Him in whose hands is

---

[1] Mohammed.

[2] I.e. they are ready to defend their false gods.

the kingdom of everything! and unto Him shall ye return.

The Chapter of the 'Ranged.'

(XXXVII. Mecca.)

In the name of the merciful and compassionate God.

By the (angels) ranged in ranks, and the drivers driving[1], and the reciters of the reminder, 'Verily, your God is one, [5] the Lord of the heavens and the earth and what is between the two, and the Lord of the sunrises!'

Verily, we have adorned the lower heaven with the adornment of the stars, and to preserve it from every rebellious devil, that they may not listen to the exalted chiefs; for they are hurled at from every side[2], driven off, and for them is lasting woe; [10] save such as snatches off a word, and there follows him a darting flame!

Ask them[3] whether they are stronger by nature or (the angels) whom we have created? We have created them of sticky clay.

Nay, thou dost wonder and they jest! and when they are reminded they will not remember; and when they see a sign they make a jest thereof, [15] and say, 'This is naught but obvious sorcery. What! when we are dead, and have become earth and bones, shall we then be raised? what! and our fathers of yore?'

Say, 'Yes, and ye shall shrink up, and it shall only

---

[1] Driving the clouds or 'scaring the devils.'

[2] See Part I, p. 50, note 2.

[3] The people of Mecca.

be one scare, and, behold, they shall look on, [20] and they shall say, 'O, woe is us! this is the day of judgment, this is the day of decision, which ye did call a lie!' Gather ye together, ye who were unjust, with their mates and what they used to serve beside God, and guide them to the way of hell, and stop them; verily, they shall be questioned. [25] 'Why do ye not help each other?' nay, on that day they shall resign themselves, and some shall draw near to others, to question each other, and they shall say, 'Verily, ye came to us from the right[1].' They shall say, 'Nay, ye were not believers, nor had we any authority over you; nay, ye were an outrageous people. [30] And the sentence of our Lord shall be due for us; verily, we shall surely taste thereof; we did seduce you—verily, we were erring too!' therefore, verily, on that day they shall share the torment: thus it is that we will do with the sinners.

Verily, when it is said to them, 'There is no god but God,' they get too big with pride, and say, [35] 'What! shall we leave our gods for an infatuated poet?' Nay, he came with the truth, and verified the apostles; verily, ye are going to taste of grievous woe, nor shall ye be rewarded save for that which ye have done!

Except God's sincere servants, [40] these shall have a stated provision of fruits, and they shall be honoured in the gardens of pleasure, upon couches facing each other[2]; they shall be served all round with a cup from a spring, [45] white and delicious to those who drink, wherein is no insidious spirit, nor shall they

---

[1] That is, with a good omen.

[2] See Chapter XV, verse 47.

be drunk therewith; and with them damsels, restraining their looks, large eyed; as though they were a sheltered egg; and some shall come forward to ask others; and a speaker amongst them shall say, 'Verily, I had a mate, [50] who used to say, "Art thou verily of those who credit? What! when we are dead, and have become earth and bones, shall we be surely judged?"' He will say, 'Are ye looking down?' and he shall look down and see him in the midst of hell. He shall say, 'By God, thou didst nearly ruin me! [55] And had it not been for the favour of my Lord, I should have been among the arraigned.'—'What! shall we not die save our first death? and shall we not be tormented?—Verily, this is mighty bliss! for the like of this then let the workers work.'

[60] Is that better as an entertainment, or the tree of Ez Zaqqûm[1]? Verily, we have made it a trial to the unjust[2]. Verily, it is a tree that comes forth from the bottom of hell; its spathe is as it were the heads of devils; verily, they shall eat therefrom, and fill their bellies therefrom. [65] Then shall they have upon it a mixture of boiling water; then, verily, their return shall be to hell.

Verily, they found their fathers erring, and they hurried on in their tracks; but there had erred before them most of those of yore, [70] and we had sent warners amongst them. Behold, then, what was the end of those who were warned, save God's sincere servants!

[1] Ez Zaqqûm is a foreign tree with an exceedingly bitter fruit, the name of which is here used for the infernal tree.

[2] The unbelievers objected that the tree could not grow in hell, where the very stones (see Part I, p. 4, note 1) were fuel for the fire.

Noah did call upon us, and a gracious answer did we give; and we saved him and his people from a mighty trouble; [75] and we made his seed to be the survivors; and we left for him amongst posterity 'peace upon Noah in the worlds; verily, thus do we reward those who do well; verily, he was of our believing servants.' [80] Then we drowned the others.

And, verily, of his sect was Abraham; when he came to his Lord with a sound heart; when he said to his father and his people, 'What is it that ye serve? with a lie do ye desire gods beside God? [85] What then is your thought respecting the Lord of the worlds?'

And he looked a look at the stars and said, 'Verily, I am sick!' and they turned their backs upon him fleeing[1]. And he went aside unto their gods and said, 'Will ye not eat? [90] What ails you that ye will not speak?' And he went aside to them smiting with the right hand.

And they[2] rushed towards him. Said he, 'Do ye serve what ye hew out, when God has created you, and what ye make?'

[95] Said they, 'Build for him a pyre, and throw him into the flaming hell!' They desired to plot against him, but we made them inferior. Said he, 'Verily, I am going to my Lord, He will guide me. My Lord! grant me (a son), one of the

---

[1] Mohammedan commentators say that he pretended to a knowledge of astrology and made as though he saw a presage of coming sickness for himself in the stars, whereupon the others fled for fear of contagion, and Abraham took the opportunity of absenting himself from the festival which was being held in honour of the idols.

[2] The people of the city.

righteous;' and we gave him glad tidings of a clement boy.

[100] And when he reached the age to work with him, he said, 'O my boy! verily, I have seen in a dream that I should sacrifice thee[1], look then what thou seest right.'

Said he, 'O my sire! do what thou art bidden; thou wilt find me, if it please God, one of the patient!'

And when they were resigned, and Abraham had thrown him down upon his forehead, we called to him, 'O Abraham! [105] thou hast verified the vision; verily, thus do we reward those who do well. This is surely an obvious trial.' And we ransomed him with a mighty victim; and we left for him amongst posterity, 'Peace upon Abraham; [110] thus do we reward those who do well; verily, he was of our servants who believe!' And we gave him glad tidings of Isaac, a prophet among the righteous; and we blessed him and Isaac;—of their seed is one who does well, and one who obviously wrongs himself.

And we were gracious unto Moses and Aaron. [115] We saved them and their people from mighty trouble, and we helped them and they had the upper hand; and we gave them both the perspicuous Book; and we guided them to the right way; and we left for them amongst posterity, [120] 'Peace upon Moses and Aaron; verily, thus do we reward those who do well; verily, they were both of our servants who believe!'

---

[1] The Mohammedan theory is that it was Ishmael and not Isaac who was taken as a sacrifice.

And verily Elyâs[1] was of the apostles; when he
said to his people, 'Will ye not fear? [125] do ye call
upon Baal and leave the best of Creators, God
your Lord and the Lord of your fathers of yore?'

But they called him liar; verily, they shall surely
be arraigned, save God's sincere servants. And we
left for him amongst posterity, [130] 'Peace upon
Elyâsîn[2]; verily, thus do we reward those who do
well; verily, he was of our servants who believe!'

And, verily, Lot was surely among the apostles;
when we saved him and his people altogether, [135]
except an old woman amongst those who lingered;
then we destroyed the others; verily, ye pass by
them in the morning and at night; have ye then no
sense?

And, verily, Jonah was amongst the apostles;
[140] when he ran away[3] into the laden ship; and
he cast lots and was of those who lost; and a fish
swallowed him, for he was to be blamed; and had
it not been that he was of those who celebrated

---

[1] Supposed by the Mohammedans to be the same as Al '*Hidh*r and Idrîs.

[2] This is probably another form of the word Elyâs, on the model of many Hebrew words which have survived in the later Arabic dialect. The Mohammedan commentators however conjecturally interpret it in various ways, some consider it to be a plural form, including Elias and his followers; others divide the word and read it Âl-ya-sîn, i.e. 'the family of Ya-sin,' namely, Elias and his father. Others imagine it to mean Mohammed or the Qur'ân. Most probably however the final syllable -în was nothing more than a prolonged utterance of the case-ending, here improperly used in order to preserve the rhyme or final cadence of the verse. The modern Bedawîn frequently do the same, and I have heard them singing a song commencing 'Zaidûn, Zaidûn, Zaidûn,' when they should say, Zaidu, 'O Zaid!' &c. Trans.

[3] The word used in the text is always applied to runaway slaves.

God's praises he would surely have tarried in the belly thereof to the day when men shall be raised.

[145] But we cast him on to the barren shore; and he was sick; and we made to grow over him a gourd tree; and we sent him to a hundred thousand or more, and they believed; and we gave them enjoyment for a season.

Ask them [1], 'Has thy Lord daughters while they have sons [2]? [150] or have we created the angels females while they were witnesses?' is it not of their lie that they say, 'God has begotten?' verily, they are liars.

Has he preferred daughters to sons? what ails you? how ye judge! [155] will ye not be mindful, or have ye obvious authority? then bring your Book if ye do speak the truth.

And they made him to be related to the *g*inns, while the *g*inns know that they shall be arraigned; celebrated be God's praises from what they attribute!—[160] save God's sincere servants.

'Verily, ye and what ye worship shall not try any one concerning him, save him who shall broil in hell; there is none amongst us but has his appointed place, and, [165] verily, we are ranged, and, verily, we celebrate His praises [3].'

And yet they say, 'Had we a reminder from those of yore we should surely have been of God's sincere servants.'

[170] But they misbelieved in it [4]; but soon shall they know.

---

[1] The Meccans.

[2] See Part I, p. 256, note 2.

[3] This speech is supposed to be the words of the angel Gabriel.

[4] I. e. in the Qur'ân.

But our word has been passed to our servants who were sent that they should be helped; that, verily, our hosts should gain mastery for them.

Then turn thou thy back upon them for a time,
[175] and look upon them, for soon they too shall look.

Would they hasten on our torment? but when it descends in their court, ill will the morning be of those who have been warned!

But turn thy back upon them for a time; and look, for soon they too shall look.

[180] Celebrated be the praises of thy Lord, the Lord of glory, above what they attribute! and peace be upon the apostles and praise be to God, the Lord of the worlds!

The Chapter of S.[1]

(XXXVIII. Mecca.)

In the name of the merciful and compassionate God.

S. By the Qur'ân with its reminder! nay, but those who misbelieve are in pride, schism!

How many a generation have we destroyed before them, and they cried out, but it was no time to escape!

And they wonder that a warner has come from amongst themselves, and the misbelievers say, 'This

[1] The Arabic commentators say of this title, 'God only knows what He means by it.' All the explanations given of it are purely conjectural. See the Introduction for this and the other mysterious letters used throughout the Qur'ân.

is a magician, a liar!' What! does he make the gods to be one God? verily, this is a wondrous thing.

[5] And the chiefs of them went away: 'Go on and persevere in your gods; this is a thing designed; we never heard this in any other sect; this is nothing but a fiction! Has a reminder come down upon him from amongst us?' nay, they are in doubt concerning my reminder; nay, they have not yet tasted of my torment!

Have they the treasures of the mercy of thy mighty Lord, the giver? or have they the kingdom of the heavens and of the earth, and what is between the two?—then let them climb up the ropes thereof.

[10] Any host whatever of the confederates shall there be routed.

Before them did Noah's people, and 'Âd, and Pharaoh of the stakes[1] call the apostles liars; and Thamûd and the people of Lot, and the fellows of the Grove, they were the confederates too.

They all did naught but call the apostles liars, and just was the punishment! Do these[2] await aught else but one noise for which there shall be no pause?

[15] But they say, 'O our Lord, hasten for us our share before the day of reckoning!'

Be patient of what they say, and remember our servant David endowed with might; verily, he

[1] Some say this refers to the punishment which Pharaoh used to inflict upon those who had offended him, whom he used to tie to four stakes and then torture. Others take the expression to refer to the stability of Pharaoh's kingdom. The word in the original is applied to the pegs with which Arabs fasten their tents.

[2] The Meccans.

turned frequently to us. Verily, we subjected the mountains to celebrate with him our praises at the evening and the dawn; and the birds too gathered together, each one would oft return to him; and we strengthened his kingdom, and we gave him wisdom and decisive address.

[20] Has there come to thee the story of the antagonists when they scaled the chamber wall? when they entered in unto David, and he was startled at them, they said, 'Fear not, we are two antagonists; one of us has injured the other; judge then between us with the truth and be not partial, but guide us to a level way. Verily, this is my brother: he had ninety-nine ewes and I had one ewe; and he said, "Give her over to my charge;" and he overcame me in the discourse.' Said he, 'He wronged thee in asking for thy ewe in addition to his own ewes. Verily, many associates do injure one another, except those who believe and do what is right, and very few are they!'

And he thought that we were trying him; and he asked pardon of his Lord and fell down bowing, and did turn; and we pardoned him; for, verily, he has a near approach to us and an excellent resort.

[25] O David! verily, we have made thee a vicegerent, judge then between men with truth and follow not lust, for it will lead thee astray from the path of God. Verily, those who go astray from the path of God, for them is keen torment, for that they did forget the day of reckoning!

And we have not created the heavens and the earth, and what is between the two, in vain. That is what those who misbelieved did think, but woe from the fire to those who misbelieve!

Shall we make those who believe and do right like those who do evil in the earth? or shall we make the pious like the sinners?

A blessed Book which we have sent down to thee that they may consider its verses, and that those endowed with minds may be mindful.

And we gave to David, Solomon, an excellent servant; verily, he turned frequently to us. [30] When there were set before him in the evening the steeds that paw the ground[1], and he said, 'Verily, I have loved the love of good things better than the remembrance of my Lord, until (the sun) was hidden behind the veil; bring them back to me;' and he began to sever their legs and necks.

And we did try Solomon, and we threw upon his throne a form; then he turned repentant[2]. Said he,

[1] The word in Arabic signifies a horse that stands on three legs and just touches the ground with the fore part of the hoof of the fourth. The story is that Solomon was so lost in the contemplation of his horses one day that he forgot the time of evening prayer, and was so smitten with remorse on discovering his negligence that he sacrificed them all except a hundred of the best. God however recompensed him by giving him dominion over the winds instead.

[2] The Mohammedan legend, borrowed from the Talmud, is that having conquered the king of Sidon and brought away his daughter *Gerâdeh*, he made her his favourite. She however so incessantly mourned her father that Solomon commanded the devils to make an image of him to console her, and to this she and her maids used to pay divine honours. To punish him for encouraging this idolatry, a devil named Sakhar one day obtained possession of his ring, which he used to entrust to a concubine named Amînah when he went out for any necessary purpose. As the whole secret of his power lay in this ring, which was engraved with the Holy Name, the devil was able to personate Solomon, who, being changed in form, was not recognised by his subjects, and wandered about for the space of forty days, the time during which the image had been worshipped in his house. After this Sakhar flew away and threw

'My Lord, pardon me and grant me a kingdom that is not seemly for any one after me; verily, thou art He who grants!'

[35] And we subjected to him the wind to run on at his bidding gently wherever he directed it; and the devils—every builder and diver, and others bound in fetters—'this is our gift, so be thou lavish or withhold without account!'

And, verily, he had with us a near approach, and a good resort.

[40] And remember our servant Job when he called upon his Lord that 'the devil has touched me with toil and torment!'

'Stamp with thy foot, this is a cool washing-place and a drink.' And we granted him his family, and the like of them with them, as a mercy from us and a reminder to those endowed with minds,—'and take in thy hand a bundle, and strike therewith, and break not thy oath!' Verily, we found him patient[1], an excellent servant; verily, he turned frequently to us.

[45] And remember our servants Abraham and

---

the signet into the sea, where it was swallowed by a fish, which was afterwards caught and brought to Solomon, who by this means recovered his kingdom and power.

[1] The Mohammedan legend is that when Job was undergoing his trials, the devil appeared to his wife and promised, if she would worship him, to restore their former prosperity; this she asked her husband to allow her to do. Job was so enraged at her conduct that he swore if he recovered to give her a hundred stripes. When Job had uttered the prayer recorded on page 52, line 19, Gabriel appeared and bade him in the words of the text to strike the ground with his feet. A fountain at once gushed forth, in which he washed and was healed, his wife also becoming young and beautiful again. In order not to break his oath he was commanded to strike her with a bundle of palm leaves, giving her a hundred painless blows at once.

Isaac and Jacob, endowed with might and sight; verily, we made them sincere by a sincere quality—the remembrance of the abode; and, verily, they were with us of the elect, the best.

And remember Ishmael and Elisha and Dhu-l-kifl, for each was of the righteous[1]. This is a reminder! verily, for the pious is there an excellent resort,—[50] gardens of Eden with the doors open to them;—reclining therein; calling therein for much fruit and drink; and beside them maids of modest glance, of their own age,—'This is what ye were promised for the day of reckoning!'—'This is surely our provision, it is never spent!'

[55] This!—and, verily, for the rebellious is there an evil resort,—hell; they shall broil therein, and an ill couch shall it be! This,—so let them taste it!—hot water, and pus, and other kinds of the same sort! 'This is an army plunged in with you! there is no welcome for them! verily, they are going to broil in the fire!'

[60] They shall say, 'Nay, for you too is there no welcome! it was ye who prepared it beforehand for us, and an ill resting-place it is!'

They shall say, 'Our Lord! whoso prepared this beforehand for us, give him double torment in the fire!' And they shall say, 'What ails us that we do not see men whom we used to think amongst the wicked? whom we used to take for mockery? have our eyes escaped them?'

Verily, that is the truth; the contention of the people of the fire.

[65] Say, 'I am only a warner; and there is no

[1] See page 53.

god but God, the one, the victorious, the Lord of the heavens and the earth, and what is between the two, the mighty, the forgiving!'

Say, 'It is a grand story, and yet ye turn from it!' I had no knowledge of the exalted chiefs when they contended.

[70] I am only inspired that I am a plain warner. When thy Lord said to the angels, 'Verily, I am about to create a mortal out of clay; and when I have fashioned him, and breathed into him of my spirit, then fall ye down before him adoring.' And the angels adored all of them, save Iblîs, who was too big with pride, and was of the misbelievers.

[75] Said He, 'O Iblîs! what prevents thee from adoring what I have created with my two hands? art thou too big with pride? or art thou amongst the exalted?' Said he, 'I am better than he, Thou hast created me from fire, and him Thou hast created from clay.' Said He, 'Then go forth therefrom, for, verily, thou art pelted, and, verily, upon thee is my curse unto the day of judgment.'

[80] Said he, 'My Lord! then respite me until the day when they are raised.' Said He, 'Then thou art amongst the respited until the day of the stated time.' Said he, 'Then, by Thy might! I will surely seduce them all together, except Thy servants amongst them who are sincere!' [85] Said He, 'It is the truth, and the truth I speak; I will surely fill hell with thee and with those who follow thee amongst them all together.'

Say, 'I do not ask thee for it any hire, nor am I of those who take too much upon myself. It is but a reminder to the servants, and ye shall surely know its story after a time.'

The Chapter of the Troops.

(XXXIX. Mecca.)

In the name of the merciful and compassionate God.

The sending down of the Book from God, the mighty, the wise.

Verily, we have sent down to thee the Book in truth, then serve God, being sincere in religion unto Him. Aye! God's is the sincere religion: and those who take beside Him patrons——'We do not serve them save that they may bring us near to God——' Verily, God will judge between them concerning that whereon they do dispute.

[5] Verily, God guides not him who is a misbelieving liar.

Had God wished to take to Himself a child, He would have chosen what He pleased from what He creates;—celebrated be His praises! He is God, the one, the victorious. He created the heavens and the earth in truth! It is He who clothes the day with night; and clothes the night with day; and subjects the sun and the moon, each one runs on to an appointed time; aye! He is the mighty, the forgiving! He created you from one soul; then He made from it its mate; and He sent down upon you of the cattle four pairs[1]! He creates you in the bellies of your mothers,—creation after creation, in three darknesses[2]. That is God for you! His is the kingdom, there is no god but He; how then can ye be turned away?

[1] Camel, oxen, sheep, and goats.

[2] I.e. the belly, the womb, and the placenta.

If ye be thankless, yet is God independent of you. He is not pleased with ingratitude in His servants; but if ye give thanks, He is pleased with that in you. But no burdened soul shall bear the burden of another; then unto your Lord is your return, and He will inform you of that which ye have done. [10] Verily, He knows the natures of men's breasts!

And when distress touches a man he calls his Lord, turning repentant to Him; then when He confers on him a favour from Himself he forgets what he had called upon Him for before, and makes peers for God to lead astray from His way! Say, 'Enjoy thyself in thy misbelief a little, verily, thou art of the fellows of the Fire.'

Shall he who is devout throughout the night, adoring and standing, cautious concerning the hereafter, and hoping for the mercy of his Lord . . . ? Say, 'Shall those who know be deemed equal with those who know not? only those will remember, who are endowed with minds!'

Say, 'O my servants who believe! fear your Lord! for those who do well in this world is good, and God's earth is spacious; verily, the patient shall be paid their hire without count!'

Say, 'Verily, I am bidden to serve God, being sincere in religion to Him; and I am bidden that I be the first of those resigned.'

[15] Say, 'Verily, I fear, if I rebel against my Lord, the torment of a mighty day.' Say, 'God do I serve, being sincere in my religion to Him; serve then what ye will beside Him!' Say, 'Verily, the losers are those who lose themselves and their families on the resurrection day. Aye, that is the obvious loss.'

They shall have over them shades of fire, and under them shades; with that does God frighten His servants: O my servants! then fear me.

But those who avoid *Tâghût*[1] and serve them not, but turn repentant unto God, for them shall be glad tidings. Then give glad tidings to my servants who listen to the word and follow the best thereof; they it is whom God guides, and they it is who are endowed with minds. [20] Him against whom the word of torment is due,—canst thou rescue him from the fire?

But for those who fear their Lord for them are upper chambers, and upper chambers above them built, beneath which rivers flow; God's promise! God does not fail in His promise.

Hast thou not seen that God sends down from the heaven water, and conducts it into springs in the earth? then He brings forth therewith corn varied in kind, then it dries up, and ye see it grow yellow; then He makes it grit;—verily, in that is a reminder for those endowed with minds.

Is he whose breast God has expanded for Islâm, and who is in light from his Lord . . . . ? And woe to those whose hearts are hardened against a remembrance of God! those are in obvious error.

God has sent down the best of legends, a book uniform and repeating; whereat the skins of those who fear their Lord do creep! then their skins and their hearts soften at the remembrance of God. That is the guidance of God! He guides therewith whom He will. But he whom God leads astray there is no guide for him.

---

[1] See Part I, p. 40, note 2.

[25] Shall he who must screen himself with his own face from the evil torment on the resurrection day . . . . ? And it shall be said of those who do wrong, taste what ye have earned.

Those before them called the (prophets) liars, and the torment came to them from whence they perceived it not; and God made them taste disgrace in the life of this world. But surely the torment of the hereafter is greater, if they did but know. We have struck out for men in this Qur'ân every sort of parable, haply they may be mindful. An Arabic Qur'ân with no crookedness therein; haply they may fear!

[30] God has struck out a parable, a man who has partners who oppose each other; and a man who is wholly given up to another; shall they be deemed equal in similitude? praise be to God! nay, but most of them know not!

Verily, thou shalt die, and, verily, they shall die; then, verily, on the resurrection day before your Lord shall ye dispute.

And who is more unjust than he who lies against God, and calls the truth a lie when it comes to him? Is there not in hell a resort for those who misbelieve? but whoso brings the truth and believes in it, these are they who fear.

[35] For them is what they please with their Lord, that is the reward of those who do well; that God may cover for them their offences which they have done, and may reward them with their hire for the best of that which they have done.

Is not God sufficient for His servants? and yet they would frighten thee with those beside Him[1].

[1] By their idols.

But he whom God leads astray there is no guide for him; and he whom God guides there is none to lead him astray: is not God mighty, the Lord of vengeance?

And if thou shouldst ask them who created the heavens and the earth, they will surely say, 'God!' Say, 'Have ye considered what ye call on beside God? If God wished me harm[1], could they remove His harm? or did He wish me mercy, could they withhold His mercy?' Say, 'God is enough for me, and on Him rely those who rely.'

[40] Say, 'O my people! act according to your power; I too am going to act; and ye shall know.'

He to whom the torment comes it shall disgrace him, and there shall alight upon him lasting torment.

Verily, we have sent down to thee the Book for men in truth; and whosoever is guided it is for his own soul: but whoso goes astray it is against them, and thou art not a guardian for them.

God takes to Himself souls at the time of their death; and those which do not die (He takes) in their sleep; and He holds back those on whom He has decreed death, and sends others back till their appointed time;—verily, in that are signs unto a people who reflect.

Do they take besides God intercessors? Say, 'What! though they have no control over anything and have no sense.'

[45] Say, 'God's is the intercession, all of it; His

[1] The pronoun in Arabic is feminine, and refers to the false gods, especially to the favourite goddesses of the Qurâis.

is the kingdom of the heavens and the earth; then unto Him shall ye be sent back.'

And when God alone is mentioned the hearts of those who believe not in the hereafter quake, and when those beside Him are mentioned, lo, they are joyful!

Say, 'O God! originator of the heavens and the earth, who knowest the unseen and the visible, thou wilt judge between thy servants concerning that whereon they do dispute!'

And had those who do wrong all that is in the earth, and the like thereof with it, they would ransom themselves therewith from the evil of the torment on the resurrection day! but there shall appear to them from God that which they had not reckoned on; and the evils of what they have earned shall appear to them; but that shall close in on them at which they mocked!

[50] And when harm touches man he calls on us; then, when we grant him favour from us, he says, 'Verily, I am given it through knowledge!' nay, it is a trial,—but most of them do not know!

Those before them said it too, but that availed them not which they had earned, and there befel them the evil deeds of what they had earned: and those who do wrong of these (Meccans), there shall befall them too the evil deeds of what they had earned, nor shall they frustrate Him.

Have they not known that God extends His provision to whom He pleases, or doles it out? verily, in that are signs unto a people who believe.

Say, 'O my servants! who have been extravagant against their own souls!' be not in despair of the mercy of God; verily, God forgives sins, all of them; verily, He is forgiving, merciful.

[55] But turn repentant unto your Lord, and resign yourselves to Him, before there comes on you torment! then ye shall not be helped: and follow the best of what has been sent down to you from your Lord, before there come on you the torment suddenly, ere ye can perceive!

Lest a soul should say, 'O my sighing! for what I have neglected towards God! for, verily, I was amongst those who did jest!' or lest it should say, 'If God had but guided me, I should surely have been of those who fear!' or lest it should say, when it sees the torment, 'Had I another turn I should be of those who do well!'

[60] 'Yea! there came to thee my signs and thou didst call them lies, and wert too big with pride, and wert of those who misbelieved!'

And on the resurrection day thou shalt see those who lied against God, with their faces blackened. Is there not in hell a resort for those who are too big with pride?

And God shall rescue those who fear Him, into their safe place; no evil shall touch them, nor shall they be grieved.

God is the creator of everything, and He is guardian over everything; His are the keys of the heavens and the earth; and those who misbelieve in the signs of God, they it is who lose!

Say, 'What! other than God would you bid me serve, O ye ignorant ones? [65] When He has inspired thee and those before thee that, "If thou dost associate aught with Him, thy work will surely be in vain, and thou shalt surely be of those who lose!" Nay, but God do thou serve, and be of those who do give thanks!'

And they do not value God at His true value; while the earth all of it is but a handful for Him on the resurrection day, and the heavens shall be rolled up in His right hand! Celebrated be His praise! and exalted be He above what they associate with Him! And the trumpet shall be blown, and those who are in the heavens and in the earth shall swoon, save whom God pleases. Then it shall be blown again, and, lo! they shall stand up and look on. And the earth shall beam with the light of its Lord, and the Book shall be set forth, and the prophets and martyrs[1] shall be brought; and it shall be decreed between them in truth, and they shall not be wronged! [70] And every soul shall be paid for what it has done, and He knows best that which they do; and those who misbelieve shall be driven to hell in troops; and when they come there, its doors shall be opened, and its keepers shall say to them, 'Did not apostles from amongst yourselves come to you to recite to you the signs of your Lord, and to warn you of the meeting of this day of yours?' They shall say, 'Yea, but the sentence of torment was due against the misbelievers!' It shall be said, 'Enter ye the gates of hell, to dwell therein for aye! Hell is the resort of those who are too big with pride!'

But those who fear their Lord shall be driven to Paradise in troops; until they come there, its doors shall be opened, and its keepers shall say to them, 'Peace be upon you, ye have done well!

[1] Or witnesses.

so enter in to dwell for aye!' and they shall say, 'Praise be to God, who hath made good His promise to us, and hath given us the earth to inherit! We establish ourselves in Paradise wherever we please; and goodly is the reward of those who work!'

[75] And thou shalt see the angels circling round about the throne, celebrating the praise of their Lord; and it shall be decided between them in truth; and it shall be said, 'Praise be to God, the Lord of the worlds!'

The Chapter of the Believer.

(XL. Mecca.)

In the name of the merciful and compassionate God.

'H. M. The sending down of the Book from God, the mighty, the knowing, the forgiver of sin and accepter of repentance, keen at punishment, long-suffering! there is no god but He! to whom the journey is!

None wrangle concerning the signs of God but those who misbelieve; then let not their going to and fro in the cities deceive thee.

[5] The people of Noah before them called the prophets liars; and the confederates after them; and every nation schemed against their Apostle to catch him. And they wrangled with falsehood that they might refute the truth thereby, but I seized them, and how was my punishment!

Thus was the sentence of thy Lord due against those who misbelieved, that they are the fellows of the Fire!

Those who bear the throne and those around it celebrate the praise of their Lord, and believe in Him, and ask pardon for those who believe: 'Our Lord! thou dost embrace all things in mercy and knowledge, then pardon those who turn repentant and follow thy way, and guard them from the torment of hell! Our Lord! make them enter into gardens of Eden which thou hast promised to them, and to those who do well of their fathers, and their wives, and their seed; verily, thou art the mighty, the wise! and guard them from evil deeds, for he whom thou shalt guard from evil deeds on that day, thou wilt have had mercy on, and that is mighty bliss!'

[10] Verily, those who misbelieve shall be cried out to, 'Surely, God's hatred is greater than your hatred of each other when ye were called unto the faith and misbelieved!' They shall say, 'Our Lord! Thou hast killed us twice, and Thou hast quickened us twice[1]; and we do confess our sins: is there then a way for getting out?'

That is because when God alone was proclaimed ye did disbelieve; but when partners were joined to Him ye did believe; but judgment belongs to God, the high, the great! He it is who shows you His signs, and sends down to you from heaven provision; but none is mindful except him who turns repentant; then call on God, being sincere in your religion to Him, averse although the misbelievers be! [15] Exalted of degrees! The Lord

[1] Referring to the absence of life before birth and the deprivation of it at death, and to the being quickened at birth and raised again after death.

of the throne! He throws the spirit by His bidding upon whom He will of His servants, to give warning of the day of meeting. The day when they shall be issuing forth, naught concerning them shall be hidden from God. Whose is the kingdom on that day?—God's, the one, the dominant! to-day shall every soul be recompensed for that which it has earned. There is no wrong to-day; verily, God is quick at reckoning up!

And warn them of the day that approaches, when hearts are choking in the gullets; those who do wrong shall have no warm friend, and no intercessor who shall be obeyed. [20] He knows the deceitful of eye and what men's breasts conceal, and God decides with truth; but those they call on beside Him do not decide at all: verily, God, He both hears and looks.

Have they not journeyed on in the earth and seen how was the end of those who journeyed on before them? They were stronger than them in might, and their vestiges are in the land; but God caught them up in their sins, and they had none to guard them against God.

That is for that their apostles did come to them with manifest signs, and they misbelieved, and God caught them up; verily, He is mighty, keen to punish!

And we did send Moses with our signs, and with obvious authority, [25] unto Pharaoh and Hâmân and Qarûn. They said, 'A lying sorcerer!' and when they came to them with truth from us, they said, 'Kill the sons of those who believe with him, and let their women live!' but the stratagem of the misbelievers is only in error!

And Pharaoh said, 'Let me kill Moses; and then let him call upon his Lord! verily, I fear that he will change your religion, or that he will cause evil doing to appear in the land.'

And Moses said, 'Verily, I take refuge in my Lord and your Lord from every one who is big with pride and believes not on the day of reckoning.'

And a believing man of Pharaoh's people, who concealed his faith, said, 'Will ye kill a man for saying, My Lord is God, when he has come to you with manifest signs from your Lord? and if he be a liar, against him is his lie; and if he be truthful, there will befall you somewhat of that which he threatens you; verily, God guides not him who is an extravagant liar. [30] O my people! yours is the kingdom to-day, ye are eminent in the land, but who will help us against the violence of God, if it comes upon us?'

Said Pharaoh, 'I will only show you what I see, and I will only guide you into the way of right direction.'

And he who believed said, 'O my people! verily, I fear for you the like of the day of the confederates, the like of the wont of the people of Noah and 'Âd and Hâmân, and of those after them; for God desires not injustice for His servants. O my people! verily, I fear for you the day of crying out,—[35] the day when ye shall turn your backs, fleeing, with no defender for you against God; for he whom God leads astray, for him there is no guide!

'And Joseph came to you before with manifest signs, but ye ceased not to doubt concerning what he brought you, until, when he perished, ye said, "God will not send after him an apostle;" thus does God lead astray him who is extravagant, a doubter.

'Those who wrangle concerning the signs of God without authority having come to them are greatly hated by God and by those who believe; thus does God set a stamp upon the heart of every tyrant too big with pride!'

And Pharaoh said, 'O Hâmân! build for me a tower, haply I may reach the tracts,—the tracts of heaven, and may mount up to the God of Moses, for, verily, I think him a liar.'

[40] And thus was his evil deed made seemly to Pharaoh, and he was turned from the way; but Pharaoh's stratagem ended only in ruin, and he who believed said, 'O my people! follow me, I will guide you to the way of the right direction. O my people! verily, the life of this world is but a provision, but, verily, the hereafter, that is the abode of stability! Whoso does evil, he shall only be recompensed with the like thereof; and whoso does right, be it male or female and a believer, these shall enter into Paradise; they shall be provided therein without count. O my people! why should I call you to salvation, and you call me to the fire? [45] Ye call on me to disbelieve in God, and to join with Him what I have no knowledge of; but I call you to the mighty forgiving One! no doubt that what ye call me to, ought not to be called on in this world or in the hereafter, and that we shall be sent back to God, and that the extravagant, they are the fellows of the Fire!

'But ye shall remember what I say to you; and I entrust my affair to God, verily, God looks upon His servants!'

And God guarded him from the evils of what they plotted, and there closed in upon Pharaoh evil woe.

The fire—they shall be exposed to it morning and evening; and 'on the day the Hour shall arise,' enter, O people of Pharaoh! into the keenest torment.

[50] And when they argue together in the fire, and the weak say to those who were big with pride, 'Verily, we were followers of yours, can ye then avail us against a portion of the fire?'

Those who were big with pride shall say, 'Verily, we are all in it; verily, God has judged between His servants.'

And those who are in the fire shall say unto the keepers of hell, 'Call upon your Lord to lighten from us one day of the torment.' They shall say, 'Did not your apostles come to you with manifest signs?' They shall say, 'Yea!' They shall say, 'Then, call!'—but the call of the misbelievers is only in error.

Verily, we will help our apostles, and those who believe, in the life of this world and on the day when the witnesses shall stand up: [55] the day when their excuse shall not avail the unjust; but for them is the curse, and for them is an evil abode.

And we did give Moses the guidance; and we made the children of Israel to inherit the Book, as a guidance and a reminder to those endowed with minds.

Be thou patient, then; verily, God's promise is true: and ask thou forgiveness for thy sins, and celebrate the praise of thy Lord in the evening and in the morn.

Verily, those who wrangle concerning the signs of God without authority having come to them, there is naught in their breasts but pride; but they shall not attain it: do thou then seek refuge in God; verily, He both hears and looks!

Surely the creation of the heavens and the earth is greater than the creation of man: but most men know it not.

[60] The blind and the seeing shall not be deemed alike, nor those who believe and do right and the evildoer; little is it that they remember.

Verily, the Hour will surely come; there is no doubt therein; but most men do not believe!

And your Lord said, 'Call upon me, I will answer you; verily, those who are too big with pride to worship shall enter into hell, shrinking up.'

God it is who has made for you the night to repose therein, and the day to see by; verily, God is Lord of grace to men, but most men give no thanks!

There is God for you! your Lord! the creator of everything! there is no god but He, how then can ye lie[1]? [65] Thus did those lie who gainsaid the signs of God.

God it is who has made for you the earth as a resting-place, and a heaven as building, and has formed you and made excellent your forms; and has provided you with good things! there is God for you!—your Lord! then blessed be God, the Lord of the worlds!

---

[1] Or 'turn away.'

He is the living One, there is no god but He! then call on Him, being sincere in your religion to Him; praise be to God, the Lord of the worlds!

Say, 'Verily, I am forbidden to serve those whom ye call on beside God, since there have come to me manifest signs from my Lord, and I am bidden to be resigned unto the Lord of the worlds.'

He it is who created you from the earth, then from a clot, then from congealed blood, then He brings you forth a child; then ye reach to puberty; then do ye become old men,—though of you there are some who are taken away before,—that ye may reach an appointed time, and haply ye may have some sense.

[70] He it is who quickens and kills, and when He decrees a matter, then He only says to it, 'BE,' and it is.

Hast thou not seen those who wrangle concerning the signs of God how they are turned away? Those who call the Book, and what we have sent our apostles with, a lie, soon shall they know—when the fetters are on their necks and the chains, as they are dragged into hell!—then in the fire shall they be baked.

Then it shall be said to them, 'Where is what ye did associate beside God?' They shall say, 'They have strayed away from us; nay, we did not call before upon anything!'—thus does God lead the misbelievers astray.

[75] There! for that ye did rejoice in the land without right; and for that ye did exult; enter ye the gates of hell, to dwell therein for aye; for evil is the resort of those who are too big with pride!

But be thou patient; verily, the promise of God is true; and whether we show thee a part of what we promised them, or whether we surely take thee to ourself, unto us shall they be returned.

And we did send apostles before thee: of them are some whose stories we have related to thee, and of them are some whose stories we have not related to thee; and no apostle might ever bring a sign except by the permission of God; but when God's bidding came it was decided with truth, and there were those lost who deemed it vain!

God it is who has made for you cattle, that ye may ride on some of them;—and of them ye eat,
[80] and ye have in them advantages;—and that ye may attain thereon a want which is in your breasts; upon them and upon ships are ye borne.

He shows you His signs; which sign then of your Lord do ye deny?

Have they not journeyed on in the land and seen how was the end of those before them, who were more numerous than they and stronger in might, and in their vestiges which are still in the land? but of no avail to them was that which they had earned.

And when there came to them their apostles with manifest signs they rejoiced in what knowledge they had; but there closed in upon them that whereat they had mocked.

And when they saw our violence they said, 'We believe in God alone, and we disbelieve in what we once associated with Him.'

[85] But their faith was of no avail to them when they saw our violence—the course of God with His servants in time past, and there the misbelievers lose!

THE CHAPTER 'DETAILED.'

(XLI. Mecca.)

In the name of the merciful and compassionate God.

'H. M. A revelation from the merciful, the compassionate; a book whose signs are detailed; an Arabic Qur'ân for a people who do know; a herald of glad tidings and a warning. But most of them turn aside and do not hear, and say, 'Our hearts are veiled from what thou dost call us to, and in our ears is dulness, and between us and thee there is a veil. Act thou; verily, we are acting too!' [5] Say, 'I am but a mortal like yourselves, I am inspired that your God is one God; then go straight to Him, and ask forgiveness of Him; and woe to the idolaters, who give not alms, and in the hereafter disbelieve!'

Verily, those who believe and do right, for them is a hire that is not grudged.

Say, 'What! do ye really misbelieve in Him who created the earth in two days, and do ye make peers for Him?—that is the Lord of the worlds!'

And He placed thereon[1] firm mountains above it and blessed it, and apportioned therein its foods in four days alike for those who ask. [10] Then He made for the heaven and it was but smoke, and He said to it and to the earth, 'Come, ye two, whether ye will or no!' They said, 'We come willingly!'

And He decreed them seven heavens in two days, and inspired every heaven with its bidding: and we

[1] On the earth.

adorned the lower heaven with lamps and guardian angels; that is the decree of the mighty, the knowing One.

But if they turn aside, then say, 'I have warned you of a thunder-clap like the thunder-clap of 'Âd and Thamûd; when their apostles came to them from before them and from behind them (saying), "Serve ye none but God."' They said, 'If our Lord pleased He would send down angels; so we in what ye are sent with disbelieve.'

And as for 'Âd, they were big with pride in the land, without right, and said, 'Who is stronger than us in might?' Did they not see that God who created them He was stronger than they in might? But they did gainsay our signs. [15] And we sent upon them a cold blast in unfortunate days, that we might make them taste the torment of disgrace in the life of this world;—but the torment of the hereafter is more disgraceful, and they shall not be helped.

And as for Thamûd we guided them; but they preferred blindness to guidance, and the thunder-clap of the torment of abasement caught them for what they had earned; but we saved those who believed and who did fear.

And the day when the enemies of God shall be gathered together into the fire, marshalled along; until when they come to it, their hearing and their eyesight and their skins shall bear witness against them of that which they have done. [20] And they shall say to their skins, 'Why have ye borne witness against us?' they shall say, 'God gave us speech who has given speech to everything; He created you at first, and unto Him shall ye be returned;

and ye could not conceal yourselves that your hearing and your eyesight should not be witness against you, nor your skins; but ye thought that God did not know much of what ye do. And that thought of yours which ye thought concerning your Lord has destroyed you, and ye have now become of those who lose!'

And if they are patient, still the fire is a resort for them; and if they ask for favour again, they shall not be taken into favour.

We will allot to them mates[1], for they have made seemly to them what was before them and what was behind them; and due against them was the sentence on the nations who passed away before them; both of *g*inns and of mankind; verily, they were the losers!

[25] Those who misbelieve say, 'Listen not to this Qur'ân, but talk foolishly about it, haply ye may gain the upper hand[2].' But we will make those who misbelieve taste keen torment; and we will recompense them with the worst of that which they have done. That is, the recompense of the enemies of God,—the fire! for them is an eternal abode therein: a recompence for that they did gainsay our signs.

And those who misbelieved say, 'Our Lord, show us those who have led us astray amongst the *g*inns and mankind; we will place them beneath our feet, and they shall both be amongst those who are put down!' [30] Verily, those who say, 'Our Lord is God,' and then go straight, the angels descend upon them—'fear not and be not grieved, but receive the glad tidings of Paradise which ye were promised;

[1] Devils, opposed to the guardian angels of the believers.

[2] I. e. interrupt the reading of the Qur'ân by talking, in order to overpower the voice of the reader.

we are your patrons in the life of this world and in the next, and ye shall have therein what your souls desire, and ye shall have therein what ye call for,—an entertainment from the forgiving, the merciful!'

And who speaks better than he who calls to God and does right, and says, 'Verily, I am of those resigned?'

Good and evil shall not be deemed alike; repel (evil) with what is best, and lo! He between whom and thyself was enmity is as though he were a warm patron. [35] But none shall meet with it save those who are patient; and none shall meet with it save those who are endowed with mighty good fortune.

And if an incitement from the devil incites you, then seek refuge in God; verily, He both hears and knows.

And of His signs are the night and the day, and the sun and the moon. Adore ye not the sun, neither the moon; but adore God who created you, if it be Him ye serve.

But if they be too big with pride—yet those who are with thy Lord celebrate His praises by night and day, and they are never weary.

And of His signs (is this), that thou mayest see the earth drooping, and when we send down water upon it it stirs and swells; verily, He who quickens it will surely quicken the dead; verily, He is mighty over all.

[40] Verily, those who are inclined to oppose our signs are not hidden from us. Is he who is cast into the fire better, or he who comes safe on the resurrection day? Do what ye will: verily, He on what ye do doth look.

Verily, those who misbelieve in the reminder when it comes to them—and, verily, it is a glorious Book! falsehood shall not come to it, from before it, nor from behind it—a revelation from the wise, the praiseworthy One. Naught is said to thee but what was said to the apostles before thee, 'Verily, thy Lord is Lord of forgiveness and Lord of grievous torment!'

And had we made it a foreign Qur'ân, they would have said, 'Unless its signs be detailed. . . . What! foreign and Arabic[1]?' Say, 'It is, for those who believe, a guidance and a healing. But those who believe not, in their ears is dulness, and it is blindness to them; these are called to from a far-off place.'

[45] And we gave Moses the Book, and it was disputed about; but had it not been for thy Lord's word already passed it would have been decided between them, for, verily, they were in hesitating doubt thereon.

Whoso does right it is for his soul, and whoso does evil it is against it, for thy Lord is not unjust towards His servants.

To Him is referred the knowledge of the Hour: and no fruits come forth from their husks, and no female conceives, or is delivered, save with His knowledge.

And the day when He shall call to them, 'Where

---

[1] I. e. they would have said, 'What! is the revelation in a foreign tongue, and we who are expected to read it Arabs?' This is paraphrased by Sale: 'If we had revealed the Qur'ân in a foreign language, they had surely said, "Unless the signs thereof be distinctly explained we will not receive the same: is the Book to be written in a foreign tongue, and the person unto whom it is directed an Arabian?"'

are the partners ye did join with me?' they shall say, 'We do own to thee there is no witness amongst us!' and that on which they used to call before shall stray away from them, and they shall think there is no escape for them. Man is never tired of praying for good, but if evil touch him, then he is despairing and hopeless.

[50] But if we make him taste mercy from us after distress has touched him he will surely say, 'This is for me, and I do not think the Hour is imminent; and if I be brought back to my Lord, verily, I shall surely have good with Him[1];' but we will inform those who misbelieve of what they have done, and we will surely make them taste wretched torment.

And when we have been gracious to man, he turns away and goes aside; but when evil touches him he is one of copious prayer.

Say, 'Let us see now! if it be from God and ye disbelieve in it, who is more in error than he who is in a remote schism?'

We will show them our signs in the regions and in themselves, until it is plain to them that it is the truth. Is it not enough for thy Lord that He is witness over all? Ay, verily, they are in doubt about the meeting of their Lord! Ay, verily, He encompasses all!

---

[1] Or the words may be rendered, 'There is good with him still due to me.'

The Chapter of Counsel.

(XLII. Mecca.)

In the name of the merciful and compassionate God.

'H. M. 'H. S. Q. Thus does God, the mighty, the wise, inspire thee and those before thee.

His is what is in the heavens and what is in the earth, and He is the high, the mighty!

The heavens well-nigh cleave asunder from above them; and the angels celebrate the praises of their Lord, and ask forgiveness for those who are on the earth. Ay, verily, God, He is the forgiving and merciful! but those who take beside Him patrons, God watches over them, and thou hast not charge over them.

[5] Thus have we revealed an Arabic Qur'ân, that thou mayest warn the Mother of cities[1] and all around it; and warn them of a day of gathering, there is no doubt therein;—a part in Paradise and a part in the blaze.

But had God pleased He would have made them one nation; but He makes whom He will enter into His mercy; and the unjust have neither patron nor help. Do they take other patrons besides Him, when God He is the patron, and He quickens the dead and He is mighty over all?

But whatsoever ye dispute about, the judgment of it is God's. There is God for you!—my Lord! upon Him do I rely, and unto Him I turn repentant. The originator of the heavens and the earth, He

[1] Mecca.

has made for you from yourselves wives; and of the cattle mates; producing you thereby. There is naught like Him, for He both hears and sees.

[10] His are the keys of the heavens and the earth, He extends provision to whom He will, or doles it out; verily, He knows everything.

He has enjoined upon you for religion what He prescribed to Noah and what we inspired thee with, and what we inspired Abraham and Moses and Jesus,—to be steadfast in religion, and not to part into sects therein—a great thing to the idolaters is that which ye call them to! God elects for Himself whom He pleases and guides unto Himself him who turns repentant.

But they did not part into sects until after the knowledge had come to them, through mutual envy; and had it not been for thy Lord's word already passed for an appointed time, it would surely have been decided between them; but, verily, those who have been given the Book as an inheritance after them, are in hesitating doubt concerning it.

Wherefore call thou, and go straight on as thou art bidden, and follow not their lusts; and say, 'I believe in the Book which God has sent down; and I am bidden to judge justly between you. God is our Lord and your Lord; we have our works and ye have your works; there is no argument between us and you. God will assemble us together and unto Him the journey is.'

[15] But those who argue about God after it has been assented to[1], their arguments shall be rebutted

[1] I.e. after the faith of Islâm had been accepted by them, or after God had assented to the prophet's prayer and supported the

before their Lord; and upon them shall be wrath, and for them shall be keen torment.

God it is who has sent down the Book with truth, and the balance[1]; and what shall make thee know whether haply the Hour be nigh? Those who believe not would hurry it on; and those who believe shrink with terror at it and know that it is true. Ay, verily, those who dispute concerning the Hour are in remote error!

God is kind to His servants; He provides whom He will, and He is the mighty, the glorious.

He who wishes for the tilth of the next world, we will increase for him the tilth; and he who desires the tilth of this world, we will give him thereof: but in the next he shall have no portion.

[20] Have they associates who have enjoined any religion on them which God permits not?—but were it not for the word of decision[2] it would have been decreed to them. Verily, the unjust,—for them is grievous woe. Thou shalt see the unjust shrink with terror from what they have gained as it falls upon them; and those who believe and do right, in meads of Paradise, they shall have what they please with their Lord;—that is great grace!

That is what God gives glad tidings of to His servants who believe and do righteous acts.

Say, 'I do not ask for it a hire—only the love of my kinsfolk.' And he who gains a good action

---

faith, or after the Jews and Christians had assented to the teaching of Mohammed, for the commentaries are uncertain as to the exact meaning of the phrase.

[1] I. e. the law contained in the Qur'ân.

[2] I. e. were it not that God has promised that those things shall be decided at the day of judgment.

we will increase good for him thereby; verily, God is forgiving and grateful!

Or will they say he has forged against God a lie? But if God pleased He could set a seal upon thy heart; but God will blot out falsehood and verify truth by His word; verily, He knows the nature of men's breasts!

He it is who accepts repentance from His ser vants and pardons their offences and knows that
which ye do. [25] And He answers the prayer
of those who believe and do right, and gives them increase of His grace; but the misbelievers,—for them is keen torment.

And if God were to extend provision to His servants they would be wanton in the earth. But He sends down by measure what He pleases; verily, of His servants He is well aware and sees.

He it is who sends down the rain after they have despaired; and disperses His mercy, for He is the praiseworthy patron.

And of His signs is the creation of the heavens and the earth, and what He hath spread abroad therein of beasts; and He is able to collect them when He will.

And what misfortunes befall you it is for what your
hands have earned; but He pardons much; [30] yet
ye cannot make Him helpless in the earth, nor have ye, besides God, either a patron or a helper.

And of His signs are the ships that sail like mountains in the sea. If He will, He calms the wind, and they become motionless on the back thereof: verily, in that are signs to every patient, grateful person:—or He makes them founder for what they have earned; but He pardons much.

But let those who wrangle about our signs know that they shall have no escape!

And whatever ye are given it is but a provision of the life of this world; but what is with God is better and more lasting for those who believe and who upon their Lord rely, [35] and those who avoid great sins and abominations, and who when they are wroth forgive, and who assent to their Lord, and are steadfast in prayer, and whose affairs go by counsel amongst themselves, and who of what we have bestowed on them give alms, and who, when wrong befalls them, help themselves.

For the recompence of evil is evil like unto it; but he who pardons and does well, then his reward is with God; verily, He loves not the unjust. And he who helps himself after he has been wronged, for these—there is no way against them. [40] The way is only against those who wrong men and are wanton in the earth without right; these—for them is grievous woe.

But surely he who is patient and forgives,—verily, that is a determined affair[1].

But whomsoever God leads astray he has no patron after Him; and thou mayest see the unjust when they see the torment say, 'Is there no way to avert this[2]?' and thou mayest see them exposed to it, humbled with abasement, looking with a stealthy glance. And those who believe shall say, 'Verily, the losers are they who have lost themselves and their families too upon the resurrection day!' Ay, verily, the unjust are in lasting torment!

[1] I. e. it is a duty laid down by law.

[2] Or 'to return (to the world),' Bâi*dh*âvî.

[45] And they shall have no patrons to help them beside God, and whomsoever God leads astray, there is no way for him.

Assent to your Lord before the day comes of which there is no averting from God; there is no refuge for you on that day; and for you there is no denial.

But if they turn aside, we have not sent thee to them as a guardian, thou hast only thy message to preach.

And, verily, when we have made man taste of mercy from us he rejoices therein; but if there befall them an evil for what their hands have done before—then, verily, man is ungrateful!

God's is the kingdom of the heavens and the earth, He creates what He pleases, He grants to whom He pleases females, and He grants to whom He pleases males, or He gives them in pairs, males and females; and He makes whom He pleases barren; verily, He is knowing, powerful!

[50] It is not for any mortal that God should speak to him, except by inspiration, or from behind a veil, or by sending an apostle and inspiring, by His permission, what He pleases; verily, He is high and wise!

And thus have we inspired thee by a spirit[1] at our bidding; thou didst not know what the Book was, nor the faith: but we made it a light whereby we guide whom we will of our servants. And, verily, thou shalt surely be guided into the right way,—the way of God, whose is what is in the heavens and what is in the earth. Ay, to God affairs do tend!

[1] Gabriel.

The Chapter of Gilding.

(XLIII. Mecca.)

In the name of the merciful and compassionate God.

'H. M. By the perspicuous Book, verily, we have made it an Arabic Qur'ân; haply ye will have some sense. And it is in the Mother of the Book with us,—high and wise[1]. Shall we then push aside from you the Reminder, because ye are a people who are extravagant?

[5] How many prophets have we sent amongst those of yore? and there never came to them a prophet but they did mock at him; then we destroyed them—more valiant than these[2]; and the example of those of yore passed away.

And if thou shouldst ask them who created the heavens and the earth, they will surely say, 'The mighty, the knowing One created them,' who made for you the earth a couch and placed for you therein roads, haply ye may be guided: [10] and who sent down from the heaven water in due measure; and we raised up thereby a dead country; thus shall ye too be brought forth; and who has created all species; and has made for you the ships and the cattle whereon to ride that ye may settle yourselves on their backs; then remember the favour of your Lord when ye settled thereon, and say, 'Celebrated be the praises of Him who hath subjected this to us! We could not have got this ourselves; and, verily, unto our Lord shall we return!'

[1] See Part I, p. 2, note 2. [2] I. e. the Meccans.

Yet they make for Him of His servants offspring; verily, man is surely obviously ungrateful.

[15] Has He taken of what He creates daughters, and chosen sons for you?

Yet when the tidings[1] are given any one of that which he strikes out as a similitude for the Merciful One, his face grows black and he is choked. What! one brought up amongst ornaments, and who is always in contention without obvious cause[2]?

And have they made the angels, who are the servants of the Merciful One, females? Were they witnesses of their creation? their witness shall be written down, and they shall be questioned; and they say, 'Had the Merciful pleased we should never have worshipped them.' They have no knowledge of that, they only conjecture.

[20] Have we given them a book[3] before it to which they might hold?

Nay; they say, 'We found our fathers (agreed) upon a religion, and, verily, we are guided by their traces.'

Thus, too, did we never send before thee to a city any warner, but the affluent ones thereof said, 'Verily, we found our fathers (agreed) upon a religion, and, verily, we are led by their traces.'

Say, 'What! if I come to you with what is a better guide than what ye found your fathers agreed upon?' and they will say, 'Verily, we in what ye are sent with disbelieve!'

[1] I.e. of the birth of a daughter, see Part I, p. 256, note 2.

[2] I.e. what! do they assign children of this kind, viz. daughters, to God?

[3] I.e. a scripture authorising the practice of their religion, such as the worship of angels and the ascribing of daughters to God.

Then we took vengeance on them, and see how was the end of those who called the (apostles) liars.

[25] When Abraham said to his father and his people, 'Verily, I am clear of all that ye serve, except Him who created me; for, verily, He will guide me:' and he made it a word remaining among his posterity, that haply they might return.

Nay; but I let these (Meccans) and their fathers have enjoyment until the truth came to them, and an apostle. And when the truth came to them they said, 'This is magic, and we therein do disbelieve!'
[30] And they say, 'Unless this Qur'ân were sent down to a man great in the two cities. . . .[1]'

Is it they who distribute the mercy of thy Lord? We distribute amongst them their livelihood in the life of this world, and we exalt some of them above others in degrees, that some may take others into subjection; but the mercy of thy Lord is better than that which they amass.

And but that men would then have been one nation, we would have made for those who misbelieve in the Merciful One roofs of silver for their houses, and steps up thereto which they might mount; and to their houses doors, and bedsteads on which they might recline; and gilding,—for, verily, all that is a provision of the life of this world, but the hereafter is better with thy Lord for those who fear!

[35] And whosoever turns from the reminder of the Merciful One, we will chain to him a devil, who shall

[1] I.e. had it been sent down to some man of influence and importance in Mecca and *Tâ'if* we would have received it.

be his mate; and, verily, these shall turn them from the path while they reckon that they are guided; until when he comes to us he shall say, 'O, would that between me and thee there were the distance of the two orients[1], for an evil mate (art thou)!' But it shall not avail you on that day, since ye were unjust; verily, in the torment shall ye share!

What! canst thou make the deaf to hear, or guide the blind, or him who is in obvious error?

[40] Whether then we take thee off we will surely take vengeance on them; or whether we show thee that which we have promised them; for, verily, we have power over them.

Say, 'Dost thou hold to what is inspired thee?' verily, thou art in the right way, and, verily, it is a reminder to thee and to thy people, but in the end they shall be asked.

And ask those whom we have sent before thee amongst the prophets, 'Did we make gods beside the Merciful One for them to serve?'

[45] We did send Moses with our signs to Pharaoh and his chiefs, and he said, 'Verily, I am the apostle of the Lord of the worlds; but when he came to them with our signs, lo, they laughed at them!'

And we did not show them a sign, but it was greater than its fellow; and we seized them with the torment, haply they might turn.

And they said, 'O thou magician! pray for us to thy Lord, as He has engaged with thee: verily, we are guided.'

---

[1] I. e. the east and west, though some understand it between the two solstices.

And when we removed from them the torment, behold they broke their word.

[50] And Pharaoh proclaimed amongst his people; said he, 'O my people! is not the kingdom of Egypt mine? and these rivers that flow beneath me? What! can ye then not see? Am I better than this fellow, who is contemptible, who can hardly explain himself[1]? Unless then bracelets of gold be cast upon him, or there come with him angels as his mates . . .!'

And he taught his people levity; and they obeyed him: verily, they were an abominable people.

[55] And when they had annoyed us we took vengeance on them, and we drowned them all together, and we made them a precedent and an example to those after them.

And when the son of Mary was set forth as a parable, behold thy people turned away from him and said, 'Are our gods better, or is he?' They did not set it forth to thee save for wrangling. Nay, but they are a contentious people[2].

He is but a servant whom we have been gracious to, and we have made him an example for the children of Israel. [60] And if we please we can make of you angels in the earth to succeed you[3]. And, verily, he is a sign of the Hour[4]. Doubt not then

---

[1] See p. 36, note 1.

[2] The Arabs objected that Jesus was worshipped by Christians as a God, and that when Mohammed cursed their false gods, the ban must apply equally to him.

[3] Just as Jesus was miraculously conceived, so can miraculously conceived offspring be produced among the Meccans themselves.

[4] Some read, 'a sign,' which is perhaps better. The reference is to the predicted second advent of the Messiah, which is to precede

concerning it, but follow this right way; and let not the devil turn you away; verily, he is to you an open foe!

And when Jesus came with manifest signs he said, 'I am come to you with wisdom, and I will explain to you something of that whereon ye did dispute, then fear God, obey me; verily, God, He is my Lord and your Lord, serve Him then, this is the right way.'

[65] But the confederates disputed amongst themselves; and woe to those who are unjust from the torment of a grievous day!

Do they expect aught but that the Hour will come upon them suddenly while they do not perceive? Friends on that day shall be foes to each other, save those who fear.

O my servants! there is no fear for you on that day; nor shall ye be grieved who believe in our signs and who are resigned. [70] Enter ye into Paradise, ye and your wives, happy!

Dishes of gold and pitchers shall be sent round to them; therein is what souls desire, and eyes shall be delighted, and ye therein shall dwell for aye; for that is Paradise which ye are given as an inheritance for that which ye have done. Therein shall ye have much fruit whereof to eat.

Verily, the sinners are in the torment of hell to dwell for aye. [75] It shall not be intermitted for them, and they therein shall be confused. We have not wronged them, but it was themselves they wronged.

---

the end of the world. Some commentators, however, read 'it,' instead of 'he,' referring to the Qur'ân, instead of to Jesus.

And they shall cry out, 'O Mâlik[1]! let thy lord make an end of us;' he shall say, 'Verily, ye are to tarry here.'

We have brought you the truth, but most of you are averse from the truth. Have they arranged the affair? then will we arrange it too[2]!

[80] Or do they reckon that we did not hear their secrets and their whispering? Nay, but our messengers are with them writing down[3].

Say, 'If the Merciful One has a son then am I the first to worship him. Celebrated be the praise of the Lord of the heavens and the earth! the Lord of the throne, above all they attribute to Him!

But leave them to ponder and to play until they meet that day of theirs which they are promised.

He it is who is in the heaven a God and in the earth a God! and He is the wise, the knowing. [85] And blessed be he whose is the kingdom of the heavens and the earth, and what is between both, and His is the knowledge of the Hour, and unto Him shall ye be brought back!

And those they call on beside Him shall not possess intercession except those only who bear witness for the truth and who do know.

And if thou shouldst ask them who created them they shall surely say, 'God!' How then can they lie?

And what he[4] says, 'O Lord, verily, these are

---

[1] Mâlik is the keeper of hell, and presides over the tortures of the damned.

[2] The word used signifies twisting up the strands of a rope.

[3] I.e. the recording angel.

[4] Mohammed.

a people who do not believe; shun them then and say, "Peace!" for they at length shall know!'

The Chapter of Smoke.

(XLIV. Mecca.)

In the name of the merciful and compassionate God.

'H. M. By the perspicuous Book! verily, we have sent it down on a blessed night;—verily, we had given warning—wherein is decided every wise affair, as an order from us. Verily, we were sending (apostles)—[5] a mercy from thy Lord; verily, He both hears and knows: from the Lord of the heavens and the earth and what is between the two, if ye were but sure. There is no god but He, He quickens and He kills—your Lord and the Lord of your fathers of yore! Nay, they in doubt do play!

But expect thou the day when the heaven shall bring obvious smoke [10] to cover men—this is grievous torment!

Our Lord! remove from us the torment; verily, we are believers.

How can they have the reminder (now), when they have had a plain apostle, and when they turned their backs away from him and said, 'Taught! mad!' Verily, we will remove the torment a little, (but) ye will surely return!

[15] On the day when we will assault with the great assault, verily, we will take vengeance.

And we already tried the people of Pharaoh when there came to them a noble apostle: 'Send back to me God's servants; verily, I am to you a faithful apostle;' and, 'Exalt not yourselves above God; verily, I come to you with obvious authority. And, verily, I seek refuge in my Lord and your Lord, that ye stone me not. [20] And if ye believe not in me then let me alone!'

Then he called upon his Lord, 'Verily, these are a sinful people.' So journey with my servants by night—verily, ye will be pursued. But leave the sea in quiet—verily, they are a host to be drowned! How many gardens and springs have they left, [25] and corn lands and a noble place, and comfort wherein they did enjoy themselves!

Thus—and we gave them for an inheritance to another people. And the heaven wept not for them, nor the earth, nor were they respited.

But we saved the children of Israel from shameful woe!—[30]—from Pharaoh; verily, he was haughty, one of the extravagant! And we did choose them, wittingly, above the worlds; and we gave them signs wherein was an obvious trial!

Verily, these [1] say, 'It is but our first death [2], so bring our fathers, if ye do speak the truth!'

[35] Are they better than the people of Tubbâ'h [3], and those before them? We destroyed them—verily, they were sinners!

Nor did we create the heavens and the earth, and what is between the two in sport: we did but create them in truth, though most of them know it not!

---

[1] The Meccans. [2] I. e. we shall only die once.

[3] The Himyarite Arabs, whose kings were called Tubbâ'h, i.e. 'successors.'

[40] Verily, the day of separation is their appointed term; the day when master shall not avail client at all, nor shall they be helped; save whomsoever God shall have mercy on; verily, He is the mighty, the merciful!

Verily, the Zaqqûm tree (shall be) the food of the sinful: [45] as it were melting[1], shall it boil in their bellies like the boiling of hot water!—'Take him and hale him into the midst of hell! then pour over his head the torment of hot water!—Taste! verily, thou art the mighty, the honourable! [50] Verily, this is that whereon ye did dispute!'

Verily, the pious shall be in a safe place! in gardens and springs, they shall be clad in satin and stout silk face to face. Thus!—and we will wed them to bright and large-eyed maids! [55] They shall call therein for every fruit in safety. They shall not taste therein of death save their first death, and we will keep them from the torment of hell! Grace from thy Lord, that is the grand bliss!

And we have only made it easy for thy tongue, that haply they may be mindful. Then watch thou; verily, they are watching too!

THE CHAPTER OF THE KNEELING.

(XLV. Mecca.)

IN the name of the merciful and compassionate God.

H. M. A revelation of the Book from God, the mighty, the wise. Verily, in the heavens and the

---

[1] Or 'like the dregs of oil.'

earth are signs to those who believe; and in your creation and the beasts that are spread abroad are signs to a people who are sure; and in the alternation of night and day, and the provision that God has sent down from heaven and quickened thereby the earth after its death, and in the veering of the winds are signs unto a people who have sense.

[5] These are the signs of God which we recite to thee in truth; and in what new story after God and His signs will they believe?

Woe to every sinful liar who hears God's signs sent to him, then persists in being big with pride as though he heard them not—so give him the glad tidings of grievous woe—and when he knows something of our signs takes them for a jest! These,—for them is shameful woe, behind them is hell, and what they have earned shall not avail them aught, nor what they have taken besides God for patrons; and for them is mighty woe.

[10] This is a guidance, and those who misbelieve in the signs of their Lord, for them is torment of a grievous plague.

God it is who subjects to you the sea that the ships may sail thereon at his bidding, and that ye may crave of His grace, and that haply ye may give thanks; and He has subjected to you what is in the heavens and what is in the earth,—all from Him; verily, in that are signs unto a people who reflect.

Say to those who believe that they pardon those who hope not for God's days[1], that He may reward a people for that which they have earned.

---

[1] That is, the successful battles against the infidels, 'battles' being always spoken of by the ancient Arabs as 'days.'

Whosoever acts aright it is for his own soul, and whosoever does evil it is against it; then unto your Lord shall ye be returned.

[15] And we did bring the children of Israel the Book and judgment and prophecy, and we provided them with good things, and preferred them above the worlds. And we brought them manifest proofs of the affair, and they disputed not until after knowledge had come to them, through mutual envy. Verily, thy Lord will decide between them on the resurrection day concerning that whereon they did dispute.

Then we did set thee [1] over a law concerning the affair: follow it then, and follow not the lusts of those who do not know. Verily, they shall not avail thee against God at all; and, verily, the wrong-doers are patrons of each other, but God is the patron of those who fear.

This is an insight for men and a guidance and a mercy to a people who are sure.

[20] Do those who commit evil deeds count that we will make them like those who believe and work righteous deeds, equal in their life and their death? —ill it is they judge.

And God created the heavens and the earth in truth; and every soul shall be recompensed for that which it has earned, and they shall not be wronged.

Hast thou considered him who takes his lusts for his god, and God leads him astray wittingly, and has set a seal upon his hearing and his heart, and has placed upon his eyesight dimness? who then shall guide him after God? Will they not then mind?

---

[1] Mohammed.

They say, 'It is only our life in this world, we die and we live, and naught destroys us but time!' But they have no knowledge of this; they do but suspect.

And when our signs are rehearsed to them with evidences their only argument is to say, 'Bring our fathers, if ye speak the truth.'

[25] Say, 'God quickens you, then He kills you, then He will gather you unto the resurrection day, there is no doubt therein, but most men do not know.'

God's is the kingdom of the heavens and the earth, and on the day when the Hour shall arise on that day shall those who call it[1] vain be losers! And thou shalt see each nation kneeling, each nation summoned to its book, 'To-day are ye rewarded for that which ye have done.'

This is our Book that speaketh to you with truth; verily, we have written down what ye have done.

But as to those who believe and do righteous deeds their Lord will make them enter into His mercy: that is the obvious bliss.

[30] And as for those who misbelieve,—were not my signs recited to you and ye were too big with pride and ye were a sinful people? And when it was said, 'Verily, the promise of God is true, and the Hour there is no doubt therein;' ye said, 'We know not what the Hour is, we only suspect, and we are not sure.'

But there shall appear to them the evils of what they have done, and that shall encompass them at which they have been mocking. And it shall be said, 'To-day will we forget you as ye forgat the

[1] The Qur'ân.

meeting of this day of yours, and your resort shall be the fire, and ye shall have no helpers. That is because ye took the signs of God for a jest and the life of this world deceived you; wherefore to-day ye shall not be brought forth therefrom, neither shall ye be taken back into favour.'

[35] God's then is the praise, the Lord of the heavens and the Lord of the earth, the Lord of the worlds! His is the grandeur in the heavens and the earth, and He is the mighty and the wise!

The Chapter of El A'hqâf[1].

(XLVI. Mecca.)

In the name of the merciful and compassionate God.

'H. M. The revelation of the Book from God the mighty, the wise.

We have only created the heavens and the earth and what is between the two in truth and for an appointed time; but those who misbelieve from being warned do turn aside.

Say, 'Have ye considered what ye call on beside God?' Show me what they have created of the earth? or have they share in the heavens? Bring me a book before this or a vestige of knowledge, if ye do tell the truth!

But who is more in error than he who calls beside God on what will never answer him until the resurrection day and who are heedless of their calling,

---

[1] Name of a tract of land in *S*i'hr in Yemen.

[5] and when men are gathered together are enemies of theirs and do deny their service?

And when our evident signs are recited to them, those who misbelieve say of the truth when it comes to them, 'This is obvious magic.'

Or do they say, 'He has forged it?' Say, 'If I have forged ye cannot obtain for me aught from God; He knows best what ye utter concerning it; He is witness enough between me and you, and He is the forgiving, the merciful.'

Say, 'I am not an innovator among the apostles; nor do I know what will be done with me or with you if I follow aught but what I am inspired with; nor am I aught but a plain warner.'

Say, 'Have ye considered, if it is from God and ye have disbelieved therein, and a witness from the children of Israel testifies to the conformity of it, and he believes while ye are too big with pride? Verily, God guides not the unjust people.'

[10] And those who misbelieve say of those who believe, 'If it had been good, they would not have been beforehand with us therein;' and when they are not guided thereby, then will they say, 'This is an old-fashioned lie.'

But before it was the Book of Moses, a model and a mercy; and this is a book confirming it in Arabic language, to warn those who do wrong and as glad tidings to those who do well.

Verily, those who say, 'Our Lord is God,' and then keep straight, there is no fear for them, and they shall not be grieved. These are the fellows of Paradise to dwell therein for aye, a recompence for that which they have done.

We have prescribed for man kindness towards his

parents. His mother bore him with trouble and brought him forth with trouble; and the bearing of him and the weaning of him is thirty months; until, when he reaches puberty, and reaches forty years, he says, 'Lord! stir me up that I may be thankful for thy favours wherewith thou hast favoured me and my parents; and that I may do right to please Thee; and make it right for me in my offspring; verily, I turn repentant unto Thee, and, verily, I am of those resigned.'

[15] There are those from whom we accept the best of what they have done, and we pass over their offences—amongst the fellows of Paradise; the promise of truth which they have been promised.

But he who says to his parents, 'Fie upon you! Do ye promise me that I shall be brought forth[1] when generations have passed away before me?'—then shall they both cry to God for help. Woe to thee! Believe! Verily, the promise of God is true. Then says he, 'This is but old folks' tales.'

There are those against whom the sentence was due amongst the nations who have passed away before them of *g*inns and men; verily, they have been the losers; and for all are degrees of what they have done, so that He may repay them their works, and they shall not be wronged.

And the day when those who misbelieve shall be exposed to the fire: 'Ye made away with your good things in your worldly life, and ye enjoyed them; wherefore to-day shall ye be rewarded with the torment of disgrace, for that ye were big with

[1] I. e. from the grave.

pride in the earth without the right, and for that ye did abomination.'

[20] Remember too the brother of 'Âd[1] when he warned his people at El A'hqâf,—though warners have passed away before him and after him,—'Serve not other than God; verily, I fear for you the torment of a mighty day!'

They said, 'Hast thou come to us to turn us from our gods? then bring us what thou dost threaten us with, if thou art of those who speak the truth!' Said he, 'Knowledge is only with God: but I will preach to you that which I am sent with, though I see you are a people who are ignorant.' And when they saw a traversing cloud approaching their valleys they said, 'This is a cloud to give us rain.' 'Nay, but it is what ye sought to hasten on —a wind in which is grievous torment; it will destroy everything at the order of its Lord!' And in the morning naught was seen save their dwellings. Thus do we reward the sinful people!

[25] We had established them in what we have established you[2], and we made for them hearing and eyesight and hearts; but neither their hearing nor their eyesight nor their hearts availed them aught, since they did gainsay the signs of God, and that encompassed them whereat they had mocked.

And we destroyed the cities that are around you:—and we turned about the signs that haply they might return.

Why did not those help them, whom beside God they took for gods that could draw nigh to Him? Nay! they strayed away from them; for that was their lie and what they had forged.

[1] The prophet Hûd. [2] I. e. the Meccans.

And when we turned towards thee some of the *g*inn listening to the Qur'ân[1], and when they were present at (the reading of) it, they said, 'Be silent!' and when it was over they turned back to their people, warning them.

Said they, 'O our people! verily, we have heard a book sent down after Moses, verifying what came before it, guiding to the truth, and unto the right way. [30] O our people! respond to God's crier and believe in Him, and He will pardon you your sins and will deliver you from grievous woe.'

And whoso responds not to God's crier shall not frustrate Him in the earth, and shall not have any patrons beside Him:—these are in obvious error!

Did they not see that God who created the heavens and the earth, and was not wearied with creating them, is able to quicken the dead?—nay, verily, He is mighty over all!

And the day when those who misbelieve shall be exposed to the fire,—'Is not this the truth?' they shall say, 'Yea, by our Lord!' He shall say, 'Then taste the torment for that ye did misbelieve!'

Then do thou[2] be patient, as the apostles endowed with a purpose were patient, and hasten not on (their punishment). It shall be to them, on the day they see what they are threatened with, as though they [35] had tarried but an hour of the day. A preaching this! Shall any perish but the people who work abomination?

---

[1] See Introduction, p. xxx.

[2] Addressed to Mohammed.

The Chapter of Mohammed, also called Fight.

(XLVII. Medînah.)

In the name of the merciful and compassionate God.

Those who misbelieve and turn folk from God's way, He will make their works go wrong. But those who believe and do right and believe in what is revealed to Mohammed,—and it is the truth from their Lord,—He will cover for them their offences and set right their mind.

That is because those who misbelieve follow falsehood, and those who believe follow the truth from their Lord. Thus does God set forth for men their parables.

And when ye meet those who misbelieve—then striking off heads until ye have massacred them, and bind fast the bonds!

[5] Then either a free grant (of liberty) or a ransom until the war shall have laid down its burdens. That!—but if God please He would conquer them—but (it is) that He may try some of you by the others. And those who are slain in God's cause, their works shall not go wrong; He will guide them and set right their mind; and will make them enter into Paradise which He has told them of.

O ye who believe! if ye help God, He will help you, and will make firm your footsteps.

But as for those who misbelieve—confound them! and He will make their works go wrong.

[10] That is because they were averse from what God has revealed; but their works shall be void!

Have they not journeyed through the land and

seen how was the end of those before them? God destroyed them; and for the misbelievers is the like thereof.

That is because God is the patron of those who believe, and because the misbelievers have no patron.

Verily, God causes those who believe and do right to enter into gardens beneath which rivers flow; but those who misbelieve enjoy themselves and eat as the cattle eat; but the fire is the resort for them!

How many a city, stronger than thy city which has driven thee out, have we destroyed, and there was none to help them!

[15] Is he who rests upon a manifest sign from his Lord like him, the evil of whose works is made seemly to him, and who follow their lusts?

The similitude of Paradise which is promised to the pious,—in it are rivers of water without corruption, and rivers of milk, the taste whereof changes not, and rivers of wine delicious to those who drink; and rivers of honey clarified; and there shall they have all kinds of fruit and forgiveness from their Lord! (Is that) like him who dwells in the fire for aye? and who are given to drink boiling water that shall rend their bowels asunder?

Some of them there are who listen to thee, until when they go forth from thee they say to those who have been given the knowledge[1], 'What is this which he says now?' These are those on whose hearts God has set a stamp and who follow their lusts.

[1] To the more learned amongst the prophet's companions, such as Ibn 'Abbâs.

But those who are guided, He guides them the more, and gives them the due of their piety.

[20] Do they wait for aught but the Hour, that it should come to them suddenly? The conditions thereof have come already; how, when it has come on them, can they have their reminder?

Know thou that there is no god but God; and ask pardon for thy sin and for the believers, men and women; for God knows your return and your resort!

Those who misbelieve say, 'Why has not a sûrah been revealed?' but when a decisive sûrah is revealed and fighting is mentioned therein, thou mayest see those in whose heart is sickness[1] looking towards thee with the look of one fainting in death. Preferable for them were obedience and a reasonable speech! But when the matter is determined on, then if they believed God it were better for them.

Would ye perhaps, if ye had turned back, have done evil in the land and severed the bonds of kinship?

[25] It is these whom God has cursed, and has made them deaf, and has blinded their eyesight! Do they not peruse the Qur'ân? or are there locks upon their hearts?

Verily, those who turn their backs after the guidance that has been manifested to them—Satan induces them, but (God) lets them go on for a time!

That is for that they say to those who are averse from what God has revealed, 'We will obey you in

[1] See Introduction, p. lxiii.

part of the affair!' but God knows their secrets! How will it be when the angels[1] take their souls, smiting their faces and their backs?

[30] This is because they follow what angers God and are averse from His goodwill; and their works are void.

Do those in whose hearts is sickness reckon that God will not bring their malice forth?

But did we please we would show thee them, and thou shouldst know them by their cognisances. But thou shalt know them by their distorting their speech, and God knows their works!

But we will try you until we know those among you who fight strenuously and the patient; and we will try the reports concerning you.

Verily, those who misbelieve and turn folks off God's path, and break with the Apostle after the guidance that has been manifested to them, cannot harm God at all, and their works shall be void!

[35] O ye who believe! obey God, and obey the Apostle; and make not your works vain.

Verily, those who misbelieve and turn folks off God's path, and then die misbelievers, God will not pardon them.

Then faint not, nor cry for peace while ye have the upper hand; for God is with you and will not cheat you of your works!

The life of this world is but a play and a sport; but if ye believe and fear God, He will give you your hire.

He does not ask you for (all) your property; if

[1] Munkir and Nakîr; see Introduction, p. lxix.

He were to ask you for it and to press you, ye would be niggardly, and he would bring your malice out.

[40] Here are ye called upon to expend in God's cause, and among you are some who are niggardly; and he who is niggardly is but niggardly against his own soul: but God is rich and ye are poor, and if ye turn your backs He will substitute another people in your stead, then they will not be like you.

The Chapter of Victory.

(XLVIII. Medînah.)

In the name of the merciful and compassionate God.

Verily, we have given thee an obvious victory! that God may pardon thee thy former and later sin[1], and may fulfil His favour upon thee, and guide thee in a right way, and that God may help thee with a mighty help.

It is He who sent down His shechina[2] into the hearts of the believers that they might have faith added to their faith;—and God's are the hosts of the heavens and the earth, and God is knowing, wise—[5] to make the believers, men and women, enter into gardens beneath which rivers flow, to dwell therein for aye; and to cover for them their offences; for that with God is a grand bliss: and

---

[1] Some of the commentators take this to mean sins committed by Mohammed before his call and after; others refer the word to the liaison with the Coptic handmaiden Mary, and to his marriage with Zâinab the wife of his adopted son Zâid. See Introduction, pp. xxix and xl.

[2] Or tranquillity; see Part I, p. 38, note 2.

to torment the hypocrites, men and women, and the idolaters, men and women, who think evil thoughts of God;—over them is a turn of evil fortune, and God will be wrath with them and curse them, and has prepared for them hell, and an evil journey shall it be!

God's are the hosts of the heavens and the earth, and God is mighty, wise!

Verily, we have sent thee as a witness, and a herald of glad tidings, and a warner;—that ye may believe in God and His Apostle, and may aid Him and revere Him and celebrate His praises morning and evening!

[10] Verily, those who swear allegiance to thee do but swear allegiance to God;—God's hand is above their hands! and whoso perjures himself does but perjure himself against himself; but he who fulfils what he has covenanted with God, God shall bring him mighty hire.

The desert Arabs who were left behind[1] shall say, 'Our wealth and our people occupied us; ask pardon then for us!'—they speak with their tongues what is not in their hearts!

Say, 'Who can control for you aught from God, if He wish you harm or wish you advantage?' Nay, God of what ye do is well aware!

Nay, ye thought that the Apostle and the believers would not ever return again to their families; that was made seemly in your hearts! and ye thought evil thoughts, and ye were a corrupt people.

---

[1] Alluding to certain tribes who held aloof from the expedition of 'Hudâibîyeh.

Whoso believes not in God and His Apostle—we have prepared for the unbelievers a blaze!

God's is the kingdom of the heavens and of the earth. He pardons whom He pleases, and torments whom He pleases; and God is forgiving, merciful.

[15] Those who were left behind[1] shall say when ye have gone forth to spoils that ye may take, 'Let us follow you;' they wish to change God's words. Say, 'Ye shall by no means follow us; thus did God say before!'

They will say, 'Nay! but ye envy us!' Nay! they did not understand save a little.

Say to those desert Arabs who were left behind, 'Ye shall be called out against a people endowed with vehement valour[2], and shall fight them or they shall become Muslims. And if ye obey, God will give you a good hire; but if ye turn your backs, as ye turned your backs before, He will torment you with grievous woe!'

There is no compulsion on the blind, and no compulsion on the lame, and no compulsion on the sick, but whoso obeys God and His Apostle, He will make him enter gardens beneath which rivers flow; but whoso turns his back He will torment with grievous woe.

God was well pleased with the believers when

[1] In an expedition against the Jews of Khâibar, which Mohammed undertook shortly after his return from 'Hudâibîyeh, and obtained considerable booty, which he shared only with those who had accompanied him on the previous occasion.

[2] The followers of Musâilimah, Mohammed's rival, and the tribes that had apostatized from Islâm. Some think it refers to the Greeks and Persians.

they did swear allegiance to thee beneath the tree[1]; and He knew what was in their hearts, and He sent down His shechina[2] upon them and rewarded them with a victory nigh at hand[3], and many spoils for them to take; for God is mighty, wise!

[20] God promised you many spoils and hastened this on for you, and restrained men's hands from you; and it may be a sign for the believers and guide you in a right way;—and other (spoils) which ye could not gain; but God has encompassed them; for God is mighty over all.

And had those who misbelieved fought you, they would have turned their backs; then they would have found neither patron nor helper!—God's course which has been followed before, and thou shalt find no change in the course of God!

He it was who restrained their hands from you, and your hands from them in the mid-valley of Mecca[4] after He had given you the victory over them; for God on what ye do doth look!

[25] Those who misbelieved and turned (you) away from the Sacred Mosque, and (turned away) the offering, kept from arriving at its destined place[5]; and had it not been for believing men and believing women whom ye knew not, whom ye might have trampled on, and so a crime might have

---

[1] At 'Hudâibîyeh.

[2] See Part I, p. 38, note 2.

[3] Either the success at Khâibar or the taking of Mecca.

[4] Alluding to the truce concluded at 'Hudâibîyeh.

[5] Mohammed having only set out with the intention of peaceably performing the pilgrimage, carried cattle with him to sacrifice in the valley of Minâ, but was obliged by the Qurâis to turn back. See Introduction, pp. xxxix, xl.

occurred to you on their account without your knowledge—that God may make whomsoever He pleases enter into His mercy. Had they been distinct from one another, we would have tormented those of them who misbelieved with grievous woe.

When those who misbelieved put in their hearts pique—the pique of ignorance[1]—and God sent down His shechina upon His Apostle and upon the believers, and obliged them to keep to the word of piety[2], and they were most worthy of it and most suited for it; for God all things doth know.

God truly verified for His Apostle the vision[3] that ye shall verily enter the Sacred Mosque, if God please, in safety with shaven heads or cut hair, ye shall not fear; for He knows what ye know not, and He has set for you, beside that, a victory nigh at hand[4].

He it is who sent His Apostle with guidance

---

[1] Suhail ibn 'Amr, who concluded the truce with Mohammed at 'Hudâibîyeh, objected to the formula 'In the name of the merciful and compassionate God,' with which the prophet ordered 'Alî to commence the document, and insisted on the heathen formula 'In Thy name, O God!' He also refused to admit the words 'Mohammed, the Apostle of God,' saying, that if they had granted so much they would not have opposed him; the words 'Mohammed the son of Abdallah' were therefore substituted. These objections were so annoying to the Muslims, that it was with difficulty that Mohammed could restrain them from an immediate breach of the peace.

[2] The Mohammedan profession of faith, 'There is no god but God, and Mohammed His servant is the Apostle.' Or it may be the initial formula which the unbelieving Meccans rejected.

[3] Mohammed dreamed that he would accomplish the pilgrimage to Mecca with all its rites; the affair at 'Hudâibîyeh disappointed his followers, but in the following year it was fulfilled.

[4] I.e. that of Khâibar.

and the religion of truth to set it above all religion; for God is witness enough!

Mohammed is the Apostle of God, and those who are with Him are vehement against the misbelievers, —compassionate amongst themselves; thou mayest see them bowing down, adoring, craving grace from God and His goodwill,—their marks are in their faces from the effects of adoration;—that is their similitude in the law[1] and their similitude in the gospel; as a seedling puts forth its sprouts and strengthens it, and grows stout, and straightens itself upon its stem, delighting the sower!—that the misbelievers may be angry at them;—God has promised those of them who believe and do right—forgiveness and a mighty hire.

The Chapter of the Inner Chambers.

(XLIX. Medînah.)

In the name of the merciful and compassionate God.

O ye who believe! do not anticipate God and His Apostle, but fear God; verily, God both hears and knows.

O ye who believe! raise not your voices above the voice of the prophet, and do not speak loud to him as ye speak loud to one another[2], lest your works become vain, while ye do not perceive.

---

[1] Or the Pentateuch.

[2] Said to refer to a dispute between Abu Bekr and 'Omar, in the course of which they came to high words in the presence of the prophet.

Verily, those who lower their voice before the Apostle of God, they are those whose hearts God has proved for piety, for them is forgiveness and a mighty hire.

Verily, those who cry out to thee from behind the inner chambers[1], most of them have no sense;
[5] but did they wait until thou come out to them, it were better for them;—but God is forgiving, merciful.

O ye who believe! if there come to you a sinner with an information, then discriminate, lest ye fall upon a people in ignorance and on the morrow repent of what ye have done[2].

And know that among you is the Apostle of God; if he should obey you in many a matter ye would commit a sin[3]; God has made faith beloved by you, and has made it seemly in your hearts, and has made misbelief and iniquity and rebellion hateful to you.—These are the rightly directed—grace from God and favour! and God is knowing, wise.

And if the two parties of the believers quarrel[4],

---

[1] Two of the Arabs wishing to speak with Mohammed when he was sleeping at noon in his harîm, cried out rudely to him, 'Mohammed, come out to us!' See p. 82.

[2] Al Walîd ibn 'Hugbâ was sent by Mohammed to collect the zakât (see Introduction, p. lxxiii) from the tribe of Mustaleq, with whom he had had a feud in the time preceding Islâm. Seeing them coming out to meet him in large numbers, he grew apprehensive, and returned hastily with the information that the tribe had refused the tribute. Mohammed thereupon sent 'Halîd ibn Walîd to reduce them by force, when it was found that the former messenger's fears had been quite groundless.

[3] I. e. ye would mislead him.

[4] Alluding to one of the frequent disputes between the tribes of Aus and '*H*azrag at Medînah. See Introduction, p. xxxiv.

then make peace between them; and if one of the twain outrages the other, then fight the party that has committed the outrage until it return to God's bidding; and if it do return then make peace between them with equity, and be just; verily, God loves the just.

[10] The believers are but brothers, so make peace between your two brethren and fear God, haply ye may obtain mercy!

O ye who believe! let not one class ridicule another who are perchance better than they; nor let women ridicule other women who are perchance better than they; and do not defame each other, nor call each other bad names—an ill name is iniquity after faith[1]!

O ye who believe! carefully avoid suspicion; verily, some suspicion is a sin. And do not play the spy, nor backbite each other; would one of you like to eat his dead brother's flesh?—why! ye would abhor it! then fear God; verily, God is relentant, compassionate.

O ye folk! verily, we have created you of male and female, and made you races and tribes that ye may know each other.

Verily, the most honourable of you in the sight of God is the most pious of you; verily, God is knowing, aware!

---

[1] I. e. it is defamation to charge a person who has embraced the faith with iniquity. The passage is said to have been revealed on account of Zafîyah bint 'Huyâi, one of the prophet's wives, who complained to him that she had been taunted by the other women with her Jewish origin. Mohammed answered her, 'Canst thou not say, "Aaron is my father, Moses my uncle, and Mohammed my husband?"'

The desert Arabs say, 'We believe.' Say, 'Ye do not believe; but say, "We have become Muslims;" for the faith has not entered into your hearts: but if ye obey God and His Apostle He will not defraud you of your works at all: verily, God is forgiving, compassionate!'

[15] The believers are only those who believe in God and His Apostle, and then doubt not, but fight strenuously with their wealth and persons in God's cause—these are the truth-tellers!

Say, 'Will ye teach God your religion?' when God knows what is in the heavens and what is in the earth, and God all things doth know!

They deem that they oblige thee by becoming Muslims. Say, 'Nay! deem not that ye oblige me by your becoming Muslims! God obliges you, by directing you to the faith, if ye do speak the truth!'

Verily, God knows the unseen things of the heavens and the earth, and God on what ye do doth look.

The Chapter of Q.

(L. Mecca.)

In the name of the merciful and compassionate God.

Q. By the glorious Qur'ân! nay, they wonder that there has come to them a warner from amongst themselves; and the misbelievers say, 'This is a wondrous thing! What, when we are dead and have become dust?—that is a remote return!'

We well know what the earth consumes of them, for with us is a book that keeps (account).

[5] Nay, they call the truth a lie when it comes to them, and they are in a confused affair[1].

Do not they behold the heaven above them, how we have built it and adorned it, and how it has no flaws?

And the earth, we have stretched it out and thrown thereon firm mountains, and caused to grow thereon every beautiful kind.

An insight and a reminder to every servant who repents!

And we sent down from the heaven water as a blessing, and caused to grow therewith gardens and the harvest grain!

[10] And the tall palm trees having piled up spathes, for a provision to (our) servants; and we quickened thereby a dead land; thus shall the resurrection be!

Before them the people of Noah and the fellows of ar Rass[2] and Thamûd and 'Âd and Pharaoh called the apostles liars; and the brethren of Lot and the fellows of the Grove[3] and the people of Tubbâ'h[4] all called the prophets liars, and the threat was duly executed.

Were we then fatigued with the first creation? nay! but they are in obscurity concerning the new creation.

[15] But we created man, and we know what his

---

[1] Alluding to the various opinions expressed by the unbelievers with reference to the Qur'ân; some calling it sorcery or divination, others poetry, and some asserting it to be 'old folks' tales' or mere invention.

[2] See Part II, p. 86, note 3.

[3] See Part I, p. 249, note 3.

[4] See Chapter XLIV, verse 35, p. 219, note 3.

soul whispers; for we are nigher to him than his jugular vein!

When the two meeters meet[1], sitting the one on the right and the other on the left, not a word does he utter, but a watcher is by him ready!

And the agony of death shall come in truth!—'that is what thou didst shun!'

And the trumpet shall be blown!—that is the threatened day!

[20] And every soul shall come—with it a driver and a witness!

'Thou wert heedless of this, and we withdrew thy veil from thee, and to-day is thine eyesight keen[2]!'

And his mate shall say, 'This is what is ready for me (to attest).

'Throw into hell every stubborn misbeliever[3]!—who forbids good, a transgressor, a doubter! [25] who sets other gods with God—and throw him, ye twain, into fierce torment!'

His mate shall say, 'Our Lord! I seduced him not, but he was in a remote error.'

He shall say, 'Wrangle not before me; for I sent the threat to you before. The sentence is not changed with me, nor am I unjust to my servants.'

On the day we will say to hell, 'Art thou full?' and it will say, 'Are there any more?'

[30] And Paradise shall be brought near to the pious,—not far off.

---

[1] The two recording angels, who accompany every man and note down his every word and action.

[2] These words are supposed to be addressed by the 'driver' to the unbelieving soul.

[3] These words are spoken by God.

This is what ye are promised, to every one who turns frequently (to God) and keeps His commandments: who fears the Merciful in secret and brings a repentant heart.

'Enter into it in peace: this is the day of eternity!'

They shall have what they wish therein, and increase from us!

[35] How many a generation have we destroyed before them, mightier than they in prowess!

Pass through the land, is there any refuge[1]? Verily, in that is a reminder to whomsoever has a heart, or gives ear, and is a witness thereto.

We did create the heavens and the earth and what is between the two in six days, and no weariness touched us[2].

Be thou patient then of what they say, and celebrate the praises of thy Lord before the rising of the sun and before the setting. And through (some) of the night celebrate His praise and the additional adorations[3].

[40] And listen for the day when the crier shall cry from a near place[4];—the day when they shall hear the shout[5] in truth—that is the day of coming forth!

Verily, we quicken and we kill, and unto us the journey is!

On the day when the earth shall be cleft asunder

---

[1] I. e. from the vengeance of God.

[2] A protest against the assertion that God rested on the seventh day.

[3] Two sigdahs used at the evening prayers, but not incumbent on the worshipper.

[4] I. e. a place from which all men may hear; generally supposed by Muslims to be the temple at Jerusalem.

[5] The sound of the last trumpet.

from them swiftly;—that is a gathering together which is easy to us!

We know what they say; nor art thou over them one to compel.

[45] Wherefore remind, by the Qur'ân, him who fears the threat.

The Chapter of the Scatterers.

(LI. Mecca.)

In the name of the merciful and compassionate God.

By the scatterers[1] who scatter! and by those pregnant[2] with their burden! and by those running on[3] easily! and by the distributors[4] of affairs!—[5] verily, what ye are threatened with is surely true!

And, verily, the judgment will surely take place!

By the heaven possessed of paths; verily, ye are at variance in what ye say!

He is turned from it who is turned.

[10] Slain be the liars, who are heedless in a flood (of ignorance).

They will ask, 'When is the day of judgment?' The day when at the fire they shall be tried. —'Taste your trial! this is what ye wished to hasten on!'

[15] Verily, the pious are in gardens and springs, taking what their Lord brings them. Verily, they before that did well. But little of the night they slept; and at the dawn they asked forgiveness.

---

[1] The winds. [2] The clouds. [3] The ships.
[4] Angels or winds.

And in their wealth was what was due to him who asked, and him who was kept back from asking.

[20] And in the earth are signs to those who are sure, and in yourselves,—what! do ye not then see?

And in the heaven is your provision and that which ye are promised[1].

But by the Lord of the heaven and the earth! verily, it is the truth,—like that which ye do utter[2]!

Has the tale of Abraham's honoured guests reached thee[3]? [25] When they entered in unto him and said, 'Peace!' he said, 'Peace!—a people unrecognised.'

And he went aside unto his people and fetched a fat calf, and brought it nigh unto them; said he, 'Will ye then not eat?'

And he felt a secret fear of them: said they, 'Fear not.' And they gave him glad tidings of a knowing boy.

And his wife approached with a noise, and smote her face, and said, 'An old woman, barren!'

[30] Said they, 'Thus says thy Lord, He is knowing, wise.' Said he, 'And about what is your errand, O ye messengers?'

They said, 'Verily, we are sent unto a sinful people, to send upon them stones of clay, marked from thy Lord for the extravagant[4].'

[35] And we sent out therefrom such as were in it of the believers; but we only found therein one house of Muslims.

---

[1] I. e. rain, which produces material sustenance, and there too is the promise of the future life.

[2] I. e. unreserved and plain as ye yourselves affirm truths to each other.

[3] See Part I, pp. 212-214. [4] See Part I, p. 214, note 1.

And we left therein a sign to those who fear the grievous woe.

And in Moses; when we sent him to Pharaoh with obvious authority.

But he turned his back towards his column[1], and said, 'A sorcerer or mad!'

[40] And we seized him and his hosts and hurled them into the sea; for he was to be blamed.

And in 'Âd, when we sent against them a desolating wind, that left naught on which it came without making it ashes!

And in Thamûd, when it was said to them, 'Enjoy yourselves for a season.' But they revolted against the bidding of their Lord; and the noise caught them as they looked on. [45] And they could not stand upright, and they were not helped!

And the people of Noah of yore; verily, they were an abominable people.

And the heaven—we have built it with might, and, verily, we do surely give it ample space!

And the earth—we have spread it out; and how well we lay it out!

And of everything have we created pairs, haply ye may be mindful.

[50] Flee then to God; verily, I am a plain warner from Him to you!

And do not set with God another god; verily, I am a plain warner from Him to you!

Thus there came no apostle to those before them, but they said, 'A sorcerer, mad!'

---

[1] Either Pharaoh's forces, or one of his nobles, or something else on which he relied. See Part I, p. 214, first line, and note 1.

Do they bequeath it[1] to each other?

Yea, they are an outrageous people!

So turn thy back upon them, so thou wilt not be to blame.

[55] And remind; for, verily, the reminder shall profit the believers.

And I have not created the *g*inn and mankind save that they may worship me.

I do not desire any provision from them, and I do not wish them to feed me.

Verily, God, He is the provider, endowed with steady might.

Verily, for those who injure (the Apostle) shall be a portion like the portion of their fellows[2], but let them not hurry Me!

[60] Then woe to those who misbelieve from their day which they are threatened.

The Chapter of the Mount.

(LII. Mecca.)

In the name of the merciful and compassionate God.

By the mount! by the Book inscribed upon an
outstretched vellum! by the frequented house[3]! [5]
by the elevated roof[4]! by the swelling sea! verily,
the torment of thy Lord will come to pass;—there
is none to avert it!

The day when the heavens shall reel about,

---

[1] I. e. this taunt.

[2] I. e. like the fate of those who wronged the apostles of old.

[3] I. e. either the Kaabah itself or the model of it, said to exist in the heavens and to be frequented by the angels.

[4] I. e. of heaven.

[10] and the mountains shall move about,—then woe upon that day to those who call (the apostles) liars, who plunge into discussion for a sport!

On the day when they shall be thrust away into the fire of hell,—'This is the fire, the which ye used to call a lie!—[15] Is it magic, this? or can ye not see?—broil ye therein, and be patient thereof or be not patient, it is the same to you: ye are but rewarded for that which ye did do!'

Verily, the pious (shall be) in gardens and pleasure, enjoying what their Lord has given them; for their Lord will save them from the torment of hell.

'Eat and drink with good digestion, for that which ye have done!'

[20] Reclining on couches in rows; and we will wed them to large-eyed maids.

And those who believe and whose seed follows them in the faith, we will unite their seed with them; and we will not cheat them of their work at all;—every man is pledged for what he earns [1].

And we will extend to them fruit and flesh such as they like. They shall pass to and fro therein a cup in which is neither folly nor sin.

And round them shall go boys of theirs, as though they were hidden pearls.

[25] And they shall accost each other and ask questions, and shall say, 'Verily, we were before amidst our families shrinking with terror [2], but God has been gracious to us and saved us from the torment of the hot blast.

[1] Every man is pledged to God for his conduct, and, if he does well, redeems himself.

[2] At the thought of the next life.

'Verily, we used to call on Him before; verily, He is the righteous, the compassionate!'

Wherefore do thou[1] remind them: for thou art, by the favour of thy Lord, neither a soothsayer nor mad!

Will they say, 'A poet; we wait for him the sad accidents of fate?'

[30] Say, 'Wait ye then; for I too am of those who wait!'

Do their dreams bid them this? or are they an outrageous people?

Or will they say, 'He has invented it?'—nay, but they do not believe!

But let them bring a discourse like it, if they tell the truth!

[35] Or were they created of nothing, or were they the creators? Or did they create the heavens and the earth?—nay, but they are not sure!

Or have they the treasures of thy Lord? or are they the governors supreme?

Or have they a ladder whereon they can listen[2]?—then let their listener bring obvious authority.

Has He daughters, while ye have sons?

[40] Or dost thou ask them a hire, while they are borne down by debt?

Or have they the unseen, so that they write it down?

Or do they desire a plot?—but those who misbelieve it is who are plotted against!

---

[1] Addressed to Mohammed.

[2] I. e. a ladder reaching to the gates of heaven, upon which they may stand and listen to the angels discoursing, as the devils do. See Part I, pp. 50, 51, note 2.

Or have they a god beside God? celebrated be God's praises above what they join with Him!

But if they should see a fragment of the sky falling down, they would say, 'Clouds in masses!'

[45] But leave them till they meet that day of theirs whereon they shall swoon[1]; the day when their plotting shall avail them naught, and they shall not be helped!

And, verily, there is a torment beside that[2] for those who do wrong; but most of them do not know!

But wait thou patiently for the judgment of thy Lord, for thou art in our eyes. And celebrate the praises of thy Lord what time thou risest, and in the night, and at the fading of the stars!

The Chapter of the Star.

(LIII. Mecca.)

In the name of the merciful and compassionate God.

By the star when it falls, your comrade errs not, nor is he deluded! nor speaks he out of lust! It is but an inspiration inspired! [5] One mighty in power[3] taught him, endowed with sound understanding, and appeared, he being in the loftiest tract.

---

[1] At the sound of the last trumpet.

[2] I.e. beside the torment of the judgment day they shall be punished with defeat and loss here.

[3] The angel Gabriel, who appeared twice to Mohammed in his natural form, namely, on the occasion of the 'Night Journey,' to which this passage refers, and on the first revelation of the Qur'ân. (See Introduction, pp. xx and xxxii.)

Then drew he near and hovered o'er! until he was two bows' length off or nigher still! [10] Then he inspired his servant what he inspired him; the heart belies not what he saw! What, will ye dispute with him on what he saw?

And he saw him another time, by the lote tree none may pass; [15] near which is the garden of the Abode! When there covered the lote tree what did cover it! The sight swerved not nor wandered. He saw then the greatest of the signs of his Lord.

Have ye considered Allât and Al 'Huzzâ, [20] and Manât the other third[1]? Shall there be male offspring for Him and female for you? That were an unfair division! They are but names which ye have named, ye and your fathers! God has sent down no authority for them! They do but follow suspicion and what their souls lust after!—And yet there has come to them guidance from their Lord.

Shall man have what he desires? [25] But God's is the hereafter and the present!

How many an angel in the heaven!—their intercession avails not at all, save after God has given permission to whomsoever He will and is pleased with!

Verily, those who believe not in the hereafter do surely name the angels with female names[2]!—but they have no knowledge thereof; they do but follow suspicion, and, verily, suspicion shall not avail against the truth at all!

[30] But turn aside from him who turns his back upon our remembrance and desires naught but this

---

[1] See Introduction, p. xxvii, and Part II, p. 62, note 1.

[2] See Introduction, pp. xii and xiii.

world's life! This is their sum of knowledge; verily, thy Lord knows best who has erred from His way, and He knows best who is guided!

God's is what is in the heavens and what is in the earth, that He may reward those who do evil for what they have done; and may reward those who do good with good! those who shun great sins and iniquities,—all but venial faults,—verily, thy Lord is of ample forgiveness; He knows best about you, when He produced you from the earth, and when ye were embryos in the wombs of your mothers.

Make not yourselves out, then, to be pure; He knows best who it is that fears.

Hast thou considered him who turns his back? who gives but little [35] and then stops[1]? Has he then the knowledge of the unseen, so that he can see?

Has he not been informed of what is in the pages of Moses and Abraham who fulfilled his word?—that no burdened soul shall bear the burden of another? [40] and that man shall have only that for which he strives; and that his striving shall at length be seen? Then shall he be rewarded for it with the most full reward; and that unto thy Lord is the limit; [45] and that it is He who makes men laugh and weep; and that it is He who kills and makes alive; and that He created pairs, male

[1] This passage refers to one El Walîd ibn Mu*gh*âirah, who being abused for following Mohammed and forsaking the religion of the Qurâi*s*, answered that he had done so to escape divine vengeance. Thereupon an idolater offered to take on himself El Walîd's sin for a certain sum of money. The offer was accepted, and Walîd apostatized from El Islâm, paying down a portion of the amount agreed upon at the time. Later on he refused to pay the balance on the ground that he had already paid enough.

and female, from a clot when it is emitted; and that for Him is the next production[1]; and that he enriches and gives possession; [50] and that He is the Lord of the Dog-star[2], and that He it was who destroyed 'Âd of yore, and Thamûd, and left none of them; and the people of Noah before them,— verily, they were most unjust and outrageous!

And the overthrown (cities)[3] He threw down; [55] and there covered them what did cover them!

Which then of your Lord's benefits do ye dispute?

This is a warner, one of the warners of yore!

The approaching day approaches; there is none to discover it but God.

At this new discourse then do ye wonder? [60] and do ye laugh and not weep? and ye divert yourselves the while!

But adore God and serve (Him)[4].

The Chapter of the Moon.

(LIV. Mecca.)

In the name of the merciful and compassionate God.

The Hour draws nigh, and the moon is split

---

[1] I. e. the resurrection.

[2] Sirius, or the Dog-star, was an object of worship amongst the ancient Arabs.

[3] Sodom, Gomorrah, &c.

[4] At this verse the Qurâis, who were present at the first reading of this chapter when their gods were spoken well of, fell down adoring with Mohammed. See Introduction, p. xxxii.

asunder[1]. But if they see a sign they turn aside and say, 'Magic, continuous[2]!'

And they call it a lie and follow their lusts; but every matter is settled!

There has come to them some information[3] with restraint in it—[5] wisdŏm far-reaching—but warners avail not!

But turn thy back on them!

The day when the caller[4] shall call to an awkward thing[5].

Humbly casting down their looks shall they come forth from their graves, as though they were locusts scattered abroad!

Hurrying forwards to the caller! the misbelievers shall say, 'This is a difficult day!'

Noah's people before them called (the apostles) liars; they called our servant a liar; and they said, 'Mad!' and he was rejected.

[10] And he called upon his Lord, 'Verily, I am overcome, come then to my help!'

And we opened the gates of heaven with water pouring down!

---

[1] According to a tradition this refers to a miracle: the unbelievers having asked for a sign, the moon appeared to be cloven in twain. The tradition is, however, supported by very doubtful authority, and is directly opposed to the teaching of the Qur'ân elsewhere, for the power to comply with the demand for a sign is always distinctly disclaimed. The more usual explanation is the natural one, that the expression merely refers to one of the signs of the day of judgment.

[2] This word is interpreted by some to mean 'transient,' by others 'powerful.'

[3] The Qur'ân.

[4] The angel Isrâfîl.

[5] The last judgment.

And we made the earth burst forth in springs, and the waters met at a bidding already decreed.

But we bore him on the thing of planks and nails; sailing on beneath our eyes, a reward for him who had been disbelieved!

[15] And we left it a sign;—but is there any one who will mind?

'Âd called the apostles liars, and how was my punishment and my warning?

Verily, we sent on them a cold storm wind on a day of continuous ill-luck!

[20] It reft men away as though they had been palm stumps torn up!

We have made the Qur'ân easy as a reminder—but is there any one who will mind?

Thamûd called the warnings lies, and said, 'A mortal, one of us, alone, shall we follow him? then indeed were we in error and excitement[1]!

[25] 'Is the warning cast on him alone among us? nay, he is an insolent liar!

'They shall know to-morrow about the insolent liar!

'Verily, we are about to send the she-camel as a trial for them, then watch them and have patience! and inform them that the water is shared between them (and her); each draught shall be sought by turns.'

Then they called their companion, and he plied (a knife) and hamstrung her.

[30] Then how was my punishment and my warning? Verily, we sent against them one noise, and they were like the dry sticks of him who builds a fold.

---

[1] Or madness.

We have made the Qur'ân easy as a reminder—but is there any one who will mind?

Lot's people called the apostles liars; verily, we sent against them a heavy sand storm; all, save Lot's family, we saved them at the dawn. [35] As a favour from us; so do we reward him who gives thanks!

He indeed had warned them of our assault, but they doubted of the warning.

And they desired his guest, and we put out their eyes.—

'So taste ye my torment and warning!'

And there overtook them on the morning a settled punishment!—

'So taste ye my torment and warning!'

[40] We have made the Qur'ân easy as a reminder—but is there any one who will mind?

The warning came to Pharaoh's people; they called our signs all lies, and we seized on them with the seizing of a mighty powerful one.

Are your misbelievers better than they? or have ye an exemption in the Scriptures? Or do they say we are a victorious company?

[45] The whole shall be routed and shall turn their backs in flight[1].

Nay, the Hour is their promised time! and the Hour is most severe and bitter!

Verily, the sinners are in error and excitement. On the day when they shall be dragged to the fire upon their faces!—'Taste ye the touch of hell.'

Verily, everything have we created by decree, [50] and our bidding is but one (word), like the twinkling of an eye!

[1] This is appealed to by Muslims as a prophecy fulfilled at the battle of Bedr.

We have destroyed the like of you—but is there any who will mind?

And everything they do is in the books[1], and everything small and great is written down.

Verily, the pious shall be amid gardens and rivers,
[55] in the seat of truth, with the powerful king.

THE CHAPTER OF THE MERCIFUL.

(LV. Mecca.)

IN the name of the merciful and compassionate God.

The Merciful taught the Qur'ân;
He created man, taught him plain speech.
The sun and the moon have their appointed time;
[5] The herbs and the trees adore;
And the heavens, He raised them and set the balance, that ye should not be outrageous in the balance;
But weigh ye aright, and stint not the balance.
And the earth He has set it for living creatures;
[10] therein are fruits and palms, with sheaths; and grain with chaff and frequent shoots;
Then which of your Lord's bounties will ye twain deny?
He created men of crackling clay like the potters. And He created the *ginn* from smokeless fire.
[15] Then which of your Lord's bounties will ye twain deny?
The Lord of the two easts[2] and the Lord of the two wests!

---

[1] The books kept by the recording angels.

[2] See p. 214, note 1.

Then which of your Lord's bounties will ye twain deny?

He has let loose the two seas that meet together;
[20] between them is a barrier they cannot pass!

Then which of your Lord's bounties will ye twain deny?

He brings forth from each pearls both large and small!

Then which of your Lord's bounties will ye twain deny?

His are the ships which rear aloft in the sea like mountains.

[25] Then which of your Lord's bounties will ye twain deny?

Every one upon it[1] is transient, but the face of thy Lord endowed with majesty and honour shall endure.

Then which of your Lord's bounties will ye twain deny?

Of Him whosoever is in the heaven and the earth does beg; every day He is in (some fresh) business!

[30] Then which of your Lord's bounties will ye twain deny?

We shall be at leisure for you, O ye two weighty ones[2]!

Then which of your Lord's bounties will ye twain deny?

O assembly of *g*inns and mankind! if ye are able to pass through the confines of heaven and earth

---

[1] The earth.

[2] I. e. mankind and the *g*inn; the meaning is, that God will have leisure to judge them both.

then pass through them!—ye cannot pass through save by authority!

Then which of your Lord's bounties will ye twain deny?

[35] There shall be sent against you a flash of fire, and molten copper, and ye shall not be helped!

Then which of your Lord's bounties will ye twain deny?

And when the heaven is rent asunder and become rosy red[1]—(melting) like grease!

Then which of your Lord's bounties will ye twain deny?

On that day neither man nor *g*inn shall be asked about his crime!

[40] Then which of your Lord's bounties will ye twain deny?

The sinners shall be known by their marks, and shall be seized by the forelock and the feet!

Then which of your Lord's bounties will ye twain deny?

'This is hell, which the sinners did call a lie! they shall circulate between it and water boiling quite!'

[45] Then which of your Lord's bounties will ye twain deny?

But for him who fears the station of his Lord are gardens twain!

Then which of your Lord's bounties will ye twain deny?

Both furnished with branching trees.

Then which of your Lord's bounties will ye twain deny?

[50] In each are flowing springs.

---

[1] The word is also said to mean red leather.

Then which of your Lord's bounties will ye twain deny?

In each are, of every fruit, two kinds.

Then which of your Lord's bounties will ye twain deny?

Reclining on beds the linings of which are of brocade, and the fruit of the two gardens within reach to cull.

[55] Then which of your Lord's bounties will ye twain deny?

Therein are maids of modest glances whom no man nor *g*inn has deflowered before.

Then which of your Lord's bounties will ye twain deny?

As though they were rubies and pearls.

Then which of your Lord's bounties will ye twain deny?

[60] Is the reward of goodness aught but goodness?

Then which of your Lord's bounties will ye twain deny?

And besides these, are gardens twain [1],

Then which of your Lord's bounties will ye twain deny?

With dark green foliage.

[65] Then which of your Lord's bounties will ye twain deny?

In each two gushing springs.

Then which of your Lord's bounties will ye twain deny?

In each fruit and palms and pomegranates.

Then which of your Lord's bounties will ye twain deny?

---

[1] For the inferior inhabitants of Paradise.

[70] In them maidens best and fairest!

Then which of your Lord's bounties will ye twain deny?

Bright and large-eyed maids kept in their tents.

Then which of your Lord's bounties will ye twain deny?

Whom no man nor *ginn* has deflowered before them.

[75] Then which of your Lord's bounties will ye twain deny?

Reclining on green cushions and beautiful carpets.

Then which of your Lord's bounties will ye twain deny?

Blessed be the name of thy Lord possessed of majesty and honour!

The Chapter of the Inevitable.

(LVI. Mecca.)

In the name of the merciful and compassionate God.

When the inevitable[1] happens; none shall call its happening a lie!—abasing—exalting!

When the earth shall quake, quaking! [5] and the mountains shall crumble, crumbling, and become like motes dispersed!

And ye shall be three sorts;

And the fellows of the right hand—what right lucky fellows!

And the fellows of the left hand—what unlucky fellows!

---

[1] I. e. the day of judgment.

[10] And the foremost foremost[1]!
These are they who are brought nigh,
In gardens of pleasure!
A crowd of those of yore,
And a few of those of the latter day!
[15] And gold-weft couches, reclining on them face to face.
Around them shall go eternal youths, with goblets and ewers and a cup of flowing wine; no headache shall they feel therefrom, nor shall their wits be dimmed!
[20] And fruits such as they deem the best;
And flesh of fowl as they desire;
And bright and large-eyed maids like hidden pearls;
A reward for that which they have done!
They shall hear no folly there and no sin;
[25] Only the speech, 'Peace, Peace!'
And the fellows of the right—what right lucky fellows!
Amid thornless lote trees.
And tal'h[2] trees with piles of fruit;
And outspread shade,
[30] And water out-poured;
And fruit in abundance, neither failing nor forbidden;
And beds upraised!
Verily, we have produced them[3] a production.
[35] And made them virgins, darlings of equal age (with their spouses) for the fellows of the right!

---

[1] I.e. the foremost in professing the faith on earth shall be the foremost then.

[2] The mimosa gummifera is generally so called in Arabia; but the banana is said to be meant in this passage.

[3] The celestial damsels.

A crowd of those of yore, and a crowd of those of
the latter day!
[40] And the fellows of the left—what unlucky
fellows!
In hot blasts and boiling water;
And a shade of pitchy smoke,
Neither cool nor generous!
Verily, they were affluent ere this, [45] and did persist
in mighty crime; and used to say, 'What, when we
die and have become dust and bones, shall we
then indeed be raised? or our fathers of yore?'
Say, 'Verily, those of yore and those of the latter
day [50] shall surely be gathered together unto
the tryst of the well-known day.'
Then ye, O ye who err! who say it is a lie! shall
eat of the Zaqqûm tree! and fill your bellies with
it! and drink thereon of boiling water! [55] and
drink as drinks the thirsty camel.
This is their entertainment on the judgment day!
We created you, then why do ye not credit?
Have ye considered what ye emit?
Do we create it, or are we the creators?
[60] We have decreed amongst you death; but we
are not forestalled from making the likes of you
in exchange, or producing you as ye know not of.
Ye do know the first production—why then do ye
not mind?
Have ye considered what ye till?
Do ye make it bear seed, or do we make it bear seed?
[65] If we pleased we could make it mere grit, so that
ye would pause to marvel:
'Verily, we have got into debt[1] and we are excluded[2].'

[1] I. e. for seed and labour. [2] From reaping the fruits of it.

Have ye considered the water which ye drink?
Do ye make it come down from the clouds, or do
we make it come down?
If we pleased we could make it pungent—why then
do ye not give thanks?
[70] Have ye considered the fire which ye strike?
Do ye produce the tree that gives it[1], or do we
produce it?
We have made it a memorial and a chattel for the
traveller of the waste?
Then celebrate the grand name of thy Lord!
So I will not swear by the positions of the stars;
[75] and, verily, it is a grand oath if ye did but
know—that, verily, this is the honourable Qur'ân
—in the laid-up Book!
Let none touch it but the purified!
A revelation from the Lord of the worlds.
[80] What! this new discourse will ye despise?
And make for your provision, that you call it a
lie?
Why then—when it[2] comes up to the throat, and ye
at that time look on, though we are nearer to him
than you are, but ye cannot see,—[85] why, if ye
are not to be judged, do ye not send it back, if
ye do tell the truth?
But either, if he be of those brought nigh to
God,—then rest and fragrance and the garden
of pleasure!
Or, if he be of the fellows of the right! [90] then
'Peace to thee!' from the fellows of the right!

---

[1] The ancient Arabs produced fire by the friction of a stick in a hollow piece of wood. Cf. p. 167, line 25.

[2] The soul of a dying man.

Or, if he be of those who say it is a lie,—who err! then an entertainment of boiling water! and broiling in hell!
[95] Verily, this is surely certain truth!
So celebrate the grand name of thy Lord!

The Chapter of Iron.

(LVII. Mecca.)

In the name of the merciful and compassionate God.

Whatever is in the heavens and the earth celebrates the praises of God, for He is the mighty, the wise!

His is the kingdom of the heavens and the earth: He quickens and He kills, and He is mighty over all!

He is the first and the last; and the outer and the inner; and He all things doth know!

He it is who created the heavens and the earth in six days, then He made for the throne; and He knows what goes into the earth and what goes forth therefrom, and what comes down from the sky and what goes up therein, and He is with you wheresoe'er ye be: for God on what ye do doth look!

[5] His is the kingdom of the heavens and the earth, and unto God affairs return. He makes the night succeed the day, and makes the day succeed the night; and He knows the nature of men's breasts.

Believe in God and His Apostle, and give alms of what He has made you successors of. For those amongst you who believe and give alms—for them is mighty hire.

What ails you that ye do not believe in God and His Apostle? He calls on you to believe in your Lord; and He has taken a compact from you, if ye be believers.

He it is who sends down upon His servants manifest signs, to bring you forth from the darkness into the light; for, verily, God to you is kind, compassionate!

[10] What ails you that ye give not alms in God's cause? for God's is the inheritance of the heavens and the earth. Not alike amongst you is he who gives alms before the victory and fights,—they are grander in rank than those who give alms afterwards and fight. But to all does God promise good; and God of what ye do is well aware!

Who is there who will lend a good loan to God? for He will double it for him, and for him is a generous reward.

On the day when thou shalt see believers, men and women, with their light running on before them and on their right hand [1],—'Glad tidings for you to-day.—Gardens beneath which rivers flow, to dwell therein for aye; that is the grand bliss!'

On the day when the hypocrites, men and women, shall say to those who believe, 'Wait for us that we may kindle at your light.' It will be said, 'Get ye back, and beg a light.' And there shall be struck out between them a wall with a door; within it shall be mercy, and outside before it torment. They shall cry out to them, 'We were not with you!' they shall say, 'Yea, but ye did tempt yourselves, and did wait, and did doubt; and your vain hopes beguiled you; and the beguiler beguiled you about God.

[1] I. e. guiding them to Paradise.

'Wherefore to-day there shall not be taken from you a ransom, nor from those who misbelieved. Your resort is the fire; it is your sovereign, and an ill journey will it be!'

[15] Is the time come to those who believe, for their hearts to be humbled at the remembrance of God, and of what He has sent down in truth? and for them not to be like those who were given the Scriptures before, and over whom time was prolonged, but their hearts grew hard, and many of them were workers of abomination?

Know that God quickens the earth after its death!—we have manifested to you the signs; haply ye may have some sense!

Verily, those who give in charity, men and women, who have lent to God a goodly loan,—it shall be doubled for them, and for them is a generous hire.

And those who believe in God and His Apostle, they are the confessors and the martyrs with their Lord; for them is their hire and their light! But those who misbelieve and call our signs lies, they are the fellows of hell!

Know that the life of this world is but a sport, and a play, and an adornment, and something to boast of amongst yourselves; and the multiplying of children is like a rain-growth, its vegetation pleases the misbelievers; then they wither away, and thou mayest see them become yellow; then they become but grit.

But in the hereafter is a severe woe, [20] and forgiveness from God and His goodwill; but the life of this world is but a chattel of guile.

Race towards forgiveness from your Lord and

Paradise, whose breadth is as the breadth of the heavens and the earth, prepared for those who believe in God and His apostles! and God's grace, He gives it to whom He pleases, for God is Lord of mighty grace!

No accident befalls in the earth, or in yourselves, but it was in the Book, before we created them; verily, that is easy unto God.

That ye may not vex yourselves for what ye miss, nor be overjoyed at what He gives you; for God loves no arrogant boaster, who are niggardly and bid men be niggardly: but whoso turns his back[1], verily, God is rich, praiseworthy.

[25] We did send our apostles with manifest signs; and we did send down among you the Book and the balance, that men might stand by justice; and we sent down iron in which is both keen violence and advantages to men; and that God might know who helps Him and His apostles in secret; verily, God is strong and mighty!

And we sent Noah and Abraham; and placed in their seed prophecy and the Book; and some of them are guided, though many of them are workers of abomination!

Then we followed up their footsteps with our apostles; and we followed them up with Jesus the son of Mary; and we gave him the gospel; and we placed in the hearts of those who followed him kindness and compassion.—But monkery, they invented it; we only prescribed to them the craving after the goodwill of God, and they observed it not with due observance. But we gave to those who

[1] I. e. from almsgiving.

believe amongst them their hire; though many amongst them were workers of abomination!

O ye who believe! fear God, and believe in His Apostle: He will give you two portions of His mercy, and will make for you a light for you to walk in, and will forgive you; for God is forgiving, compassionate.

That the people of the Book may know that they cannot control aught of God's grace; and that grace is in God's hands, He gives it to whom He will; for God is Lord of mighty grace!

THE CHAPTER OF THE WRANGLER.

(LVIII. Medînah.)

GOD has heard the speech of her who wrangled with you about her husband[1], and complained to God; and God hears your gossip; verily, God both hears and sees.

Those among you who back out of their wives[2] they are not their mothers: their mothers are only those who gave them birth; and, verily, they speak a wrong speech and a false.

Verily, God both pardons and forgives. But those who back out of their wives and then would recall their speech,—then the manumission of a captive before they touch each other; that is what ye are admonished, and God of what ye do is well aware!

---

[1] Khâulah bint Tha'labah being divorced from her husband by the formula mentioned below, and which was always considered to be a final separation, appealed to Mohammed, who said he could not alter the custom. Afterwards, on the woman praying to God, this passage was revealed, abolishing the objectionable form of divorce.

[2] I. e. divorce them by the formula 'Thou art to me as my mother's back!' See Part I, p. 43, note 4.

[5] But he who finds not (the means):—then a fast for two months consecutively, before they touch each other; and he who cannot endure that:—then the feeding of sixty poor folk. That is that ye may believe in God and His Apostle; and these are the bounds of God; and for the misbelievers is grievous woe!

Verily, those who oppose God and His Apostle shall be upset, as those before them were upset.

We have sent down manifest signs: for the misbelievers is shameful woe on the day when God shall raise them all together, and shall inform them of what they have done. God has taken account of it, but they forget it; for God is witness over all!

Dost thou not see that God knows what is in the heavens and what is in the earth? and that there cannot be a privy discourse of three but He makes the fourth? nor of five but He makes the sixth? nor less than that nor more, but that He is with them wheresoe'er they be? then He will inform them of what they have done upon the resurrection day; verily, God all things doth know!

Dost thou not look at those who were prohibited from privy talk, and then returned to that they were forbidden? and they too discourse together with sin and enmity and rebellion against the Apostle; and when they come to thee they greet thee with what God greets thee not[1]; and they say in themselves, Why does not God torment us for what we say? Hell is enough for them! they shall broil therein, and an ill journey shall it be!

---

[1] Instead of saying, Es salâm 'halaika, 'peace be upon thee!' they used to say, Es sâm 'halaika, 'mischief be upon thee!'

[10] O ye who believe! when ye discourse together, then discourse not in sin and enmity and rebellion against the Apostle; but discourse together in righteousness and piety; and fear God, for unto Him ye shall be gathered!

Privy talk is only from the devil, and those who do believe may grieve: it cannot hurt them at all, except by the permission of God: and upon God let the believers rely.

O ye who believe! when it is said to you, 'Make room in your assemblies,' then make room; God will make room for you; and when it is said to you, 'Rise up,' then rise up; God will raise all you who believe, as well as those who are given knowledge, in rank; for God of what ye do is well aware!

O ye who believe! when ye address the Apostle, then give in charity before addressing him; that is better for you, and more pure. But if ye find not the means,—then God is forgiving, compassionate. What! do ye shrink from giving in charity before addressing him? then if ye do it not, and God relents towards you, then be steadfast in prayer, and give alms, and fear God and His Apostle; for God is well aware of what ye do!

[15] Dost thou not look at those who take for patrons a people[1] God is wrath with? they are neither of you nor of them, and they swear to you a lie the while they know; for them God has prepared severe torment; verily, evil is it they have done!

They take their faith for a cloak; and they turn men aside from the path of God; and for them is shameful woe!

---

[1] The Jews.

Their wealth shall not avail them, nor their children at all, against God; they are the fellows of the Fire, and they shall dwell therein for aye!

On the day when God raises them all together, then will they swear to Him as they swore to you; and they will think that they rest on somewhat.—Ay, verily, they are liars!

[20] Satan hath overridden them, and made them forget the remembrance of God: they are the crew of Satan; ay, the crew of Satan, they are the losers!

Verily, those who oppose God and His Apostle are amongst the most vile.

God has written, 'I will surely prevail, I and my apostles;' verily, God is strong and mighty!

Thou shalt not find a people who believe in God and the last day loving him who opposes God and His Apostle, even though it be their fathers, or their sons, or their brethren, or their clansmen.

He has written faith in their hearts, and He aids them with a spirit from Him; and will make them enter into gardens beneath which rivers flow, to dwell therein for aye! God is well pleased with them, and they well pleased with Him: they are God's crew; ay, God's crew, they shall prosper!

The Chapter of the Emigration.

(LIX. Medînah.)

In the name of the merciful and compassionate God.

What is in the heavens and in the earth celebrates God's praises; He is the mighty, the wise!

He it was who drove those of the people of the Book who misbelieved forth from their houses, at the first emigration[1]; ye did not think that they would go forth, and they thought that their fortresses would defend them against God; but God came upon them from whence they did not reckon, and cast dread into their hearts! They ruined their houses with their own hands and the hands of the believers; wherefore take example, O ye who are endowed with sight!

Had it not been that God had prescribed for them banishment, He would have tormented them in this world[2]; but for them in the next shall be the torment of the Fire! that is because they opposed God and His Apostle: and whoso opposes God, verily, God is keen to punish!

[5] What palm trees ye did cut down or what ye left standing upon their roots was by God's permission, and to disgrace the workers of abomination; and as for the spoils that God gave to His Apostle from these (people) ye did not press forward after them with horse or riding camel; but God gives His Apostle authority over whom He pleases, for God is mighty over all[3]!

---

[1] The Jews of en Na*dh*îr, near Medînah, who at first promised to stand neuter between him and the idolaters. After his success at Bedr they came over to his side, but turned again after the defeat of Ohod. For this offence they were forced to leave the country.

[2] Like those of Qurâi*dh*ah, who were slaughtered. See Introduction, p. xxxix.

[3] The Muslims did not use cavalry on the occasion, Mohammed himself being the only mounted member of the expedition. For this reason the spoils were assigned to the prophet alone, and not divided in the usual manner as prescribed in Chapter VIII, verse 42, Part I, pp. 167, 168.

What God gave as spoils to His Apostle of the people of the cities is God's, and the Apostle's, and for kinsfolk, orphans, and the poor, and the wayfarer, so that it should not be circulated amongst the rich men of you.

And what the Apostle gives you, take; and what he forbids you, desist from; and fear God, verily, God is keen to punish!

And (it is) for the poor who fled[1], who were driven forth from their houses and their wealth, who crave grace from God and His goodwill, and help God and the Apostle; they are the truthful.

And those who were settled in the abode[2] and the faith before them, love those who fled to them[3]; and they do not find in their breasts a need of what has been given to them; preferring them to themselves, even though there be poverty amongst them; and whoso is preserved from his own covetousness, these are the prosperous!

[10] And those who came after them say, 'Our Lord, forgive us and our brethren who were beforehand with us in the faith, and place not in our hearts ill-will towards those who believe—our Lord! verily, thou art kind, compassionate!'

Dost thou not look on those who were hypocritical, saying to their brethren who misbelieved amongst the people of the Book[4], 'If ye be driven forth we will go forth with you; and we will never obey any one concerning you; and if ye be fought

[1] The poorer Muhâgerîn were allowed to participate in the spoils, but not the Ansârs.

[2] The Ansârs at Medînah.

[3] The Muhâgerîn.

[4] The Jews.

against we will help you.' But God bears witness that they are surely liars!

If they be driven forth, these will not go forth with them; and if they be fought against, these will not help them; or if they do help them, they will turn their backs in flight;—then shall they not be helped!

Ye indeed are a keener source of fear in their hearts than God; that is because they are a people who do not understand! They will not fight against you in a body save in fortified cities, or from behind walls; their valour is great amongst themselves;—thou dost reckon them as one body, but their hearts are separated. This is because they are a people who have no sense!

[15] Like unto those before them, recently[1]; they tasted the evil result of their affair, and for them is grievous woe.

Like unto the devil when he said to man, 'Disbelieve.' But when he disbelieved, he said, 'Verily, I am clear of thee! Verily, I fear God the Lord of the worlds!' And the end of them both shall be that they shall both be in the Fire, to dwell therein for aye! for that is the reward of the unjust!

O ye who believe! fear God; and let each soul look to what it sends on for the morrow; and fear God; verily, God is well aware of what ye do!

And be ye not like those who forget God, and He makes them forget themselves; they are the workers of abomination!

[20] Not deemed alike shall be the fellows of the

[1] Either the idolaters slain at Bedr, or the Jews of Qâinuqâh, or those of Na*dh*îr.

Fire and the fellows of Paradise: the fellows of Paradise they are the blissful!

Had we sent down this Qur'ân upon a mountain, thou wouldst have seen it humbling itself, splitting asunder from the fear of God! These parables do we strike out for men; haply they may reflect!

He is God than whom there is no god; who knows the unseen and the visible; He is the merciful, the compassionate! He is God than whom there is no god; the King, the Holy, the Peace-Giver, the Faithful, the Protector, the Mighty, the Repairer, the Great!—celebrated be the praises of God above what they join with Him.

He is God, the Creator, the Maker, the Fashioner; His are the excellent names[1]! His praises, whatever are in the heavens and the earth do celebrate; for God is the mighty, the wise!

The Chapter of the Tried.

(LX. Medînah.)

In the name of the merciful and compassionate God.

O ye who believe! take not my enemy and your enemy for patrons, encountering them with love for they misbelieve in the truth that is to come to you; they drive out the Apostle and you for that ye believe in God your Lord[2]!

---

[1] See Introduction, p. lxvii.

[2] 'Hâ*t*ib ibn abi Balta'hah had given the Meccans warning of an

If ye go forth fighting strenuously in my cause and craving my good pleasure, and secretly show love for them, yet do I know best what ye conceal and what ye display! and he of you who does so has erred from the level path.

If they find you they will be enemies to you, and they will stretch forth against you their hands and their tongues for evil, and would fain that ye should disbelieve; neither your kindred nor your children shall profit you upon the resurrection day; it will separate you! but God on what ye do doth look!

Ye had a good example in Abraham and those with him, when they said to their people, 'Verily, we are clear of you and of what ye serve beside God. We disbelieve in you: and between us and you is enmity and hatred begun for ever, until ye believe in God alone!'

But not[1] the speech of Abraham to his father, 'Verily, I will ask forgiveness for thee, though I cannot control aught from God!' O our Lord! on thee do we rely! and unto thee we turn! and unto thee the journey is!

[5] Our Lord! make us not a trial for those who misbelieve; but forgive us! Our Lord! verily, thou art mighty, wise!

Ye had in them a good example for him who

---

intended surprise by Mohammed, and on his letter being intercepted, excused himself by saying that he had only done so in order to make terms for his family, who were at Mecca, and that he knew that the information would be of no avail. Mohammed pardoned him, but the verse in the text prohibits such conduct for the future.

[1] I.e. they are not to imitate Abraham's speech to his father, and ask forgiveness for their infidel friends. Cp. Part I, p. 189, verse 115.

would hope in God and the last day. But whoso turns his back, verily, God, He is rich and to be praised.

Mayhap that God will place love between you and between those of them ye are hostile towards[1]: for God is powerful, and God is forgiving, compassionate.

God forbids you not respecting those who have not fought against you for religion's sake, and who have not driven you forth from your homes, that ye should act righteously and justly towards them; verily, God loves the just!

He only forbids you to make patrons of those who have fought against you for religion's sake, and driven you forth from your homes, or have aided in your expulsion; and whoever makes patrons of them, they are the unjust!

[10] O ye who believe! when there come believing women who have fled, then try them: God knows their faith. If ye know them to be believers do not send them back to the misbelievers;—they are not lawful for them, nor are the men lawful for these;—but give them[2] what they have expended[3], and it shall be no crime against you that ye marry them, when ye have given them their hire. And do not ye retain a right over misbelieving women; but ask for what ye have spent, and let them ask for what they have spent. That is God's judgment: He judges between you, for God is knowing, wise!

And if any of your wives escape from you to the

[1] I. e. by their becoming converted to Islâm.

[2] I. e. to their infidel husbands.

[3] The dowries.

misbelievers, and your turn comes, then give to those whose wives have gone away the like of what they have spent; and fear God, in whom it is that ye believe.

O thou prophet! when believing women come to thee and engage with thee that they will not associate aught with God, and will not steal, and will not fornicate, and will not kill their children, and will not bring a calumny which they have forged between their hands and feet[1], and that they will not rebel against thee in what is reasonable, then engage with them and ask forgiveness for them of God;—verily, God is forgiving, compassionate.

O ye who believe! take not for patrons a people whom God is wroth against; they despair of the hereafter, as the misbelievers despair of the fellows of the tombs[2]!

The Chapter of the Ranks.

(LXI. Mecca.)

In the name of the merciful and compassionate God.

What is in the heavens and what is in the earth celebrates the praises of God, for He is the mighty, the wise!

O ye who believe! say not what ye do not. It is most hateful to God that ye say what ye do not.

---

[1] This is said by some commentators to mean foisting spurious children on to their husbands.

[2] I. e. of the resurreetion of the dead.

Verily, God loves those who fight in His cause in ranks as though they were a compact building[1].

[5] When Moses said to his people, 'O my people! why do ye hurt me, when ye know that I am the apostle of God to you?' and when they swerved, God made their hearts to swerve; for God guides not the people who work abomination!

And when Jesus the son of Mary said, 'O children of Israel! verily, I am the apostle of God to you, verifying the law that was before me and giving you glad tidings of an apostle who shall come after me, whose name shall be A'hmed[2]!'—but when he did come to them with manifest signs, they said, 'This is manifest sorcery!'

And who is more unjust than he who forges against God a lie when called unto Islâm? but God guides not the unjust people.

They desire to put out the light of God with their mouths; but God will perfect His light, averse although the misbeliever be!

He it is who sent His Apostle with guidance and the religion of truth to set it above all religion; averse although the idolaters may be.

[10] O ye who believe! shall I lead you to a merchandise which will save you from grievous woe?

To believe in God and His Apostle, and to fight strenuously in God's cause with your property and

---

[1] Who fight in close and unbroken lines.

[2] A'hmed is equivalent in meaning to Mohammed, and means 'Praised,' 'Laudable.' The allusion is to the promise of the Paraclete in John xvi. 7, the Muslims declaring that the word παράκλητος has been substituted in the Greek for περικλυτός, which would mean the same as A'hmed. See Introduction, p. xlix.

your persons; that is better for you if ye did but know!

He will pardon you your sins, and bring you into gardens beneath which rivers flow, and goodly dwellings in gardens of Eden;—that is the mighty bliss!

And other things which ye love,—help from God and victory nigh! so do thou give the glad tidings unto the believers!

O ye who believe! be ye the helpers[1] of God! as Jesus son of Mary said to the apostles, 'Who are my helpers for God?' Said the apostles, 'We are God's helpers[2]!'

And a party of the children of Israel believed, and a party misbelieved. And we aided those who believed against their enemies, and they were on the morrow superior!

THE CHAPTER OF THE CONGREGATION.

(LXII. Medînah.)

In the name of the merciful and compassionate God.

What is in the heavens and what is in the earth celebrates the praises of God the King, the holy, the mighty, the wise!

He it is who sent unto the Gentiles[3] a prophet amongst themselves to recite to them His signs and to purify them, and to teach them the Book and

---

[1] Ansâr.

[2] See Part I, p. 53 (Chapter III, verse 45).

[3] See Introduction, p. xlvii, and Part I, p. 156, note.

the wisdom, although they were before in obvious error.

And others of them have not yet overtaken them[1]; but He is the mighty, the wise!

That is God's grace, He gives it to whomsoever He will; for God is Lord of mighty grace.

[5] The likeness of those who were charged with the law and then bore it not is as the likeness of an ass bearing books: sorry is the likeness of the people who say God's signs are lies! but God guides not an unjust people.

Say, 'O ye who are Jews! if ye pretend that ye are the clients of God, beyond other people; then wish for death if ye do speak the truth!'

But they never wish for it, through what their hands have sent before! but God knows the unjust.

Say, 'Verily, the death from which ye flee will surely meet you; then shall ye be sent back to Him who knows the unseen and the visible, and He will inform you of that which ye have done!'

O ye who believe! when the call to prayer is made upon the Congregation Day[2], then hasten to the remembrance of God, and leave off traffic; that is better for you, if ye did but know!

[10] And when prayer is performed, then disperse abroad in the land, and crave of God's grace; and remember God much; haply ye may prosper!

But when they see merchandise or sport they flock to it and leave thee standing[3]! Say, 'What is

---

[1] I.e. by embracing Islâm.

[2] Friday, called before this 'Harûbah. It was the day on which Mohammed entered Medînah for the first time.

[3] It is said that one Friday a caravan entered the town while Mohammed was conducting the public prayers, and the congrega-

with God is better than sport and than merchandise, for God is the best of providers!'

The Chapter of the Hypocrites[1].

(LXIII. Medînah.)

In the name of the merciful and compassionate God.

When the hypocrites come to thee, they say, 'We bear witness that thou art surely the Apostle of God;' but God knows that thou art His Apostle: and God bears witness that the hypocrites are liars!

They take their faith[2] for a cloak, and then they turn folks from God's way:—evil is that which they have done! That is because they believed and then disbelieved, wherefore is a stamp set on their hearts so that they do not understand!

And when thou seest them, their persons please thee[3]; but if they speak, thou listenest to their speech: they are like timber propped up[4]: they reckon every noise against them! They are the foe, so beware of them!—God fight against them, how they lie!

---

tion hearing the drums beat rushed out to see the sight, with the exception of about twelve of them.

[1] The disaffected portion of the inhabitants of Medînah. See Introduction, p. xxxiv.

[2] Or, by a various reading, 'their oaths.'

[3] Abdallah ibn Ubai, the leader of the 'Hypocrites' (see Introduction, p. xxxv), was a man of fine presence and eloquent address.

[4] I.e. though of tall and imposing presence, they are really like mere logs.

[5] And when it is said to them, 'Come, and the Apostle of God will ask forgiveness for you!' they turn away their heads, and thou mayest see them turning away since they are so big with pride!

It is the same to them whether thou dost ask forgiveness for them, or whether thou dost not ask forgiveness for them,—God will not forgive them; verily, God guides not a people who work abomination!

They it is who say, 'Expend not in alms upon those who are with the Apostle of God, in order that they may desert him!'—but God's are the treasures of the heavens and the earth; but the hypocrites have no sense!

They say, 'If we return to el Medînah, the mightier will surely drive out the meaner therefrom;' but to God belongs the might, and to His Apostle and to the believers; but the hypocrites do not know!

O ye who believe! let not your property nor your children divert you from the remembrance of God,—for whosoever does that, they are those who lose!

[10] But expend in alms of what we have bestowed upon you before death come on ahy one of you, and he says, 'My Lord! wouldst thou but have respited me till an appointed time nigh at hand, then would I surely give in charity and be among the righteous!' But God will never respite a soul when its appointed time has come: and God of what ye do is well aware!

The Chapter of Cheating.

(LXIV. Place of origin doubtful.)

In the name of the merciful and compassionate God.

What is in the heavens and what is in the earth celebrates God's praises; His is the kingdom, and His is the praise, and He is mighty over all!

He it is who created you, and of you is (one) a misbeliever and (one) a believer; and God on what ye do does look.

He created the heavens and the earth in truth; and has formed you and made excellent your forms; and unto Him the journey is!

He knows what is in the heavens and the earth, and knows what ye conceal and what ye display; for God knows the nature of men's breasts!

[5] Has there not come to you the story of those who misbelieved before, and tasted the evil result of their affair, and for them was grievous woe?

That is because their apostles came to them with manifest signs, and they said, 'Shall mortals guide us?' and they misbelieved and turned their backs. But God was independent of them; for God is rich and to be praised!

Those who misbelieve pretend that they shall surely not be raised: say, 'Yea! by my Lord! ye shall surely be raised: then ye shall be informed of that which ye have done;' for that is easy unto God.

So believe in God and His Apostle and the light which we have sent down; for God of what ye do is well aware!

On the day when he shall gather you to the day

of gathering, that is the day of cheating[1]! but whoso believes in God and acts aright, He will cover for him his offences, and will bring him into gardens beneath which rivers flow, to dwell therein for aye! that is the mighty bliss!

[10] But those who misbelieve and say our signs are lies, they are the fellows of the Fire, to dwell therein for aye! and evil shall the journey be!

No calamity befalls but by the permission of God: and whoso believes in God, He will guide his heart; for God all things doth know!

So obey God and obey the Apostle[2]: but if ye turn your backs—our Apostle has only his plain message to preach!

God, there is no god but He; and upon Him let the believers rely!

O ye who believe! verily, among your wives and children are foes of yours: so beware of them! But if ye pardon, and overlook it, and forgive,—verily, God is forgiving, compassionate!

[15] Your property and your children are but a trial; and God, with Him is mighty hire!

Then fear God as much as ye can! and hear, and obey, and expend in alms: it is better for yourselves. But whosoever is saved from his own covetousness—these are the prosperous!

If ye lend to God a goodly loan, He will double it for you, and will forgive you; for God is grateful, clement!

---

[1] I. e. both the righteous and the wicked will disappoint each other by reversing their positions, the wicked being punished while the righteous are in bliss.

[2] This expression seems to indicate that this verse at least was revealed at Medînah.

He knows the unseen and the visible; the mighty, the wise!

The Chapter of Divorce.

(LXV. Medînah.)

In the name of the merciful and compassionate God.

O thou prophet! when ye divorce women, then divorce them at their term[1], and calculate the term and fear God your Lord. Do not drive them out of their houses unless they have committed manifest adultery. These are God's bounds, and whoso transgresses God's bounds has wronged himself. Thou knowest not whether haply God may cause something fresh to happen after that[2].

And when they have reached their appointed time, then retain them with kindness, or separate from them with kindness; and bring as witnesses men of equity from among you; and give upright testimony to God. That is what He admonishes him who believes in God and the last day; and whosoever fears God, He will make for him a (happy) issue, and will provide for him from whence he reckoned not.

And whosoever relies on God, He is sufficient for him: verily, God will attain His purpose:—God has set for everything a period.

And such of your women as despair of menstrua-

---

[1] When they have had three periods of menstruation; or, if they prove with child, after their delivery. See Part I, p. 34.

[2] I. e. whether God may not reconcile them again.

tion,—if ye doubt, then their term is three months; and such as have not menstruated too.

And those who are heavy with child their appointed time is when they have laid down their burden; and whosoever fears God, He will make for him an easy affair.

[5] That is God's command, He has sent it down to you; and whosoever fears God He will cover for him his offences and will make grand for him his hire.

Let them[1] dwell where ye dwell, according to your means, and do not harm them, to reduce them to straits; and if they be heavy with child, then pay for them until they lay down their burdens; and if they suckle (the child) for you, then give them their hire, and consult among yourselves in reason; but if ye be in difficulties, and another woman shall suckle the child for him, let him who has plenty expend of his plenty; but he whose provision is doled out, let him expend of what God has given him; God will not compel any soul beyond what He has given it;—God will make after difficulty ease!

How many a city has turned away from the bidding of its Lord and His apostles; and we called them to a severe account, and we tormented them with an unheard-of torment!

And they tasted the evil results of their conduct; and the end of their conduct was loss!

[10] God prepared for them severe torment;—then fear God, ye who are endowed with minds!

Ye who believe! God has sent down to you a

[1] The divorced women.

reminder;—an apostle to recite to you God's manifest signs;—to bring forth those who believe and act aright from darkness into light! and whoso believes in God and acts right He will bring him into gardens beneath which rivers flow, to dwell therein for ever and for aye! God has made goodly for him his provision!

God it is who created seven heavens, and of the earth the like thereof. The bidding descends between them, that ye may know that God is mighty over all, and that God has encompassed all things with His knowledge!

THE CHAPTER OF PROHIBITION[1].

(LXVI. Medînah.)

IN the name of the merciful and compassionate God.

O thou prophet! wherefore dost thou prohibit what God has made lawful to thee, craving to please thy wives? but God is forgiving, compassionate!

God has allowed you to expiate your oaths; for

[1] This chapter was occasioned by Mohammed's liaison with the Coptic girl Mary (see Introduction, p. xl), with whom he lay on the day due to 'Âyeshah or 'Hafsah. The latter was greatly enraged, and Mohammed to pacify her swore never to touch the girl again, and enjoined 'Hafsah to keep the matter secret from the rest of his wives. She, however, revealed it in confidence to 'Âyeshah; when Mohammed, annoyed at finding his confidence betrayed, not only divorced her, but separated himself from his other wives for the space of a month, which time he passed in Mary's apartment. The chapter is intended to free him from his oath respecting Mary, and to reprove his wives for their conduct.

God is your sovereign, and He is the knowing, the wise!

And when the prophet told as a secret to one of his wives a recent event, and when she gave information thereof and exposed it, he acquainted her with some of it and avoided part of it. But when he informed her of it, she said, 'Who told thee this?' he said, 'The wise one, the well-aware informed me.

'If ye both turn repentant unto God,—for your hearts have swerved!—but if ye back each other up against him,—verily, God, He is the sovereign; and Gabriel and the righteous of the believers, and the angels after that, will back him up.

'[5] It may be that his Lord if he divorce you will give him in exchange wives better than you, Muslims, believers, devout, repentant, worshipping, given to fasting—such as have known men and virgins too.'

O ye who believe! save yourselves and your families from the fire, whose fuel is men and stones; —over it are angels stout and stern; they disobey not God in what He bids them, but they do what they are bidden!

O ye who disbelieve! excuse not yourselves today;—ye shall only be rewarded for that which ye have done.

O ye who believe! turn repentant to God with sincere repentance; it may be that thy Lord will cover for you your offences and will bring you into gardens beneath which rivers flow!—the day God will not disgrace the Prophet nor those who believe with him; their light shall run on before them, and at their right hands! they shall say, 'Our Lord! perfect for us our light and forgive us; verily, Thou art mighty over all!'

O thou prophet! fight strenuously against the misbelievers and hypocrites and be stern towards them; for their resort is hell, and an evil journey shall it be!

[10] God strikes out a parable to those who misbelieve: the wife of Noah and the wife of Lot; they were under two of our righteous servants, but they betrayed them: and they availed them nothing against God; and it was said, 'Enter the fire with those who enter.'

And God strikes out a parable for those who believe: the wife of Pharaoh, when she said, 'My Lord, build for me a house with Thee in Paradise, and save me from Pharaoh and his works, and save me from the unjust people!'

And Mary, daughter of Imrân, who guarded her private parts, and we breathed therein of our spirit and she verified the words of her Lord and His books, and was of the devout.

The Chapter of the Kingdom.

(LXVII. Mecca.)

In the name of the merciful and compassionate God.

Blessed be He in whose hand is the kingdom, for He is mighty over all!

Who created death and life, to try you, which of you does best; for He is the mighty, the forgiving!

Who created seven heavens in stories; thou canst not see any discordance in the creation of the Merciful!

Why, look again! canst thou see a flaw? Then

look again twice!—thy look shall return to thee driven back and dulled!

[5] And we have adorned the lower heaven with lamps; and set them to pelt the devils with[1]; and we have prepared for them the torment of the blaze!

And for those who disbelieve in their Lord is the torment of hell, and an evil journey shall it be!

When they shall be cast therein they shall hear its braying[2] as it boils—it will well-nigh burst for rage!

Whenever a troop of them is thrown in, its treasurers shall ask them, 'Did not a warner come to you?'

They shall say, 'Yea! a warner came to us, and we called him liar, and said, "God has not sent down aught; ye are but in great error!"'

[10] And they shall say, 'Had we but listened or had sense we had not been amongst the fellows of the blaze!'

And they will confess their sins; but 'Avaunt to the fellows of the blaze!'

Verily, those who fear their Lord in secret, for them is forgiveness and a great hire!

Speak ye secretly or openly, verily, He knows the nature of men's breasts!

Ay! He knows who created! for He is the subtle, the well-aware!

[15] He it is who made the earth flat for you; so walk in the spacious sides thereof and eat of His provision; for unto Him the resurrection is!

---

[1] See Part I, pp. 50, 51, note 2.

[2] Cf. Chapters XXV, verse 12, and XXXI, verse 18.

Are ye sure that He who is in the heaven will not cleave the earth with you, and that it then shall quake?

Or are ye sure that He who is in the heaven will not send against you a heavy sand storm, and that ye then shall know how the warning was?

But those before them did call the apostles liars, and what a change it was!

Or have they not looked at the birds above them expanding their wings or closing them?—none holds them in except the Merciful One; for He on everything doth look.

[20] Or who is this who will be a host for you, to help you against the Merciful?—the misbelievers are only in delusion!

Or who is this who will provide you if He hold back His provision?—Nay, but they persist in perverseness and aversion!

Is he who walks prone upon his face more guided than he who walks upright upon a straight path?

Say, 'It is He who produced you and made for you hearing and sight and hearts'—little is it that ye give thanks.

Say, 'It is He who sowed you in the earth, and unto Him shall ye be gathered!'

[25] They say, 'When shall this threat be, if ye do speak the truth?'

Say, 'The knowledge is only with God; and I am but a plain warner!'

And when they see it nigh, sorry shall be the faces of those who misbelieve; and it shall be said, 'This is that for which ye used to call!'

Say, 'Have ye considered, whether God destroy me and those with me, or whether we obtain mercy, yet who will protect the misbelievers from grievous torment?'

Say, 'He is the Merciful; we believe in Him, and upon Him do we rely; and ye shall shortly know who it is that is in obvious error!'

[30] Say, 'Have ye considered if your waters on the morrow should have sunk, who is to bring you flowing water?'

The Chapter of the Pen.

(LXVIII. Mecca.)

In the name of the merciful and compassionate God.

N.[1] By the pen, and what they write, thou art not, by God's grace, mad! and, verily, thine is a hire that is not grudged! [5] and, verily, thou art of a grand nature[2]!

But thou shalt see and they shall see which of you is the infatuated.

Verily, thy Lord He knows best who errs from His way; and He knows best those who are guided.

Then obey not those who call thee liar; they would fain that thou shouldst be smooth with them, then would they be smooth with thee!

[10] And obey not any mean swearer[3], a back-

---

[1] The Arabic name of the letter nûn signifies both 'a fish' and 'an inkstand;' the symbol is by some supposed to refer to Jonah, mentioned in verse 48, and by others to writing on the eternal tablets (see Part I, p. 2, note 2), to which the first words of the chapter apply.

[2] For bearing so meekly the insults of the misbelievers.

[3] The person meant is, probably, Walîd ibn Mug*h*âirah, the inveterate enemy of the prophet.

biter, a walker about with slander; a forbidder of good, a transgressor, a sinner; rude, and base-born too; though he have wealth and sons!

[15] When our signs are recited to him he says, 'Old folks' tales!'

We will brand him on the snout!

Verily, we have tried them as we tried the fellows of the garden when they swore, 'We will cut its fruit at morn!'

But they made not the exception[1]; and there came round about it an encompassing calamity from thy Lord the while they slept; [20] and on the morrow it was as one the fruit of which is cut.

And they cried to each other in the morning, 'Go early to your tilth if ye would cut it!'

So they set off, saying privily to each other, 'There shall surely enter it to-day unto you no poor person!'

[25] And they went early deciding to be stingy[2].

And when they saw it they said, 'Verily, we have erred! Nay, we are forbidden (its fruit)!'

Said the most moderate of them, 'Said I not to you, "unless ye celebrate God's praises!"'

Said they, 'Celebrated be the praises of our Lord! verily, we were unjust!'

[30] And they approached each other with mutual blame.

Said they, 'O woe to us! verily, we have been outrageous! Haply our Lord may give us instead a better than it; verily, we unto our Lord do yearn.'

---

[1] I. e. they did not add, 'If God please!'

[2] Or, according to another interpretation, 'with a determined purpose.'

Thus is the torment, but, verily, the torment of the hereafter is greater, if ye did but know!

Verily, for the pious with their Lord are gardens of pleasure!

[35] Shall we then make the Muslims like the sinners? What ails you? how ye judge!

Or have ye a book in which ye can study, that ye are surely to have what ye may choose?

Or have ye oaths binding on us until the judgment day that ye are surely to have what ye may judge?

[40] Ask them, which of them will vouch for this?

Or have they partners, then let them bring their partners if they do speak the truth?

On the day when the leg shall be bared[1]; and they shall be called to adore and shall not be able!

Lowering their looks, abasement shall attack them, for they were called to adore while yet they were safe!

But let me alone with him who calls this new discourse a lie. We will surely bring them down by degrees from whence they do not know.

[45] And I will let them have their way! for my device is sure.

Or dost thou ask them a hire for it while they are burdened with debts?

Or have they the knowledge of the unseen, so that they write?

But wait patiently for the judgment of thy Lord, and be not like the fellow of the fish[2], when he cried out as he was choking with rage.

---

[1] An expression signifying any great calamity or battle, because the non-combatants gird up their loins to be ready for flight.

[2] Jonah.

Had it not been that grace from his Lord reached him, he would have been cast out on the naked (shore) and blamed the while!

[50] But his Lord elected him, and made him of the pious.

The misbelievers well-nigh upset thee with their looks when they hear the reminder, and they say, 'Surely he is mad!'

And yet it is but a reminder to the worlds!

The Chapter of the Infallible.

(LXIX. Mecca.)

In the name of the merciful and compassionate God.

The Infallible, what is the Infallible? and what should make thee know what the Infallible is?

Thamûd and 'Âd called the Striking[1] Day a lie;
[5] but as for Thamûd they perished by the shock; and as for 'Âd they perished with the violent cold blast of wind, which He subjected against them for seven nights and eight days consecutively. Thou mightest see the people therein prostrate as though they were palm stumps thrown down, and canst thou see any of them left?

And Pharaoh and those before him of the overturned cities[2] committed sins,
[10] and they rebelled against the apostle of their Lord, and He seized them with an excessive punishment.

Verily, we, when the water surged, bore you on

[1] Cf. Chapter XIII, verse 31, Part I, p. 236.

[2] Sodom and Gomorrah; cf. Part I, p. 183, note 1.

it in a sailing ship, to make it a memorial for you, and that the retentive ear might hold it.

And when the trumpet shall be blown with one blast, and the earth shall be borne away, and the mountains too, and both be crushed with one crushing; [15] on that day shall the inevitable happen; and the heaven on that day shall be cleft asunder, for on that day shall it wane! and the angels upon the sides thereof; and above them on that day shall eight bear the throne of thy Lord!

On the day when ye shall be set forth no hidden thing of yours shall be concealed.

And as for him who is given his book in his right hand, he shall say, 'Here! take and read my book. [20] Verily, I thought that I should meet my reckoning;' and he shall be in a pleasing life, in a lofty garden, whose fruits are nigh to cull—'Eat ye and drink with good digestion, for what ye did aforetime in the days that have gone by!'

[25] But as for him who is given his book in his left hand he shall say, 'O, would that I had not received my book! I did not know what my account would be. O, would that it[1] had been an end of me! my wealth availed me not! my authority has perished from me!' [30] 'Take him and fetter him, then in hell broil him! then into a chain whose length is seventy cubits force him! verily, he believed not in the mighty God, nor was he particular to feed the poor: [35] therefore he has not here to-day any warm friend, nor any food except foul ichor, which none save sinners shall eat!'

I need not swear by what ye see or what ye do

[1] I. e. death.

not see, [40] verily, it is the speech of a noble apostle; and it is not the speech of a poet:—little is it ye believe!

And it is not the speech of a soothsayer,—little is it that ye mind!—a revelation from the Lord of the worlds.

Why if he had invented against us any sayings, [45] we would have seized him by the right hand, then we would have cut his jugular vein; nor could any one of you have kept us off from him.

Verily, it is a memorial to the pious; and, verily, we know that there are amongst you those who say it is a lie; [50] and, verily, it is a source of sighing to the misbelievers; and, verily, it is certain truth!

Therefore celebrate the name of thy mighty Lord!

The Chapter of the Ascents.

(LXX. Mecca.)

In the name of the merciful and compassionate God.

An asker[1] asked for torment that must befall, for the unbelievers; there is no repelling it; from God the Lord of the ascents[2], whereby ascend the angels

---

[1] The person referred to is said to have been either Abu *G*ahl, who challenged Mohammed to cause a portion of the heaven to fall on them, see Chapter XXVI, verse 187, p. 97, or one Na*dh*r ibn el 'Hâreth, who said of Islâm, 'If this be the truth from Thee, then rain down on us stones from heaven!'

[2] Either steps by which the prayers of the righteous or the angels ascend to heaven; or the word may refer to the various degrees of the angels, or to the seven heavens themselves. See Introduction, p. lxx.

and the Spirit unto Him in a day whose length is fifty thousand years[1].

[5] Wherefore be patient with fair patience; verily, they see it as afar off, but we see it nigh!

The day when the heaven shall be as molten brass, and the mountains shall be like flocks of wool; [10] when no warm friend shall question friend; they shall gaze on each other, and the sinner would fain give as a ransom from the torment of that day his sons and his mate, and his brother and his kin who stand by him, and all who are in the earth, that yet it might rescue him!

[15] Nay, verily, it is a flame,—dragging by the scalp! it shall call those who retreated and turned their backs and who amassed and hoarded!

Verily, man is by nature rash[2]! [20] when evil touches him, very impatient; when good touches him, niggardly; all save those who pray, who remain at their prayers, and in whose wealth is a reasonable due (set aside) [25] for him who asks and him who is kept from asking, and those who believe in a day of judgment, and those who shrink in terror from the torment of their Lord;—verily, the torment of their Lord is not safe;—and those who guard their private parts, [30] except for their wives or the (slave girls) whom their right hands possess, for they are not to be blamed; but whoso craves beyond this, they are the transgressors; and those who observe their trusts and their compacts, and those who are upright in their testimonies, and those who keep their prayers, [35] these shall dwell in gardens honoured.

---

[1] Cf. Chapter XXXII, verse 4, p. 135.

[2] Cf. Chapter XVII, verse 12, p. 2.

What ails the misbelievers that they hurry on before thee, crowding together on the right and on the left[1]? Does every man of them wish to enter the garden of pleasure?

Nay, we created them of what they know!

[40] And I need not swear by the Lord of the easts and the wests[2]; verily, we are able to change them for others better, nor are we prevented!

So leave them to plunge in discussion, and to play until they meet that day of theirs which they are threatened with, the day when they shall come forth in haste from the graves, as though they flock to a standard! with their looks abashed; meanness shall cover them! That is the day which they were promised!

The Chapter of Noah.

(LXXI. Mecca.)

In the name of the merciful and compassionate God.

Verily, we sent Noah to his people, 'Warn thy people before there come to them a grievous torment!'

Said he, 'O my people! verily, I am to you an obvious warner, that ye serve God and fear Him and obey me. He will pardon you your sins, and will defer you unto an appointed time; verily, God's

---

[1] Cf. pp. 262, 263.

[2] I. e. of the east and the west; or of the various points of the horizon at which the sun rises and sets in the course of the year.

appointed time when it comes will not be deferred, did ye but know!'

[5] Said he, 'My Lord! verily, I have called my people by night and day, and my call did but increase them in flight; and, verily, every time I called them, that Thou mightest pardon them, they placed their fingers in their ears and tried to cover themselves with their garments and persisted, and were very big with pride. Then I called them openly; then I published to them and I spoke to them in secret, and I said, "Ask forgiveness of your Lord, verily, He is very forgiving. [10] He will send the rain upon you in torrents, and will extend to you wealth and children, and will make for you gardens, and will make for you rivers. What ails you that ye hope not for something serious from God, when He has created you by steps[1]? Do ye not see how God has created the seven heavens in stories, [15] and has set the moon therein for a light, and set the sun for a lamp? and God has made you grow out of the earth, and then He will make you return thereto, and will make you come forth therefrom; and God has made for you the earth a carpet that ye may walk therein in broad paths."'

[20] Said Noah, 'My Lord! verily, they have rebelled against me, and followed him whose wealth and children have but added to his loss, and they have plotted a great plot, and said, "Ye shall surely not leave your gods: ye shall surely neither leave Wadd, nor Suwâ'h, nor Ya*gh*ûth, nor Ya'ûq, nor Nasr[2], and they led astray many."' And thou

[1] See Chapter XXII, verse 5, p. 56.

[2] For these five idols, see Introduction, p. xii.

(Mohammed) wilt only increase the unjust in their error—[25] because of their sins they were drowned and made to enter into the fire, and they found no helpers against God!

And Noah said, 'My Lord! leave not upon the earth one dweller of the misbelievers. Verily, Thou, if Thou shouldst leave them, they will lead astray Thy servants, and they will only bear for children sinners and misbelievers. My Lord! pardon me and my two parents, and whomsoever enters my house believing, and (pardon) the believers men and women—but Thou shalt only increase the unjust in loss.'

THE CHAPTER OF THE *G*INN.

(LXXII. Mecca.)

IN the name of the merciful and compassionate God.

Say, 'I have been inspired that there listened a company of the *g*inn[1], and they said, "We have heard a marvellous Qur'ân that guides to the right direction; and we believe therein, and we join no one with our Lord, for, verily, He—may the majesty of our Lord be exalted!—has taken to Himself neither consort nor son.

'"And, verily, a fool among us spake against God wide of the mark!

'"[5] And we thought that men and *g*inn would never speak a lie against God.

---

[1] See Introduction, pp. xiii–xiv. The occasion of Mohammed's preaching to the *g*inn was on his returning from his unsuccessful errand to *T*â'if; see Introduction, p. xxx.

'"And there are persons amongst men who seek for refuge with persons amongst the ginn[1]; but they increase them in their perverseness. And they thought, as ye thought, that God would not raise up any one from the dead.

'"But we touched the heavens and found them filled with a mighty guard and shooting-stars; and we did sit in certain seats thereof to listen; but whoso of us listens now finds a shooting-star for him on guard.

'"[10] And, verily, we know not whether evil be meant for those who are in the earth, or if their Lord means right by them.

'"And of us are some who are pious, and of us are some who are otherwise: we are in separate bands.

'"And we thought that we could not frustrate God in the earth, and could not frustrate Him by flight.

"' But, verily, when we heard the guidance we believed therein, and he who believes in his Lord shall fear neither diminution nor loss.

'"And, verily, of us are some who are Muslims, and of us some are trespassers; but those of us who are Muslims they strive after right direction; [15] and as for the trespassers they are fuel for hell."'

And if they[2] will go right upon the way, we will irrigate them with copious water to try them thereby; and whoso turns from the remembrance of his Lord He will drive him to severe torment.

And (say) that the mosques are God's, and that ye

[1] The pagan Arabs when they found themselves in a lonely place, such as they supposed the ginn to haunt, used to say, 'I take refuge in the Lord of this valley from the foolish among his people!'

[2] The Meccans.

should not call on any one with God, and that when God's servant[1] stood up to pray they[2] called out to him and well-nigh crowded upon him. [20] Say, 'I only call upon my Lord, and I join no one with Him.'

Say, 'Verily, I cannot control for you either harm, or right direction.'

Say, 'Verily, as for me none can protect me against God, nor do I find any refuge beside Him,—except delivering the message from God and His errands: and whoso rebels against God and His Apostle, verily, for him is the fire of hell for them to dwell therein for ever and for aye!'

[25] Until when they see what they are threatened with, then shall they surely know who is most weak at helping and fewest in numbers!

Say, 'I know not if what ye are threatened with be nigh, or if my Lord will set for it a term. He knows the unseen, and He lets no one know His unseen, save such apostle as He is well pleased with: for, verily, He sends marching before him and behind him a guard!'

That He may know that they have delivered the errands of their Lord, for He compasses what they have, and reckons everything by number.

The Chapter of the Enwrapped.

(LXXIII. Mecca.)

In the name of the merciful and compassionate God.

O thou who art enwrapped! rise by night except a little—the half, or deduct therefrom a little, or

---

[1] Mohammed. [2] The ginn.

add thereto, and chant the Qur'ân chanting. [5]
Verily, we will cast on thee a heavy speech.

Verily, the early part of the night is stronger in impressions and more upright in speech!

Verily, thou hast by day a long employment; but mention the name of thy Lord and devote thyself thoroughly to Him, the Lord of the east and the west; there is no god but He; then take Him for a guardian!

[10] And endure patiently what they say, and flee from them with a decorous flight.

And leave me and those who say it is a lie, who are possessed of comfort; and let them bide for a while.

Verily, with us are heavy fetters and hell-fire, and food that chokes, and mighty woe!

On the day when the earth and the mountains shall tremble and the earth shall be as a crumbling sand-hill!

[15] Verily, we have sent unto you an apostle bearing witness against you, as we sent an apostle unto Pharaoh.

But Pharaoh rebelled against the apostle, and we seized him with an overpowering punishment.

Then how will ye shield yourselves if ye misbelieve from the day which shall make children grey-headed, whereon the heaven cleaves—its promise shall be fulfilled!

Verily, this is a memorial, and whoso will, let him take unto his Lord a way[1].

---

[1] From verse 20 the rest of the sûrah seems from its style to belong to the Medînah period; and there is a tradition ascribed to 'Âyeshah that it was revealed a year later than the earlier part of the chapter.

[20] Verily, thy Lord knows that thou dost stand up to pray nearly two-thirds of the night, or the half of it or the third of it, as do part of those who are with thee; for God measures the night and the day; He knows that ye cannot calculate it, and He turns relentant towards you.

So read what is easy of the Qur'ân. He knows that there will be of you some who are sick and others who beat about in the earth craving the grace of God, and others who are fighting in the cause of God. Then read what is easy of it and be steadfast in prayer, and give alms, and lend to God a goodly loan, for what ye send forward for yourselves of good ye will find it with God. It is better and a greater hire; and ask ye pardon of God: verily, God is forgiving, merciful!

THE CHAPTER OF THE 'COVERED [1].'

(LXXIV. Mecca.)

IN the name of the merciful and compassionate God.

O thou who art covered! rise up and warn!
And thy Lord magnify!
[5] And thy garments purify!
And abomination shun!
And grant not favours to gain increase!
And for thy Lord await!
And when the trump is blown,—for that day is a

---

[1] The first five verses of this chapter form the second revelation by the angel Gabriel in person, and the first after the Fatrah, or period of 'Intermission.' See Introduction, p. xxii.

difficult day! [10] for the misbelievers aught but easy!

Leave me alone with him I have created, and for whom I have made extensive wealth[1], and sons that he may look upon, and for whom I have smoothed things down. [15] Then he desires that I should increase! nay, verily, he is hostile to our signs! I will drive him up a hill! Then he reflected and planned! May he be killed,—how he planned! [20] Again, may he be killed,—how he planned! Then he looked; then he frowned and scowled; then he retreated and was big with pride and said, 'This is only magic exhibited! [25] this is only mortal speech!'—I will broil him in hell-fire! and what shall make thee know what hell-fire is? It will not leave and will not let alone. It scorches the flesh; [30] over it are nineteen (angels).

We have made only angels guardians of the fire, and we have only made their number a trial to those who misbelieve; that those who have been given the Book may be certain, and that those who believe may be increased in faith; and that those who have been given the Book and the believers may not doubt; and that those in whose hearts is sickness, and the misbelievers may say, 'What does God mean by this as a parable?'

Thus God leads astray whom He pleases, and guides him He pleases: and none knows the hosts of thy Lord save Himself; and it is only a reminder to mortals!

[35] Nay, by the moon!
And the night when it retires!

[1] The person meant is generally supposed to be Walîd ibn Mu*gh*âirah, one of the chiefs of the Qurâi*s*.

And the morning when it brightly dawns!

Verily, it is one of the greatest misfortunes; a
warning to mortals; [40] for him amongst you who
wishes to press forward or to tarry!

Every soul is pledged[1] for what it earns; except the fellows of the right: in gardens shall they ask each other about the sinners!—'What drove you into hell-fire?'

They shall say, 'We weren't[2] of those who prayed;
[45] we didn't feed the poor; but we did plunge into discussion with those who plunged, and we called the judgment day a lie until the certainty[3] did come to us!'

But there shall not profit them the intercession of the intercessors.

[50] What ailed them that they turned away from the memorial as though they were timid asses fleeing from a lion?

Nay, every man of them wished that he might have given him books spread open!

Nay, but they did not fear the hereafter!

Nay, it is a memorial! and let him who will re-
member it; [55] but none will remember it except
God please. He is most worthy of fear; and he is most worthy to forgive!

The Chapter of the Resurrection.

(LXXV. Mecca.)

In the name of the merciful and compassionate God.

I need not swear by the resurrection day!

[1] See Chapter LII, verse 21, p. 249, note 1.

[2] See Part I, p. 78, note 1.

[3] I.e. death.

Nor need I swear by the self-accusing soul!

Does man think that we shall not collect his bones? Able are we to arrange his finger tips!

[5] Nay, but man wishes to be wicked henceforward! he asks, When is the resurrection day?

But when the sight shall be dazed, and the moon be eclipsed, and the sun and the moon be together, [10] and man shall say upon that day, 'Where is a place to flee to?'—nay, no refuge! and to thy Lord that day is the sure settlement: He will inform man on that day of what He has sent forward or delayed!

Nay, man is an evidence against himself, [15] and even if he thrusts forward his excuses—.

Do not move thy tongue thereby to hasten it[1]. It is for us to collect it and to read it; and when we read it then follow its reading. And again it is for us to explain it.

[20] Nay, indeed, but ye love the transient life, and ye neglect the hereafter!

Faces on that day shall be bright, gazing on their Lord!

And faces on that day shall be dismal!

[25] Thou wilt think that a back-breaking calamity has happened to them!

Nay, but when the [soul] comes up into the throat, and it is said, 'Who will charm it back?' and he will think that it is his parting [hour]. And leg shall be pressed on leg[2]; [30] unto thy Lord on that day shall the driving be.

For he did not believe[3] and did not pray; but

---

[1] I.e. the revelation; see p. 16, note 2, and p. 43, note 2. The words are addressed to Mohammed by the angel Gabriel.

[2] I.e. in the death struggle.

[3] Or did not give in charity.

he said it was a lie, and turned his back! Then he went to his people haughtily—woe to thee, and woe to thee! again woe to thee, and woe to thee!

Does man think that he shall be left to himself?

Wasn't[1] he a clot of emitted seed? Then he was congealed blood, and (God) created him, and fashioned him, and made of him pairs, male and female.

[35] Is not He able to quicken the dead?

The Chapter of Man.

(LXXVI. Mecca.)

In the name of the merciful and compassionate God.

Does there not come on man a portion of time when he is nothing worth mentioning[2]?

Verily, we created man from a mingled clot, to try him; and we gave him hearing and sight. Verily, we guided him in the way, whether he be grateful or ungrateful.

Verily, we have prepared for those who misbelieve chains and fetters and a blaze!

[5] Verily, the righteous shall drink of a cup tempered with Kâfûr[3], a spring from which God's servants shall drink and make it gush out as they please!

They who fulfil their vows, and fear a day, the evil

---

[1] See Part I, p. 78, note 1.

[2] While in the womb.

[3] Name of a river in Paradise, so called because it is white, cool, and sweet-smelling, as camphor is.

which shall fly abroad, and who give food for His love to the poor and the orphan and the captive. 'We only feed you for God's sake; we desire not from you either reward or thanks; [10] we fear from our Lord a frowning, calamitous day!'

And God will guard them from the evil of that day and will cast on them brightness and joy; and their reward for their patience shall be Paradise and silk! reclining therein upon couches they shall neither see therein sun nor piercing cold[1]; and close down upon them shall be its shadows; and lowered over them its fruits to cull; [15] and they shall be served round with vessels of silver and goblets that are as flagons—flagons of silver which they shall mete out! and they shall drink therein a cup tempered with Zin*g*abîl[2], a spring therein named Silsabîl! and there shall go round about them eternal boys; when thou seest them thou wilt think them scattered pearls; [20] and when thou seest them thou shalt see pleasure and a great estate! On them shall be garments of green embroidered satin and brocade; and they shall be adorned with bracelets of silver; and their Lord shall give them to drink pure drink! Verily, this is a reward for you, and your efforts are thanked.

Verily, we have sent down upon thee the Qur'ân. Wherefore wait patiently for the judgment of thy Lord, and obey not any sinner or misbeliever amongst them. [25] But remember the name of thy Lord morning, and evening, and through the

---

[1] Zamharîr, the word here rendered 'piercing cold,' is by some authorities interpreted to mean 'the moon.'

[2] Zin*g*abîl signifies 'ginger.'

night, and adore Him, and celebrate His praises the whole night long.

Verily, these love the transitory life, and leave behind them a heavy day!

We created them and strengthened their joints; and if we please we can exchange for the likes of them in their stead. Verily, this is a memorial, and whoso will, let him take unto his Lord a way.

[30] But ye will not please except God please! Verily, God is knowing, wise.

He makes whomsoever He pleases to enter into His mercy; but the unjust He has prepared for them a grievous woe!

The Chapter of those Sent.

(LXXVII. Mecca.)

In the name of the merciful and compassionate God.

By those sent in a series[1]!

And by those who speed swiftly!

And by the dispensers abroad!

And by the separators apart!

[5] And by those who instil the reminder, as an excuse or warning!

Verily, what ye are threatened with shall surely happen!

And when the stars shall be erased!

And when the heaven shall be cleft!

[10] And when the mountains shall be winnowed!

And when the apostles shall have a time appointed for them!

---

[1] Either angels or winds, or as some interpret the passage, the verses of the Qur'ân.

For what day is the appointment made?

For the day of decision! and what shall make thee know what the decision is?

[15] Woe on that day for those who say it is a lie!

Have we not destroyed those of yore, and then followed them up with those of the latter day? Thus do we with the sinners.

Woe on that day for those who say it is a lie!

[20] Did we not create you from contemptible water, and place it in a sure depository unto a certain decreed term? for we are able and well able too!

Woe on that day for those who say it is a lie!

[25] Have we not made for them the earth to hold the living and the dead? and set thereon firm mountains reared aloft? and given you to drink water in streams?

Woe on that day for those who say it is a lie!

Go off to that which ye did call a lie!
[30] Go off
to the shadow of three columns, that shall not shade nor avail against the flame! Verily, it throws off sparks like towers,—as though they were yellow camels!

Woe on that day for those who say it is a lie!

[35] This is the day when they may not speak,—when they are not permitted to excuse themselves!

Woe on that day for those who say it is a lie!

This is the day of decision! We have assembled you with those of yore; if ye have any stratagem employ it now!

[40] Woe on that day for those who say it is a lie!

Verily, the pious are amid shades and springs and

fruit such as they love.—'Eat and drink with good digestion, for that which ye have done!'

Verily, thus do we reward those who do well.

[45] Woe on that day for those who say it is a lie!

'Eat and enjoy yourselves for a little; verily, ye are sinners!'

Woe on that day for those who say it is a lie!

And when it is said to them bow down, they bow not down.

Woe on that day for those who say it is a lie!

[50] And in what new discourse after it will they believe?

THE CHAPTER OF THE INFORMATION.

(LXXVIII. Mecca.)

IN the name of the merciful and compassionate God.

Of what do they ask each other?—Of the mighty
information whereon they do dispute[1]? nay, they
shall know too well! [5] Again, nay, they shall
know too well!

Have we not set the earth as a couch, and the
mountains as stakes, and created you in pairs, and
made your sleep for rest, [10] and made the night
a garment, and made the day for livelihood, and
built above you seven solid (heavens) and set a
burning lamp, and, sent down from the rain-express-
ing clouds water pouring forth, [15] to bring out

[1] I. e. the news of the resurrection.

thereby the grain and herb and gardens thickly planted?

Verily, the day of decision is an appointed time; and the day when the trumpet shall be blown, and ye shall come in troops, and the heavens shall be opened, and shall be all doors, [20] and the mountains shall be moved, and shall be like a mirage!

Verily, hell is an ambuscade; a reward for the outrageous, to tarry therein for ages. They shall not taste therein cool nor drink, [25] but only boiling water and pus;—a fit reward!

Verily, they did not hope for the account; but they ever said our signs were lies.

Everything have we remembered in a book.

[30] 'Then taste, for we will only increase your torment!'

Verily, for the pious is a blissful place,—gardens and vineyards, and girls with swelling breasts of the same age as themselves, and a brimming cup; [35] they shall hear therein no folly and no lie;—a reward from thy Lord, a sufficient gift! The Lord of the heavens and the earth, and what is between them both,—the Merciful,—they cannot obtain audience of Him!

The day when the Spirit and the angels shall stand in ranks, they shall not speak save to whom the Merciful permits, and who speaks aright.

That is the true day; and whoso pleases let him take to a resort unto his Lord!

[40] Verily, we have warned you of a torment that is nigh: on a day when man shall see what his two hands have sent forward; and the misbeliever shall say, 'Would that I were dust!'

The Chapter of those who Tear Out.

(LXXIX. Mecca.)

In the name of the merciful and compassionate God.

By those who tear out violently!

And by those who gaily release[1]!

And by those who float through the air!

And the preceders who precede[2]!

[5] And those who manage the affair!

On the day when the quaking[3] quakes which the following one shall succeed! Hearts on that day shall tremble; eyes thereon be humbled!

[10] They say, 'Shall we be sent back to our old course?—What! when we are rotten bones?' they say, 'That then were a losing return!'

But it will only be one scare, and lo! they will be on the surface!

[15] Has the story of Moses[4] come to you? when his Lord addressed him in the holy valley of Tuvâ, 'Go unto Pharaoh, verily, he is outrageous; and say, "Hast thou a wish to purify thyself, and that I may guide thee to thy Lord, and thou mayest fear?"'

[20] So he showed him the greatest signs; but

[1] Referring to the angel of death and his assistants, who tear away the souls of the wicked violently, and gently release the souls of the good.

[2] The angels who precede the souls of the righteous to Paradise.

[3] The trumpet blast at the last day, which shall make the universe quake.

[4] See Chapter XX, verse 12, p. 35.

he called him a liar and rebelled. Then he retreated hastily, and gathered, and proclaimed, and said, 'I am your Lord most High!' [25] but God seized him with the punishment of the future life and of the former.

Verily, in that is a lesson to him who fears!

Are ye harder to create or the heaven that He has built? He raised its height and fashioned it; and made its night to cover it, and brought forth its noonday light; [30] and the earth after that He did stretch out. He brings forth from it its water and its pasture.

And the mountains He did firmly set, a provision for you and for your cattle.

And when the great predominant calamity shall come, [35] on the day when man shall remember what he strove after, and hell shall be brought out for him who sees!

And as for him who was outrageous and preferred the life of this world, verily, hell is the resort!

[40] But as for him who feared the station of his Lord, and prohibited his soul from lust, verily, Paradise is the resort!

They shall ask thee about the Hour, for when it is set. Whereby canst thou mention it? Unto thy Lord its period belongs.

[45] Thou art only a warner to him who fears it.

On the day they see it, it will be as though they had only tarried an evening or the noon thereof.

The Chapter 'He Frowned.'

(LXXX. Mecca.)

In the name of the merciful and compassionate God.

He frowned and turned his back, for that there came to him a blind man[1]!

But what should make thee know whether haply he may be purified? or may be mindful and the reminder profit him?

[5] But as for him who is wealthy, thou dost attend to him; and thou dost not care that he is not purified; but as for him who comes to thee earnestly fearing the while, [10] from him thou art diverted!

Nay! verily, it is a memorial; and whoso pleases will remember it.

In honoured pages exalted, purified, [15] in the hands of noble, righteous scribes!

May man be killed! how ungrateful he is!

Of what did He create him? Of a clot. He created him and fated him; [20] then the path He did make easy for him; then He killed him, and laid him in the tomb; then when He pleases will He raise him up again.

---

[1] One Abdallah ibn Umm Maktûm, a poor blind man, once interrupted Mohammed while the latter was in conversation with Walîd ibn Mu*gh*âirah and some others of the Qurâis chiefs. The prophet taking no notice of him, the blind man raised his voice and earnestly begged for religious instruction, but Mohammed, annoyed at the interruption, frowned and turned away. This passage is a reprimand to the prophet for his conduct on the occasion. Afterwards, whenever he saw the blind Abdallah, Mohammed used to say, 'Welcome to him on whose account my Lord reproved me!' and subsequently made him governor of Medînah.

Nay, he has not fulfilled his bidding!

But let man look unto his foods. [25] Verily, we have poured the water out in torrents: then we have cleft the earth asunder, and made to grow therefrom the grain, and the grape, and the hay, and the olive, and the palm, [30] and gardens closely planted, and fruits, and grass,—a provision for you and for your cattle!

But when the stunning noise shall come, on the day when man shall flee from his brother [35] and his mother and his father and his spouse and his sons! Every man among them on that day shall have a business to employ him.

Faces on that day shall be bright,—laughing, joyous! [40] and faces shall have dust upon them,—darkness shall cover them! those are the wicked misbelievers!

The Chapter of the Folding up.

(LXXXI. Mecca.)

In the name of the merciful and compassionate God.

When the sun is folded up,
And when the stars do fall,
And when the mountains are moved,
And when the she-camels ten months' gone with young shall be neglected [1],
[5] And when the beasts shall be crowded together [2],

---

[1] Such camels being among the most valuable of an Arab's possessions, neglect of them must imply some terribly engrossing calamity.

[2] The terrors of the judgment day will drive all the wild beasts together for mutual shelter.

And when the seas shall surge up,
And when souls shall be paired with bodies,
And when the child who was buried alive shall be asked for what sin she was slain [1],
[10] And when the pages shall be spread out,
And when the heaven shall be flayed,
And when hell shall be set ablaze,
And when Paradise shall be brought nigh,
The soul shall know what it has produced!
[15] I need not swear by the stars that slink back, moving swiftly, slinking into their dens!
Nor by the night when darkness draws on!
Nor by the morn when it first breathes up!
Verily, it is the speech of a noble apostle, [20]
mighty, standing sure with the Lord of the throne, obeyed and trusty too!
Your comrade is not mad; he saw him [2] on the plain horizon [3], nor does he grudge to communicate the unseen [4].
[25] Nor is it the speech of a pelted devil [5].
Then whither do ye go?
It is but a reminder to the worlds, to whomsoever of you pleases to go straight:—but ye will not please, except God, the Lord of the world, should please.

---

[1] See Part I, p. 132, note 3, and p. 256, note 2. See also Introduction, p. x.

[2] Gabriel.

[3] See Chapter LIII, verses 1–19, pp. 251, 252.

[4] Some copies have a various reading, 'suspicious of.'

[5] See Part I, note 2, pp. 50, 51.

The Chapter of the Cleaving asunder.

(LXXXII. Mecca.)

In the name of the merciful and compassionate God.

When the heaven is cleft asunder,
And when the stars are scattered,
And when the seas gush together,
And when the tombs are turned upside down,
[5] The soul shall know what it has sent on or kept back!

O man! what has seduced thee concerning thy generous Lord, who created thee, and fashioned thee, and gave thee symmetry, and in what form He pleased composed thee?

Nay, but ye call the judgment a lie! [10] but over you are guardians set[1],—noble, writing down! they know what ye do!

Verily, the righteous are in pleasure, and, verily, the wicked are in hell; [15] they shall broil therein upon the judgment day; nor shall they be absent therefrom!

And what shall make thee know what is the judgment day? Again, what shall make thee know what is the judgment day? a day when no soul shall control aught for another; and the bidding on that day belongs to God!

The Chapter of those who give short Weight.

(LXXXIII. Mecca.)

In the name of the merciful and compassionate God.

Woe to those who give short weight! who when

---

[1] See p. 243, note 1.

they measure against others take full measure; but when they measure to them or weigh to them, diminish!

Do not these think that they shall be raised again [5] at the mighty day? the day when men shall stand before the Lord of the worlds!

Nay, verily, the book of the wicked is in Siggîn[1]; and what shall make thee know what Siggîn is?—a book inscribed!

[10] Woe on that day for those who say it is a lie!

Who call the judgment day a lie! but none shall call it a lie except every sinful transgressor, who, when our signs are read to him, says, 'Old folks' tales!'

Nay, but that which they have gained has settled upon their hearts.

Nay, verily, [15] from their Lord on that day are they veiled; and then, verily, they shall broil in hell; then it shall be said, 'This is what ye once did call a lie!'

Nay, verily, the book of the righteous is in 'Illiyûn[2]; and what shall make thee know what 'Illiyûn is?—[20] a book inscribed! those nigh to God shall witness it.

Verily, the righteous shall be in pleasure; upon couches shall they gaze; thou mayest recognise in their faces the brightness of pleasure; [25] they shall be given to drink wine that is sealed, whose seal is musk; for that then let the aspirants aspire!

---

[1] Siggîn, the 'prison' of hell, whence the register of the wicked is named.

[2] 'Illiyûn means 'high places.'

—and it shall be tempered with Tasnîm[1],—a spring from which those nigh to God shall drink.

Verily, those who sin do laugh at those who believe; [30] and when they pass by they wink at one another, and when they return to their family they return ridiculing them; and when they see them they say, 'Verily, these do go astray!'—but they are not sent as guardians over them!

But to-day those who believe shall at the misbelievers laugh! [35] Upon couches shall they gaze; are the misbelievers rewarded for what they have done?

The Chapter of the Rending asunder.

(LXXXIV. Mecca.)

In the name of the merciful and compassionate God.

When the heaven is rent asunder and gives ear unto its Lord, and is dutiful!

And when the earth is stretched out and casts forth what is in it, and is empty, [5] and gives ear unto its Lord, and is dutiful!

O man! verily, thou art toiling after thy Lord, toiling; wherefore shalt thou meet Him!

And as for him who is given his book in his right hand, he shall be reckoned with by an easy reckoning; and he shall go back to his family joyfully.

[10] But as for him who is given his book behind his back[2], he shall call out for destruction, but he

---

[1] Name of a fountain in Paradise, so called because it is conveyed to the highest apartments there.

[2] I.e. in the left hand, which will be chained behind the back, the right hand being fettered to the neck.

shall broil in a blaze! Verily, he was amongst his family joyful. Verily, he thought that he should never return to God.

[15] Yea, verily, his Lord on him did look!
I need not swear by the evening glow,
Or by the night, and what it drives together,
Or by the moon when it is at its full,
Ye shall be surely transferred from state to state[1]!
[20] What ails them that they do not believe?
and, when the Qur'ân is read to them, do not adore?
Nay, those who misbelieve do say it is a lie, but
God knows best the (malice) that they hide.
So give them the glad tidings of grievous woe!
[25] save those who believe and act aright, for them
is hire that is not grudged!

THE CHAPTER OF THE ZODIACAL SIGNS.

(LXXXV. Mecca.)

In the name of the merciful and compassionate God.
By the heaven with its zodiacal signs[2]!
And the promised day!
And the witness and the witnessed[3]!
The fellows of the pit were slain;
[5] And the fire with its kindling,
When they sat over it
And witnessed the while what they were doing with those who believed[4].

---

[1] From life to death, and from death to the future life.

[2] Literally, 'towers.'

[3] Various interpretations are given of these words, the most probable perhaps being that 'the witness' is Mohammed, and 'the witnessed' the faith.

[4] Alluding to the persecution of the Christians at Negrân by

And they took not vengeance on them save for their belief in God,
The mighty, the praiseworthy,
Whose is the kingdoms of the heavens and the earth;
For God is witness over all!

[10] Verily, those who make trial of the believers, men and women, and then do not repent, for them is the torment of hell, and for them is the torment of the burning!

Verily, those who believe and act aright, for them are gardens beneath which rivers flow,—that is the great bliss!

Verily, the violence of thy Lord is keen!

Verily, He produces and returns, and He is the forgiving, the loving, [15] the Lord of the glorious throne; the doer of what He will!

Has there come to thee the story of the hosts of Pharaoh and Thamûd?

Nay, those who misbelieve do say it is a lie; [20] but God is behind them—encompassing!

Nay, it is a glorious Qur'ân in a preserved tablet[1].

The Chapter of the Night Star.

(LXXXVI. Mecca.)

In the name of the merciful and compassionate God.

By the heaven and by the night star! And what

Dhu 'n Navvâs, king of Yemen, who had embraced the Jewish religion, and who commanded all his subjects who would not do the same to be flung into a pit filled with fire, and burnt to death.

[1] See Part I, p. 2, note 2.

shall make thee know what the night star is?—The star of piercing brightness.

Verily, every soul has a guardian over it.

[5] Then let man look from what he is created: he is created from water poured forth, that comes out from between the loins and the breast bones[1].

Verily, He is able to send him back again, on the day when the secrets shall be tried, [10] and he shall have no strength nor helper.

By the heaven that sends back the rain!

And the earth with its sprouting!

Verily, it is indeed a distinguishing speech, and it is no frivolity!

[15] Verily, they do plot a plot!

But I plot my plot too! let the misbelievers bide; do thou then let them bide awhile!

The Chapter of the Most High.

(LXXXVII. Mecca.)

In the name of the merciful and compassionate God.

Celebrated the name of thy Lord most High, who created and fashioned, and who decreed and guided, and who brings forth the pasture, [5] and then makes it dusky stubble!

We will make thee recite, and thou shalt not forget[2], save what God pleases. Verily, He knows the open and what is concealed; and we will send

---

[1] From the loins of the man and the breast bones of the woman.—Al Bâi*dh*âvî.

[2] See Chapter II, verse 100, Part I, p. 14.

thee easily to ease; wherefore remind, for, verily, the reminder is useful.

[10] But he who fears will be mindful; but the wretch will avoid it; he who will broil on the great fire, and then therein shall neither die nor live!

Prosperous is he who purifies himself, [15] and remembers the name of his Lord and prays!

Nay! but ye prefer the life of this world, while the hereafter is better and more lasting.

Verily, this was in the books of yore,—the books of Abraham and Moses.

The Chapter of the Overwhelming[1].

(LXXXVIII. Mecca.)

In the name of the merciful and compassionate God.

Has there come to thee the story of the overwhelming?

Faces on that day shall be humble, labouring, toiling,—shall broil upon a burning fire; [5] shall be given to drink from a boiling spring! no food shall they have save from the foul thorn, which shall not fatten nor avail against hunger!

Faces on that day shall be comfortable, content with their past endeavours,—[10] in a lofty garden wherein they shall hear no foolish word; wherein is a flowing fountain; wherein are couches raised on high, and goblets set down, [15] and cushions arranged, and carpets spread!

---

[1] Another name of the last day.

Do they not look then at the camel how she is created[1]?

And at the heaven how it is reared?

And at the mountains how they are set up?

[20] And at the earth how it is spread out?

But remind: thou art only one to remind; thou art not in authority over them; except such as turns his back and misbelieves, for him will God torment with the greatest torment.

[25] Verily, unto us is their return, and, verily, for us is their account!

THE CHAPTER OF THE DAWN.

(LXXXIX. Mecca.)

IN the name of the merciful and compassionate God.

By the dawn and ten nights[2]!

And the single and the double!

And the night when it travels on!

Is there in that an oath for a man of sense?

[5] Hast thou not seen how thy Lord did with 'Âd?—with Iram of the columns[3]? the like of which has not been created in the land?

---

[1] So useful an animal as a camel being to an Arab a singular instance of divine wisdom.

[2] The first ten nights of the sacred months of DHU 'l Heggeh.

[3] Sheddâd, the son of 'Âd, is related to have ordered the construction of a terrestrial paradise in the desert of Aden, ostensibly in rivalry of the celestial one, and to have called it Irem, after the name of his great-grandfather Irem (Aram). On going to take possession of it, he and all his people were struck dead by a noise from heaven, and the paradise disappeared. Certain Arab travellers are declared to have come across this mysterious garden.

And Thamûd when they hewed the stones in the valley?

And Pharaoh of the stakes[1]?

[10] Who were outrageous in the land, and did multiply wickedness therein, and thy Lord poured out upon them the scourge of torment.

Verily, thy Lord is on a watch tower! and as for man, whenever his Lord tries him and honours him and grants him favour, then [15] he says, 'My Lord has honoured me;' but whenever he tries him and doles out to him his subsistence, then he says, 'My Lord despises me!'

Nay, but ye do not honour the orphan, nor do ye urge each other to feed the poor, [20] and ye devour the inheritance (of the weak) with a general devouring[2], and ye love wealth with a complete love!

Nay, when the earth is crushed to pieces, and thy Lord comes with the angels, rank on rank, and hell is brought on that day,—on that day shall man be reminded! but how shall he have a reminder?

[25] He will say, 'Would that I had sent something forward for my life!'

But on that day no one shall be tormented with a torment like his, and none shall be bound with bonds like his!

O thou comforted soul! return unto thy Lord, well pleased and well pleased with!

And enter amongst my servants, [30] and enter my Paradise!

---

[1] Cf. p. 176, note 1.

[2] Cf. Part I, p. 72, note 1.

The Chapter of the Land.

(XC. Mecca.)

In the name of the merciful and compassionate God.

I need not swear by the Lord of this land[1], and thou a dweller in this land[2]!

Nor by the begetter and what he begets!

We have surely created man in trouble.

[5] Does he think that none can do aught against him?

He says, 'I have wasted wealth in plenty;' does he think that no one sees him?

Have we not made for him two eyes and a tongue, and two lips? [10] and guided him in the two highways? but he will not attempt the steep!

And what shall make thee know what the steep is? It is freeing captives, or feeding on the day of famine, [15] an orphan who is akin, or a poor man who lies in the dust; and again (it is) to be of these who believe and encourage each other to patience, and encourage each other to mercy,—these are the fellows of the right[3]!

But those who disbelieve in our signs, they are the fellows of the left, [20] for them is fire that closes in!

---

[1] I. e. the sacred territory of Mecca.

[2] Or, 'art at liberty to act as thou pleasest.'

[3] See pp. 263, 264.

The Chapter of the Sun.

(XCI. Mecca.)

In the name of the merciful and compassionate God.

By the sun and its noonday brightness!
And the moon when it follows him!
And the day when it displays him!
And the night when it covers him!
[5] And the heaven and what built it!
And the earth and what spread it!
And the soul and what fashioned it, and taught it its sin and its piety!
Prosperous is he who purifies it!
[10] And disappointed is he who corrupts it!

Thamûd called the apostle a liar[1] in their outrage, when their wretch rose up and the apostle of God said to them, 'God's she-camel! so give her to drink.'

But they called him a liar, and they ham-strung
her; but their Lord destroyed them in their sins,
and served them all alike; [15] and He fears not
the result thereof!

The Chapter of the Night.

(XCII. Mecca.)

In the name of the merciful and compassionate God.

By the night when it veils!
And the day when it is displayed!
And by what created male and female!
Verily, your efforts are diverse!

---

[1] See Part I, p. 147, note 1.

[5] But as for him who gives alms and fears God,
And believes in the best,
We will send him easily to ease!
But as for him who is niggardly,
And longs for wealth,
And calls the good a lie,
[10] We will send him easily to difficulty!
And his wealth shall not avail him
When he falls down (into hell)!
Verily, it is for us to guide;
And, verily, ours are the hereafter and the former life!
And I have warned you of a fire that flames!

[15] None shall broil thereon, but the most wretched, who says it is a lie and turns his back.

But the pious shall be kept away from it, he who gives his wealth in alms, and who gives no favour to any one for the sake of reward, [20] but only craving the face of his Lord most High; in the end he shall be well pleased!

The Chapter of the Forenoon.

(XCIII. Mecca.)

In the name of the merciful and compassionate God.

By the forenoon!

And the night when it darkens!

Thy Lord has not forsaken thee, nor hated thee!
and surely the hereafter is better for thee than the
former; [5] and in the end thy Lord will give thee,
and thou shalt be well pleased!

Did He not find thee an orphan, and give thee

shelter? and find thee erring, and guide thee? and find thee poor with a family, and nourish thee?

But as for the orphan oppress him not; [10] and as for the beggar drive him not away; and as for the favour of thy Lord discourse thereof.

The Chapter of 'Have we not expanded?'

(XCIV. Mecca.)

In the name of the merciful and compassionate God.

Have we not expanded for thee thy breast[1]? and set down from thee thy load which galled thy back? and exalted for thee thy renown?

[5] Verily, with difficulty is ease! verily, with difficulty is ease!

And when thou art at leisure then toil, and for thy Lord do thou yearn!

The Chapter of the Fig.

(XCV. Place of origin doubtful.)

In the name of the merciful and compassionate God.

By the fig!

And by the olive!

---

[1] I.e. expanded it for the reception of the truth. Taking the words literally some Muslims have supposed it to refer to the legend, that the angel Gabriel appeared to Mohammed while he was a child, and having cut open his breast took out his heart, and cleansed it from the black drop of original sin. This explanation is, however, rejected by the more sensible of the orthodox Muslim divines.

And by Mount Sinai!

And by this safe land[1]!

We have indeed created man in the best of symmetry. [5] Then we will send him back the lowest of the low; save those who believe and act aright; for theirs is a hire that is not grudged.

But what shall make thee call the judgment after this a lie!

Is not God a most just of judges?

THE CHAPTER OF CONGEALED BLOOD[2].

(XCVI. Mecca.)

IN the name of the merciful and compassionate God.

READ, in the name of thy Lord!

Who created man from congealed blood!

Read, for thy Lord is most generous!

[5] Who taught the pen!

Taught man what he did not know!

Nay, verily, man is indeed outrageous at seeing himself get rich!

Verily, unto thy Lord is the return!

Hast thou considered him who forbids [10] a servant[3] when he prays[4]?

---

[1] Alluding to the inviolable character of the sacred territory of Mecca.

[2] The five opening verses of the chapter are generally allowed to have been the first that were revealed. See Introduction, p. xx, and note 1, idem.

[3] I.e. Mohammed.

[4] The allusion is to Abu *G*ahl, who threatened to set his foot on Mohammed's neck if he caught him in the act of adoration.

Hast thou considered if he were in guidance or bade piety?

Hast thou considered if he said it was a lie, and turned his back?

Did he not know that God can see?

[15] Nay, surely, if he do not desist we will drag him by the forelock!—the lying sinful forelock!

So let him call his counsel: we will call the guards of hell!

Nay, obey him not, but adore and draw nigh!

The Chapter of Power[1].

(XCVII. Place of origin doubtful.)

In the name of the merciful and compassionate God.

Verily, we sent it down on the Night of Power!

And what shall make thee know what the Night of Power is?—the Night of Power is better than a thousand months!

The angels and the Spirit descend therein, by the permission of their Lord with every bidding.

[5] Peace it is until rising of the dawn!

The Chapter of the Manifest Sign.

(XCVIII. Place of origin doubtful.)

In the name of the merciful and compassionate God.

Those of the people of the Book and the idolaters

---

[1] The word el Qadr signifies 'power,' 'worth,' 'measure,' and 'the divine decree.'

who misbelieve did not fall off until there came to them the manifest sign,—

An apostle from God reading pure pages wherein are right scriptures:

Nor did those who were given the Book divide into sects until after there came to them the manifest sign.

But they were not bidden aught but to worship God, being sincere in religion unto Him as 'Hanîfs, and to be steadfast in prayer, and to give alms: for that is the standard religion.

[5] Verily, those who disbelieve amongst the people of the Book and the idolaters shall be in the fire of hell, to dwell therein for aye; they are wretched creatures!

Verily, those who believe and act aright, they are the best of creatures; their reward with their Lord is gardens of Eden, beneath which rivers flow, to dwell therein for aye; God shall be well pleased with them, and they with Him! that is for him who fears his Lord!

The Chapter of the Earthquake.

(XCIX. Place of origin doubtful.)

In the name of the merciful and compassionate God.

When the earth shall quake with its quaking!

And the earth shall bring forth her burdens, and man shall say, 'What ails her!'

On that day she shall tell her tidings, [5] because thy Lord inspires her.

On the day when men shall come up in separate

bands to show their works: and he who does the weight of an atom of good shall see it! and he who does the weight of an atom of evil shall see it!

The Chapter of the Chargers.

(C. Mecca.)

In the name of the merciful and compassionate God.

By the snorting chargers!

And those who strike fire with their hoofs!

And those who make incursions in the morning,

And raise up dust therein,

[5] And cleave through a host therein!

Verily, man is to his Lord ungrateful; and, verily, he is a witness of that.

Verily, he is keen in his love of good.

Does he nôt know when the tombs are exposed,
[10] and what is in the breasts is brought to light?

Verily, thy Lord upon that day indeed is well aware.

The Chapter of the Smiting.

(CI. Mecca.)

In the name of the merciful and compassionate God.

The smiting!

What is the smiting?

And what shall make thee know what the smiting is?

The day when men shall be like scattered moths; and the mountains shall be like flocks of carded wool!

[5] And as for him whose balance is heavy, he shall be in a well-pleasing life.

But as for him whose balance is light, his dwelling shall be the pit of hell[1].

And who shall make thee know what it is?—a burning fire!

The Chapter of the Contention about Numbers.

(CII. Place of origin doubtful.)

In the name of the merciful and compassionate God.

The contention about numbers deludes you till ye visit the tombs[2]!

Not so! In the end ye shall know! And again not so! In the end ye shall know!

[5] Not so! Did ye but know with certain knowledge!

Ye shall surely see hell! And again ye shall surely see it with an eye of certainty.

Then ye shall surely be asked about pleasure[3]!

The Chapter of the Afternoon[4].

(CIII. Mecca.)

In the name of the merciful and compassionate God.

By the afternoon! verily, man is in loss! save

[1] El Hâwiyeh, see Introduction, p. lxx.

[2] The commentators say that in one of the frequent contentions about the respective nobility of the Arab tribes, that the Abu Menaf clan disputed with that of Sahm, which was the most numerous, and the latter, having lost many men in battle, declared that their dead should be taken into account as well as the living.

[3] That is, the pleasures of this life.

[4] Or, 'the age.'

those who believe and do right, and bid each other be true, and bid each other be patient.

The Chapter of the Backbiter.

(CIV. Mecca.)

In the name of the merciful and compassionate God.

Woe to every slanderous backbiter, who collects wealth and counts it.

He thinks that his wealth can immortalize him.

Not so! he shall be hurled into El 'Hutamah!

[5] And what shall make thee understand what El 'Hutamah[1] is?—the fire of God kindled; which rises above the hearts. Verily, it is an archway over them on long-drawn columns.

The Chapter of the Elephant.

(CV. Mecca.)

In the name of the merciful and compassionate God.

Hast thou not seen what thy Lord did with the fellows of the elephant[2]?

Did He not make their stratagem lead them astray, and send down on them birds in flocks, to throw down on them stones of baked clay, [5] and make them like blades of herbage eaten down?

---

[1] See Introduction, p. lxx.

[2] Abrahat el Asram, an Abyssinian Christian, and viceroy of the king of Sanaa in Yemen in the year in which Mohammed was born, marched with a large army and some elephants upon Mecca, with the intention of destroying the Kaabah. He was defeated and his army destroyed in so sudden a manner as to have given rise to the

THE CHAPTER OF THE QURÂIS.

(CVI. Mecca.)

IN the name of the merciful and compassionate God.

For the uniting of the Qurâis; uniting them for the caravan of winter and summer.

So let them serve the Lord of this house who feeds them against hunger and makes them safe against fear[1].

THE CHAPTER OF 'NECESSARIES.'

(CVII. Place of origin doubtful.)

IN the name of the merciful and compassionate God.

Hast thou considered him who calls the judgment a lie? He it is who pushes the orphan away; and urges not (others) to feed the poor.

But woe to those who pray [5] and who are careless in their prayers,

Who pretend and withhold necessaries[2].

THE CHAPTER OF EL KÂUTHAR.

(CVIII. Mecca.)

IN the name of the merciful and compassionate God.

Verily, we have given thee El KÂUTHAR[3];

---

legend embodied in the text. It is conjectured that small-pox broke out amongst his men.

[1] See Introduction, p. xvi. Some connect the first sentence with the last chapter.

[2] Or, 'alms.' The word might be rendered 'resources.'

[3] The word signifies 'abundance.' It is also the name of a river in Paradise.

So pray to thy Lord and slaughter (victims).
Verily, he who hates thee shall be childless[1].

The Chapter of Misbelievers.

(CIX. Mecca.)

In the name of the merciful and compassionate God.

Say, 'O ye misbelievers! I do not serve what ye serve; nor will ye serve what I serve; nor will I serve what ye serve; [5] nor will ye serve what I serve;—ye have your religion, and I have my religion!'

The Chapter of Help.

(CX. Mecca.)

In the name of the merciful and compassionate God.

When there comes God's help and victory,
And thou shalt see men enter into God's religion by troops,
Then celebrate the praises of thy Lord, and ask forgiveness of Him, verily, He is relentant!

The Chapter of Abu Laheb[2].

(CXI. Mecca.)

In the name of the merciful and compassionate God.

Abu Laheb's two hands shall perish, and he shall perish!

[1] This is directed against Âs ibn Wail, who, when Mohammed's son El Qâsim died, called him abtar, which means 'docktailed,' i.e. childless.

[2] See Introduction, p. xxviii. Abu Laheb, 'the father of the flame,'

His wealth shall not avail him, nor what he has earned!

He shall broil in a fire that flames[1], and his wife carrying faggots!—[5] on her neck a cord of palm fibres.

THE CHAPTER OF UNITY[2].

(CXII. Place of origin doubtful.)

In the name of the merciful and compassionate God.

Say, 'He is God alone!
God the Eternal!
He begets not and is not begotten!
Nor is there like unto Him any one!'

THE CHAPTER OF THE DAYBREAK.

(CXIII. Place of origin doubtful.)

In the name of the merciful and compassionate God.

Say, 'I seek refuge in the Lord of the daybreak, from the evil of what He has created; and from the evil of the night when it cometh on[3]; and from the evil of the blowers upon knots[4]; [5] and from the evil of the envious when he envies.'

---

was the nickname of 'Abd el 'Huzzâ, uncle of Mohammed, and a bitter opponent of Islâm.

[1] A pun upon his name.

[2] The chapter is generally known in Arabic by the name of El I'hlâs, 'clearing oneself,' i.e. of belief in any but one God.

[3] Or, according to a traditional explanation given by the prophet to 'Âyeshah, 'the moon when it is eclipsed.'

[4] Witches who make knots in string and blow upon them, uttering at the same time some magical formula and the name of the persons they wish to injure.

The Chapter of Men.

(CXIV. Place of origin doubtful.)

In the name of the merciful and compassionate God.

Say, 'I seek refuge in the Lord of men, the King of men, the God of men, from the evil of the whisperer[1], who slinks off, [5] who whispers into the hearts of men!—from *g*inns and men!'

[1] The devil.

INDEX.

(al) Aarâf, bridge of, Int. p. lxix; Part I, p. 143; Part II, p. 32 note 1.
Aaron, I, 38, 94, 125, 152, 154, 201; II, 29 n, 36, 39, 41, 50, 51, 68, 86, 91, 92, 110, 172, 240 n.
Abbâs, xxxii, xli, xlii.
'Abd ad Dar, xvii, xviii.
'Abdallah ibn Sa'hd ibn Abî Sar'h, Mohammed's secretary, lvii; I, 126 n.
'Abdallah ibn Ubai, xxxv.
'Abdallah ibn Ubbai, chief of the 'Hypocrites,' lxiii; II, 74 n 2, 77 n 4, 284 n.
Abdallah ibn Umm Maktûm, II, 320 n.
'Abd al 'Hareth, one of Adam's sons, I, 161 n 1.
'Abd al Huzzâ, lx; II, 344 n.
'Abd al Mu*tt*alib, xvii, xviii.
'Abd ar Rahmân ibn Auf, xxiii.
'Abd Menâf, xvii, xviii.
— clan of, II, 341 n.
'Abd Shems, xviii.
Abraham, xiii, xvi, xlvii, l, liii, lxxiv; I, 17, 18, 19, 40, 40 n 3, 41, 50, 50 n 2, 54, 57, 58, 59, 80, 90, 94, 125, 133 n 1, 137, 183, 189, 212, 213, 219, 223, 242, 247, 263; II, 30, 31, 65, 93, 120, 124, 139, 179, 206, 246, 253, 269, 278, 329.
— is cast into the fiery furnace, II, 171, 172.
— station of, xvi, xvii, lxxiv.
— surnamed, '*H*alîla 'llâh, the Friend of God, lxxi.
Abrahat al A*s*ram, II, 341 n.
— attacks the Kaabah, II, 341 n.
Abrogation of verses, lvii.
Abu'l 'Abbas, I, 175.
Abu Bekr, xix, xxiii, xxiv, xxv, xxxiii, xliv, xlvi; I, 68 n 1.
— hides with Mohammed in a cave, lvii; I, 179 n 1; II, 75 n 1.
Abu *G*ahl, xxxiii; II, 300, 336 n.
— challenges Mohammed to cause a portion of the heavens to fall on the Qurâi*s*, II, 300 n.
Abu 'Hâmir, I, 188 n 1.
Abu Lahed, xxix, lx; II, 144, 343.
Abu Sufiyân, xxxv, xxxvii; I, 164 n 1.
Abu Tâlib, xviii, xxiv, xxv, xxviii, xxix, xli, xlii.
Abyssinia, xxvi, xxvii, xl; I, 214 n 3; II, 341 n.
'Âd, xlviii; I, 145, 146, 183, 210, 211, 239; II, 61, 86, 95, 121, 176, 193, 200, 227, 242, 247, 254, 256, 298, 330.
Adam, I, 5 n, 50, 54, 101, 138, 139, 140; II, 8, 9, 19, 31, 43, 44.
— children of, I, 141, 159, 161 n 1.
Adam, Zafîy allâh, the Chosen of God, lxxi.
Adrian, persecution of, xv.
Æsop. See Loqmân.
A'hmed, prophecy of, xlix; II, 281.
A'*h*nas ibn *S*urâiq eth ṭhaqafi, I, 29 n 3.
(al) A'hqâf, II, 227.
— chapter of, II, 224.
Akabeh, xxxi.
— pledge given at, by a deputation from the inhabitants of Medînah, xxxii; I, 9 n 1, 98 n 1.
Al 'asmâ'u l'husnâ, II, 13 n 1.
Alexander the Great, his prime minister, II, 23 n 3.
'Ali ibn Ali Tâlib, xxxiii; II, 74 n 2, 143.
Allâh, xii, xiii, xiv, xxiv, lxv, lxvi; I, 132 n 2; II, 13 n 1.
— meaning of name, lxvi.
Allâh ta'âlah, xii, lxvi.
Allâhu akbar, II, 13 n 2.
Allât, xii, xiii, xxvii, xliii; I, 160 n 1; II, 9 n 1, 62 n 1, 252.
Alms, lxxi, lxxiii; I, 180, 181.
Amanuensis, employed by Mohammed, lvii.
Amînah, Mohammed's mother, xviii.
Amînah, one of Solomon's concubines, II, 178 n.
'Amr, xli.
Amram, I, 50, n 1.
'Amr ibn La'hy, xvii.

Angel of death, II, 136.
— fallen, xiv.
Angels, lii, lxviii, lxx; I, 161 n 1, 164, 169; II, 139, 145, 155, 168, 174, 181, 200, 205, 232, 245, 252, 300, 315, 317.
— chapter of, II, 157.
— 'daughters of God,' xiii, lxi; I, 256 n 2.
— guardian, I, 233.
— recording, I, 195 n 1.
Ant, chapter of, II, 99.
Antichrist, lxxi; I, 94 n 2.
Antioch, II, 164 n.
Antistes, I, 17 n 1.
Apes, Sabbath-breakers turned into, I, 9.
Apostle of the Gentiles, I, 156 n 1.
Apostles, the twelve, II, 282.
Arab orators, l.
Arab writers, I, 257 n 1.
Arabia, I, 191 n 1; II, 263.
— boundaries of, ix.
Arabian prophets, I, 159 n 1.
Arabs, I, 256 n 2; II, 13 n 1.
— ancient, I, 27, 40 n, 48, 64 n, 79, 176 n 1.
— — beacon fires, I, 106 n 1.
— — character, x.
— — Christian tribes, xiv.
— — formula for avoiding the evil influence of *g*inns in lonely places, II, 305 n.
— — formula of deprecation of hostilities during the sacred months, II, 85.
— — idols, xii.
— — Jewish tribes, xiv, xv.
— — manners, ix, x.
— — position of women amongst, xi.
— — pride of birth, x.
— — religion, xi, xiv, xv.
— — superstitions, xi, xii.
— — tribes of, I, 145 n 1.
— — vices, x.
— battles, II, 221.
— desert, I, 216 n 1, 259 n 1; II, 36 n 3, 234, 235, 241.
— desert, ask to be excused from fighting, I, 185, 187.
— desert and town, ix.
— dislike of female offspring, II, 212.
— disregard of treaties if they are themselves of superior strength to their enemy, I, 260 n 2.
— Himyarite, II, 219 n.
Arabs, hospitality, II, 147 n.
— hypocrisy, I, 186, 190.
— Jewish, xxx.
— pagan, burying female children alive, I, 132 n.
— — mutilate the ears of cattle, I, 89 n 1.
— — offerings to idols, I, 132 n.
— — superstitions, I, 132 n, 134 n.
— — superstitious customs respecting cattle, I, 112, 115 n 1.
— practice of divination amongst, II, 2 n 2.
— relations to their adopted children, II, 144.
— sacred months not to be put off, I, 178 n 1.
— superstitious, II, 7 n 1.
— superstitious about entering houses by the doors on their return from Mecca, I, 27 n 1.
'Arafât, lxxiv; I, 29.
Arafât, Mount, xliv.
Archangels, lxix.
'Arîsh, I, 133 n 2.
Ark, I, 38; II, 164 n.
Ar Rahman, lxi; II, 13 n 1.
Ashram, Abraha, the, xviii; II, 341 n.
Athar, I, 124.
Athar Nâgat en Nebî, I, 147 n 1.
Aus, xxx, xxxiv, xxxix; I, 59 n 1; II, 217, 239, 258.
Âyatu 'l Kursîy, I, 40 n 1.
'Âyeshah, xliv; II, 74 n 2, 75 n 1, 77 n 5, 290, 307 n, 344 n.
Âzar, I, 124.

Baal, priests of, I, 68 n 2.
Babel, tower of, I, 253.
Babylon, I, 14, 14 n 2.
Babylonia, ix.
Ba'hîrah, I, 112, 112 n 1.
Ba'*h*tnazr, I, 41 n 1.
Bâi*dh*âvî, lxxx; I, 33 n 1, 177 n 1; II, 328 n.
Bait allâh, xiii; I, 17 n 2.
Balaam, I, 159 n 1.
Bedawîn, modern, xiv; I, 147 n 1, 256 n 2.
Bedr, battle of, xxxvi, xxxvii; I, 47 n 1, 61, 66 n 1, 86 n 1, 165 n 1, 171 n 1; II, 20 n 1, 62 n 2, 70 n 2, 257, 274 n, 276.
Bee, similitude of, I, 4 n 3.
Bekkah, xvi; I, 58.
Benu Bakr, xvii.

Benu Ghanm, I, 188 n 1, 189 n 1.
Benu '*H*uzâ'hah, xvii.
Benu Kenânah, xvii.
Bethel, xiii; I, 17 n 2.
Bilâl, the first Muezzin, xxiii.
Bismillah, lxviii; I, 24 n 2, 172 n.
Byzantium, ix, xl.

Cain, I, 161 n 1.
Calf, golden, I, 6, 7, 12, 13, 155.
Camels, II, 321.
Captives, ransom of, I, 171.
Carmel, Mount, I, 68 n 2.
Cave, fellows of the, II, 14.
Chaldea, xi.
Christianity, x, xiv, xv, li, lii, lix, lxi.
Christians, I, 8, 15, 19, 54, 99, 105, 107, 109; II, 16 n 1, 58.
— accused of perverting the Scriptures, I, 250 n 3.
Christian traditions, xlvii.
Confederates, the, siege of Medînah by, xxxix; II, 138, 138 n 1, 140 n, 142 n.
Constantinople, II, 125 n.
Creator, the, I, 128.

(ed) Da*gg*âl, lxxi.
Dan, xii n 1; I, 13 n 2.
Dâr al Qarâr (Chapter xl, 42), the Abode of Rest, lxx.
Dâr as Salâm (Chapter vi, 127), the Abode of Peace, lxx.
David, I, 9 n 1, 39, 52, 52 n, 94, 108, 125; II, 7, 100.
— taught to make coats of mail, II, 151.
— the parable of the ewe lamb, II, 177, 178.
Death, angel of, II, 136.
Deluge, Mohammedan account of the, I, 209 n 1.
Demons, lii.
Denarius, I, 55 n 2.
Deputations, year of, xliii.
Dervishes, I, 53 n 4.
Deuteronomy xxi. 1–9, I, 9 n 2.
Devil, the, I, 162.
— tempts man, II, 276.
Devils, II, 168 n, 179 n.
— appointed to watch unbelievers, II, 201.
— are not allowed to listen at the gate of heaven, II, 98, 99, 250 n.
— do not descend with the Qur'ân, II, 98.
Devils, on whom they do descend, II, 98.
— pelted with shooting-stars, I, 51 n; II, 293, 305, 330 n.
Dhu 'l 'He*gg*eh, xxxix; II, 59 n 1.
Dhu 'l Kifl, II, 53, 180.
Dhu 'l Qa'hdah, xxxix, xl; I, 27 n 4.
Dhu 'l Qarnâin, II, 24, 24 n 1, 25.
Dhu 'n Navvâs, II, 327 n.
Dhu 'nnûn, II, 53.
Dinâr = denarius.
Diodorus, xvi.
Dioscuri, liv.
Discrimination, the, I, 7, 26, 46, 55, 55 n 2, 166, 168; II, 50, 83.
Divorce, II, 138, 146, 270 n, 288, 289.
— chapter of, II, 288.
Dog-star, II, 254.
Dolmens, I, 97 n 2.
Dualism, lii; I, 115 n 2.
Duwâr, xiii.

Eden, gardens of, I, 183, 235, 253; II, 160, 180, 191, 282, 338.
Edom, II, 147 n.
Egypt, ix, xl; I, 8, 202, 220 n 1, 221, 227 n 1, 230.
Egyptian, II, 91.
Eidolon of Jesus crucified instead of him, I, 53 n 3.
Elath, I, 9 n 1.
Elephant, chapter of, I, 214 n 3; II, 341.
— year of, xviii; II, 341.
Elias, I, 41 n 1, 125, 147 n 1; II, 23 n 3, 53 n 1.
Elijah, I, 68 n 2.
Elisha, I, 125; II, 180.
Elyâs, II, 172.
Enoch, xi; II, 31 n.
Enquirer, the, xv.
Ephesus, Seven Sleepers of, II, 14 n 1.
Esdras, I, 41 n 1.
Eusebius, I, 124.
Eutychians, li.
Eve, I, 161 n 1.
Exodus, II, 36 n 1.
— ch. x. ver. 9, p. lxxv.
— ch. xiv. ver. 30, I, 203 n 2.
— ch. xxxii. ver. 20, I, 13 n 1.
— ch. xxxii. vers. 24, 26, 27, I, 7 n 1.
—'Desert of the,' I, 147 n 1; II, 36 n 1.
Ezekiel, vision of, I, 37 n 2.
— ch. xxxvii. vers. 1–10, I, 37 n 2.
Ezra, Mohammedan legend of, I, 177, 177 n.

Farewell pilgrimage, xliv.
(al) Farqân, lvii.
Fasting, lxxi, lxxiii.
Fâtimah, II, 143 n 1.
Fatrah, the, xxii; II, 308.
Female children buried alive, I, 132 n 2; II, 212, 322.
Firdâus, II, 26 n 1.
Firdausî, II, 131 n 3.
Fire, how produced, II, 167, 265 n.
Flight, the, I, 176 n 1.
Friday, the day of public prayer, lxxii; II, 283.
(al) Furqân, II, 83 n 1.
Future life, belief in, xiv.

Gabriel, xxxvi, lxv, lxix; I, 2 n 2, 13, 13 n 2, 99, 179 n, 203 n 1, 221 n 2, 261 n 2; II, 10 n 1, 28 n 1, 41 n 1, 62 n 1, 98, 164 n, 174 n; 291, 308, 311, 322, 335.
— appears to Mohammed in natural form, II, 251 n.
*G*ahîm (Chapter ii, 113), the Fierce Fire, lxx.
Gâlût = Goliath, I, 39.
*G*annat al Firdaus (Chapter xviii, 107), the Garden of Paradise, lxx.
*G*annat al 'Hilliyûn (Chapter lxxxiii, 18), the Garden of the Most High, lxx.
*G*annat al '*H*uld (Chapter xxv, 16), the Garden of Eternity, lxx.
*G*annat al Mâ'wâ (Chapter xxxii, 19), the Garden of Resort, lxx.
*G*annat an Na'hîm (Chapter vi, 70), the Garden of Pleasure, lxx.
*G*annat 'Hadn (Chapter ix, 72), the Garden of Eden, lxx.
*G*ehennum (Chapter xix, 44), Gehenna, lxx.
Genesis ch. i. ver. 2, I, 205.
— ch. vi. ver. 2, I, 14 n 2.
— ch. ix. vers. 20–25, I, 209 n 2.
— ch. xi. ver. 13, I, 147 n 1.
— ch. xv. ver. 9, I, 41 n 2.
— ch. xxviii. vers. 18–19, p. xiii.
Gentiles, I, 48, 56; II, 282.
— prophet of, xlvii.
George, St., II, 23 n 3.
*G*erâdeh, one of Solomon's wives, II, 178 n 2.
Ghassan, xiv.
(al) Ghazzâli, lxx.
*G*ibt, ancient Arab idol, I, 79.
Gideon, I, 38 n 4.
*G*ihâd, I, 32 n 2; II, 7 n 1.
*G*inns, xii; I, 127, 131, 142, 160, 160 n 3; II, 7 n 1, 69, 156, 259 n, 260, 305 n, 306, 345.
— listen to Mohammed's preaching, lxx; II, 304.
— serve Solomon, II, 102, 151.
— their creation, lxix.
Giordi. See *G*ûdî.
Gnat, similitude of, I, 4.
God, names of, lxvii; II, 277.
Goddesses of the Qurâis, II, 186 n, 252.
Gog, lxxi; II, 25 n 1, n 2, n 3.
Goliath, I, 39 n 1; II, 1 n 4.
Gomorrah, I, 183 n 1; II, 255, 298.
Gordyæi. See Giordi.
Gospels, I, 254 n 1; II, 86 n 1.
Goyîm, I, 48 n 1.
Greeks, II, 42 n 1, 235 n.
— chapter of, II, 124.
— prophecy of the victory of, II, 125, 125 n.
Grove, the, I, 249; II, 67, 242.
*G*ûdî, Mount, where the ark rested, I, 210, 210 n 2.
Gulf of Oman, ix.
Gulf, Persian, ix.

*H*abbâb, II, 33 n 1.
'Hab'hab, xiii.
Habîb, II, 164 n.
'Hadab, II, 54 n 2.
'Hadhramaut, II, 86 n 3.
'*H*adî*g*ah, xix, xxi, xxii, xxiii, xxiv, xxix, xlix, lxxvi.
Hadîth, lxvi.
'Hafsah, II, 290 n.
'Ha*gg*, xvii, liii, lxxvi; I, 29 n 1 and 2.
— meaning of word, lxxv.
— pilgrims, I, 50 n 2.
— rites of, xiii, lxxiii, lxxiv, lxxv.
(al) 'Hagr, I, 244, 249.
— chapter of, I, 244.
— meaning of name, I, 244 n.
'Hâlid ibn Walîd, xxxviii, xli, xlii; II, 239.
Hâmân, Pharaoh's vizier, II, 108, 108 n 1, 112, 121 n.
'Hâmî, I, 112, 112 n 1.
'Hamr, includes all intoxicating drinks, I, 32 n 3.
'Hamzah, Mohammed's uncle, xxxviii; I, 264 n 1; II, 192, 193, 194.

'Hanîf, xv, xxiv, lii; I, 19, 54, 90, 124, 133 n 1, 137, 204, 263; II, 59, 338.
Harîrî, Maqâmat of, lvi; II, 16 n 3.
'Harûbah, II, 283 n.
Hârût, xiv; I, 14.
'Hasan, II, 74 n 2.
Hâshim, xvi, xviii, lx.
'Hâsî ibn Wâil, II, 33 n 1.
'Hâtib ibn abi Balta'hah, warns the Meccans of an intended attack by Mohammed, II, 277 n 2
'Havârîyûn, I, 53 n 1.
Hâwiyeh (Chapter cl, 8), the Abyss, lxx.
'Hazrag, tribe of, xxx, xxxi, xxxiv; I, 59 n 1; II, 239 n.
Heaven, names of, lxx :—
Dâr al Qarâr (Chapter xl, 42), the Abode of Rest, lxx.
Dâr as Salâm (Chapter vi, 127), the Abode of Peace, lxx.
Gannat al 'Huld (Chapter xxv, 16), the Garden of Eternity, lxx.
Gannat al 'Hilliyûn (Chapter lxxxiii, 18), the Garden of the Most High, lxx.
Gannat al Firdaus (Chapter xviii, 107), the Garden of Paradise, lxx.
Gannat al Mâ'wâ (Chapter xxxii, 19), the Garden of Resort, lxx.
Gannat an Na'hîm (Chapter vi, 70), the Garden of Pleasure, lxx.
Gannat 'Hadn (Chapter ix, 72), the Garden of Eden, lxx.
Heifer, chapter of, xlii; I, 2.
Hell, I, 70, 80, 165, 182, 183, 184, 186; II, 293, 301, 309, 317, 322, 329, 337, 340.
Hell, names of, lxx :—
Hâwiyeh (Chapter cl, 8), the Abyss, lxx.
Hutamah (Chapter civ, 4), the Raging Fire that splits everything to pieces, lxx.
Gahîm (Chapter ii, 113), the Fierce Fire, lxx.
Gehennum (Chapter xix, 44), Gehenna, lxx.
Latbâ (Chapter lxx, 15), the Flaming Fire, lxx.
Sa'hîr (Chapter iv, 11), the Blaze, lxx.
Saqar (Chapter liv, 58), the Scorching Fire, lxx.
'Hîd al Az'hâ, lxxiv.
(al) 'Hidbr, I, 41; II, 23 n 3.
Higâz, ix.
Higrah, the, xxxiv; I, 16 n 1, 20 n 2, 32 n 1.
Hind, xxxvii.
Hirâ, Mount, xxii.
Hittatun, I, 7, 7 n 4; II, 157.
Holy Ghost, I, 113.
Holy Name, the, II, 178 n.
Homer, liv.
Homicide, I, 135.
Homoiousians, li.
Honein, xlii, xliii; I, 176 n 1.
Hour, the, I, 161, 249, 258; II, 16, 33, 56, 57, 62, 84, 126, 130, 135, 148, 150, 195, 204, 215, 231, 254, 257, 319.
House, the, I, 17, 18, 58, 111, 163, 243; II, 59, 60, 143.
Hubal, xii.
Hûd, I, 145, 145 n 2, 210, 211, 215; II, 95, 227.
Hudâibîyeh, I, 97 n 1; II, 236, 237 n.
— expedition of, II, 234 n, 235 n.
— house of, xl, xli; II, 237 n.
— oath of fealty at, xliii.
Husein, II, 74 n 2.
'Hutamah, II, 341.
'Hutamah (Chapter civ, 4), the Raging Fire that splits everything to pieces, lxx.
'Hutbah, lxxii.
'Huzair ibn Sara'hyâ, I, 41 n 1.
(al) 'Huzzâ, xii, xiii, xxvii; II, 62 n 1, 252.
Hypocrites, xxxiv, xxxvii, lxiii; I, 169, 182, 183, 184; II, 140, 142, 145, 148, 149, 234, 265, 284.

Iblîs, lxix; I, 5, 50 n 2, 138, 246; II, 8, 20, 44, 94, 181.
Ibn Abbâs, II, 230.
Idols of the Arabs, xii, xiii, xv; I, 4 n 1; II, 185 n, 186 n.
Idrîs, II, 31, 53.
Idumæa, I, 146 n 1.
Ifrît, lxx.
Igmâ'h, lxvi.
I'hfâ'un, meaning of word, II, 35 n 2.
(el) I'hlâs, chapter of, II, 344 n.
I'hrâm, II, 59 n 2.
Iliad, liv.
'Illiyûn, II, 324.
Imâm, I, 17 n 1.
Imâmam, meaning of word, I, 263 n 2.
Immunity, chapter of, I, 172.

Imrân, I, 50.
Iram, terrestrial paradise of, II, 330.
Iron, chapter of, I, 266.
Isaac, lxxiv; I, 18, 19, 50 n 2, 57, 125, 213, 219, 223; II, 30, 51, 180.
Isâf, xiii.
Isaiah, murder of, II, 1 n 4.
Isfendiâr, II, 131 n.
Ishmael, xiii, xvii, lxxiv; I, 17, 19, 57, 94, 125; II, 31, 53, 172, 180.
Islâm, li; I, 15 n 1, 19 n 1, 30 n 1, 55 n 1, 57, 59 n 1, 60 n 1, 74 n 1, 97, 131, 147 n 1, 175 n 1, 181 n 1, 183, 188 n 1; II, 184, 206.
— conquests of, I, 237 n 2.
— meaning of word, li, lxv.
— position of women under, lxxv.
— practical duties of, lxxi.
Israel, I, 17, 30, 37, 58, 100; II, 31.
— children of, I, 6, 37 n 2, 107, 108, 113, 153, 202, 203 n 2; II, 1, 1 n 1, 12, 37, 38 n 3, 91, 106, 137, 195, 215, 219, 282.
Israfîl shall sound the last trumpet, II, 255.

Jacob, I, 18, 19, 57, 94, 125, 213, 219, 223, 226 n 2, 227; II, 27, 30, 51, 180.
Jacobites, li.
Jebel Musa, I, 147 n 1.
(al) Jelâlâin, commentary of, lxv.
Jeremiah, imprisonment of, II, 1 n 4.
Jericho, I, 7 n 2.
Jerusalem, I, 7 n 2, 20 n 2, 41 n 1; II, 244 n.
— taken by Persians, liii; II, 125 n.
— temple at, II, 1 n 4.
Jesus, xxvi, li; I, 12, 19, 39, 53, 53 n 3, 57, 94, 95, 104, 108, 113, 114, 125; II, 29, 139, 164 n, 206, 216 n, 269, 282.
— an eidolon crucified instead of, I, 53 n 3.
— Rû'ha 'llâh, the Spirit of God, lxxi.
Jethro, I, 149 n 1, 249 n 3.
Jews, xiv, xlvii, l, lix; I, 8, 10 n 1 and 2, 15, 19, 20 n 2, 48 n 1, 54, 55 n 1, 103, 105, 106, 107, 134, 263; II, 42 n 1, 58, 272 n, 275, 282.
— accused of perverting the Scriptures, I, 125 n, 250 n 3.
— of Qurâi*th*ah, II, 142.
— of YaTHrib, xxxi.
— sins of the, II, 1 n 4.
Jewish tradition, xlvii.
Job, I, 94, 125; II, 52, 179, 179 n.
John, I, 51, 125; II, 28.
St. John ch. xvi. ver. 7, quoted II, 281 n.
— ch. xx. ver. 16, quoted I, 56 n.
John the Baptist, murder of, II, 1 n 4.
Jonas, I, 94, 125, 173, 202; II, 53, 295, 297.
Jordan, I, 52 n 1.
Jorhamites, xvii.
Joseph, xxi; I, 219, 220, 220 n 1, 221, 222, 224, 224 n, 225, 227, 227 n 1, 228, 229; II, 13 n 2, 77 n 5, 193.
Joshua, II, 53 n 1.
Judaism, xiv, xv, xxxv, li.
Judges vi, I, 38 n 4.
Judgment day, II, 106, 107, 255, 262, 297, 298, 311, 314, 315, 318, 319, 321, 323, 325, 329, 338, 339.
— signs preceding, lxxi.

Kaabah, xiii, xvi, xvii, xviii, xxvi, xxviii, xxxix, xli, xlii, liii, lxxiv, lxxv; I, 16 n 1, 17 n 1, 2, and 3, 20 n 2, 111, 165 n 2, 243 n 1; II, 1 n 2, 69 n 2, 248 n.
— model of the, in heaven, xvi; II, 248 n.
Kâfûr, II, 312.
Kalîmu 'llâh, I, 39 n 2.
KauTHar, II, 342.
Khâibar, Jews of, II, 235 n, 236 n, 237 n.
Khâulah bint THa'labah, II, 270 n.
Khorassan, veiled prophet of, xlv.
Khosrou, xl.
Kifl, II, 53 n 1.
Kindeh, xiv.
Korah, II, 116, 116 n, 121.

Lailat el Qadr, lxxiii.
Land, the Holy, I, 100.
La*th*â (Chapter lxx, 15), the Flaming Fire, lxx.
(al) Lau'h el Ma'hfû*th*, lxxv.
Loqmân, II, 131, 132.
Lord's Prayer, liv.
Lot, xxv; I, 61, 125, 148, 213, 214, 215, 248; II, 20 n 1, 27 n 1, 51, 97, 104, 120, 173, 176, 242.
— wife of, II, 292.
Lote tree, the celestial, II, 252.
— trees, II, 152, 152 n.

Magicians, I, 151.
Magog, lxxi; II, 25 n 1, n 2, n 3.
Mâgûg, II, 25, 54.
(al) Mâisar, games of chance, I, 32, 32 n 4, 52 n 1, 97 n 2, 110.
Mâlik, the keeper of hell, lxix; II, 217.
Manât, xii, xiii, xxvii; II, 62 n 1, 252.
Manichæans, lii.
Manna, I, 7.
Maqâm Ibrâhîm, lxxiv.
Maqauqas, xl.
Mârab, bursting of the dyke of, II, 151, 153 n.
Marriage among the Arabs, xi.
— with whom lawful, II, 146.
— with women who have come out from the infidel ranks, II, 279, 280.
Mârût, xiv; I, 14.
Marwâ, Mount, xiii.
Mary, Coptic slave, xl; II, 290.
Mary, daughter of Imran, II, 292.
Mary, son of, li; I, 12, 39, 51, 52, 93, 95, 100, 104, 108, 113, 114, 177; II, 28, 29, 68, 215, 269, 282.
Mary, Virgin, I, 50 n 1; II, 292.
Mecca, ix, xiii, xvi, xxiv, xxvi, xxx, xxxi, xxxiii, xxxv, xxxvii, xli, xliii, xliv, xlv, xlviii, xlix, liii, lix, lxiii, lxxiii, lxxiv; I, 16, 17 n 3, 20 n 2, 22 n 2, 27 n 1, 30 n 1, 58 n 1, 82 n 1, 97 n 1, 126 n 1, 164 n 1, 165 n 2, 176 n 1, 187 n 1, 188 n 1, 192 n 1, 214 n 3, 242 n 1, 260 n 1, 264 n 1; II, 9 n 1, 44 n 1, 70 n 1, 87, 123, 168 n, 213, 236, 275, 332 n, 336 n, 341.
— invasion of, by the Abyssinians, xviii.
Medayen, II, 125.
Medînah, ix, xviii, xxxi, xxxiv, xxxvii, xxxix, xli, xliv, xlviii, lix, lxiii, lxxv; I, 20 n 2, 30 n 1, 32 n 1, 163, 183 n 2, 187, 187 n 2, 188 n 1; II, 123 n 1, 140, 239, 284, 285, 287, 320.
— Jews of, xxxv.
Mehdi, coming of, lxxi.
Merciful, II, 317.
Merwah, Mount, near Mecca, I, 22.
Messiah, xxx, li; I, 52, 93, 95, 100, 108, 177.
Michael, xiii; I, 13 n 2.
Midian, I, 148, 183, 214, 216, 249 n 4; II, 37, 61, 86 n 3, 109, 110, 121.
Minâ, lxxiv; I, 50 n 1; II, 236 n.
— vale of, II, 59 n 1 and 3.
Miracle, alleged at Bedr, I, 165 n 1.
Miriam, I, 50 n 1.
Mista'h, a relation of Abu Bekr, who had assisted in spreading the scandal about 'Âyeshah, II, 75 n 1.
Moab, II, 147 n.
Mohammed, lxv; I, 13 n 2, 15 n 1, 32 n 1, 50 n 1, 97 n 1, 126 n 2, 165 n 2, 175 n 1, 183 n 2, 188 n 1, 197 n 1; II, 229, 236 n, 238.
— accused of unfair division of the spoils, II, 149.
— adopts Mecca as his qiblah, I, 20 n 2.
— amour of, with the Coptic handmaiden Mary, II, 233, 290.
— ancestors, xvi, xvii.
— attempts the pilgrimage to Mecca, xxxix; II, 236.
— bidden not to hasten the revelation of the Qur'ân, II, 311.
— bidden to pray by night, II, 308.
— birth, xviii.
— 'black drop' taken out of his heart, II, 335 n.
— chapter of, II, 229.
— character of, xlvi.
— children of, xix.
— compromise with the idolatrous Meccans, II, 62 n 1.
— concludes truce at 'Hudâibîyeh, II, 237 n.
— conspiracy to murder him, xxxiii.
— death of, xliv.
— death of his wife '*H*adîgah, xxix.
— defeated at Ohod, xxxvii, xxxviii.
— destroys the idols, xiii.
— early life of, xix.
— expedition of, against the Jews of Khâibar, I, 16 n 1.
— first call of, xx.
— first collision of, with the Meccan army, xxxv; I, 164 n 1.
— first converts of, xxiii.
— flight of, to Medînah, xxxiii; I, 187 n 1.
— hysterical symptoms of, xxi.
— inspired through Gabriel, I, 2 n 2.
— invited to Medînah, xxxi.
— marriage of, with the divorced wife of Zâid, II, 139 n.

Mohammed marries 'Hadîgah, xix.
— mental struggles, xxii.
— 'night journey' of, to heaven, II, 137 n 2.
— oath of fealty sworn by him at 'Akabah, I, 98 n 1.
— pedigree, xviii.
— personal description of, xix.
— persons supposed to have helped him in compiling the Qur'ân, I, 261, 261 n 4.
— prophecies concerning him, xlix; I, 21 n 1, 99 n 2; II, 281 n 1.
— proscribed by the Qurâis, xxvii, xxviii.
— put out to nurse, xviii.
— receives a check at 'Honein, I, 176 n 1.
— removal of the ban, xxviii.
— reproved for neglecting a poor convert, II, 320.
— repulses a poor blind man, II, 320.
— 'seal of the prophets,' lxxi.
— second revelation, xxii.
— secret of his success, xlv.
— sent to both men and ginns, xix.
— takes Mecca, xlii.
— takes refuge with Abu Bekr in a cave, xxxiii, xxxiv; I, 178 n.
— takes revenge on the Jews, xxxvii.
— tomb of, at Medînah, lxxv.
— victorious at the battle of Bedr, xxxvi.
— vindicated from the charge of being a mere poet, II, 167.
— vision of the congregation of the ginns listening to the recitation of the Qur'ân, xxx.
— vision of the 'night journey,' xxxi, xxxii.
— visits Tâ'if, xxv.
— wives of, II, 142 n 5, 147.
— wounded at the battle of Ohod, xxxviii; I, 61 n 1.
Mohammed, Rusûl allâh, the Apostle of God, lxxi.
Mohammedan commentators, I, 121 n 1.
Monophysites, li.
Monotheism, xv, xlix.
Monothelites, li.
Month, sacred, I, 27.
Moon, chapter of, II, 254.
— alleged miracle of its being cleft asunder, II, 255 n.
Mosaic law, I, 9 n 2.
Moses, I, 6, 7, 8, 12, 15, 19, 37, 38, 39 n 2, 57, 93, 94, 100, 125, 136, 147 n 1, 151, 152, 154, 155, 156, 157, 201, 202, 206, 216, 217, 238, 239; II, 1, 12, 21, 22, 23, 30, 35, 36, 36 n 1, 37, 38, 39, 40, 41, 50, 61, 68, 86, 90, 92, 93, 100, 107, 108, 109, 112, 113, 121, 137, 139, 149 n, 172, 193, 194, 195, 203, 206, 214, 225, 228, 240 n, 247, 253, 281, 318, 329.
— mother of, II, 108.
Mosque, I, 16, 176; II, 306.
— meaning of word, lxxii.
— 'Remote,' II, 1.
— 'Sacred,' xxxi, lxxiv; I, 20, 21, 27, 28, 31, 97, 167, 173, 175; II, 1, 58, 237.
Mother of cities, II, 205.
Mother of the Book, the, see Umm al Kitâb, I, 211, 237.
Mu'edhdhin, lxxii.
(al) Mughâirah, lxv.
Muhagerîn, xxxiv; I, 172 n, 187 n 1; II, 139, 275.
Mu'harram, I, 96.
(al) Mukanna', xlv.
Munâfiqîn, xxxiv, lxiii.
Munkir, lxix; II, 232 n.
Muqâm Ibrahîm, I, 17 n 3.
Mûsâ allâh, II, 18.
Musâilimah, a false prophet, xlv; II, 235 n.
Muslims, I, 14 n 1, 18 n 1, 24 n 2, 32 n 1, 110 n 3, 127, 152 n 1, 164 n 2, 176 n 1; II, 65.
— their flight to Abyssinia, xxvi.
— they prepare for flight to Medînah, xxxiii.
Mûta, xli.
Mutanebbi, xlv.
(al) Muttalib, xviii.
Muz'hab, xxxii.

(an) Nadhîr, Jews of, II, 274 n, 276 n.
(an) Nadhîr ibn el Hareth, II, 300.
— prefers the Persian legends to the Qur'ân, II, 131 n.
Naggâsî, xxvi, xl.
Nagrân, xiv.
— persecution of Christians at, II, 326 n.
Na'ha'h tribe, patois, I, 236 n 2.
Nakîr, lxix; II, 232 n.

Names, the excellent, lxvii.
Nasr, xii; II, 303.
Nâufel, xviii.
Nebi Sâleh, I, 147 n 1.
(an) Nebîy el' ummîy, xlvii.
Nebuchadnezzar, I, 41 n 1; II, 1 n 4.
Nebuk, II, 152 n.
Negd, ix.
Nehemiah ii. 13, I, 41 n 1.
Night journey, xxi; II, 1 n 1, 251 n.
Nights, Arabian, I, 128 n 1.
Nimrod, I, 40 n 3.
Noah, xxv; I, 50, 94, 125, 144, 145, 183, 200, 201 n 2, 207, 208, 209, 210, 215, 239; II, 1, 3, 20 n 1, 31, 51, 61, 66, 86, 94, 119, 139, 164 n, 171, 176, 190, 193, 242, 247, 255, 269, 302.
— chapter of, II, 302, 303, 304.
— wife of, II, 292.
Noah, Nabîy allâh, the Prophet of God, lxxi.
Noah's son, I, 209 n 2.
Nöldeke, lvi, lx.
Numberers, the, II, 72.
Nûn, meaning of word, II, 295 n 1.

'Obed Adâma, I, 161 n 1.
Offspring, female, buried alive, I, 132 n 3, 256 n 2.
Ohod, battle of, xxxvii, xli; I, 61 n 1, 66 n 1, 264 n 1.
'Omâiyyat ibn Abi Zalt, I, 159 n 1.
'Omar ibn el 'Hattâb, xxiv, xlvi, lvii.
Ommaîyat ibn '*H*alf, II, 17 n 1.
Ommaiyeh, family of, xviii.
Orators, Arab, l.
Osamer, xliv.
Othman, Caliph, xxiii, lix; I, 172 n 3.

Parables, liv.
Paradise, xlii, lxx; I, 15, 31, 62, 63, 69, 89, 139, 140, 142, 143, 155, 207, 237, 253; II, 31, 65, 85, 123, 164, 166, 169, 205, 207, 216, 225, 226, 229, 230, 242, 243, 267, 277, 292, 299, 312, 316, 317, 322, 325 n, 329, 331, 342 n.
παράκλητος, xlix; II, 281 n.
Paul, St., liv.
Pen, chapter of, II, 295.
Pentateuch, li; I, 254 n 1; II, 86 n 1, 113 n.
περικλυτός, xlix; II, 281 n.
Persia, ix, xl, lii; II, 125 n, 235 n.
Persian Gulf, ix.
Persian invasion, II, 1 n 4.
Petra, I, 244 n 1.
Pharaoh, xxv; I, 6, 47, 151, 152, 153, 154, 169, 170, 201, 202, 216, 226 n 2; II, 36, 37, 38, 39 n 1, 40, 68, 90, 91, 92, 92 n 1, 93, 100, 107, 108, 110, 112, 121, 176, 192, 193, 194, 195, 214, 215, 218, 219, 242, 247, 247 n, 257, 298, 307, 318, 327, 331.
— Mohammedan legend of, I, 203 n 2.
— surnamed 'of the stakes,' II, 176.
— wife of, II, 108, 292.
Phineas ibn Azûra, I, 68 n 1.
Pilgrimage, lxxi; I, 28, 173; II, 59. See 'Ha*gg*.
— ceremonies of, liii.
— farewell, xliv.
Pit, fellows of, II, 326.
Poets, II, 98.
Power, night of, II, 337.
Prayer, lxxi.
— call to, lxxii.
— enjoined at night, II, 308.
— incumbent and supererogatory, lxxii.
— times of, lxxii.
Prophet, 'The Righteous,' I, 147 n 1.
Psalm xxxvii. 29, p. xlviii; II, 55 n 2.
— cxlviii, II, 52.
Psalms, the, I, 7, 94; II, 55.
Ptolemy, works of, I, 145 n 2.

Qadr, meaning of word, II, 337 n.
Qâf, Mount, lxx.
Qâinuqâh, Jews of, xxxvii; I, 68 n 1: II, 276 n.
Qarûn, II, 192. See Korah.
(al) Qâsim, Mohammed's son, II, 343 n.
Qiblah, liii; I, 20, 202.
Qin*t*âr=talent, I, 55 n 2.
Qiyâs, lxvi.
Quails, I, 7.
Qubâ', Mosque of, I, 188 n.
Qurâi*dh*ah, Jews of, xxxviii; II, 274 n.
— fall of the, xxxix.
Qurâi*s*, xvi, xxvi, xxviii, xxxiii, xlix, liii, lix, lxi; I, 97 n, 165 n 1, 254 n; II, 17 n 1, 62 n 1, 69 n 2, 236, 254, 320 n, 342.
— compromise with, xxvii.
— idiom of, lxxvi; II, 35 n 2.
— territory of, I, 249 n 2.

Qur'ân, I, 147 n 1; II, 307, 308.
— abrupt changes of persons in, I, 195 n 2.
— Arabic, I, 219.
— chronological arrangement of, lix, lxiv.
— division into Mecca and Medînah, l.
— divisions of sûrahs, lx, lxv.
— English translations of, lxxix.
— language of, lxxvi.
— meaning of name, lvii.
— names of, lxv.
— on what written, lvii.
— persons supposed to have assisted in the composition of, xlviii.
— recensions of, lix.
— revelation of, not to be hurried, II, 311.
— style of, liv, lv, lxxvii.
— various dialects incorporated in, lix.
— verses of, annulled, lvii.
Quzai, xvii.

Rabbânîyîn, I, 56 n 1.
Rabbi, I, 177 n 2.
Rabbinic legends, li.
Rabbis, Jewish, I, 68 n 1, 159 n 1.
Rabboni, I, 56 n 1.
Rama*dh*ân, lxxiii; I, 26, 26 n 2, 27 n 3.
(ar-)Raqîm, II, 14, 14 n 1.
(ar) Rass, II, 86, 86 n 3, 242.
Razwân, keeper of Paradise, lxix.
Red Sea, ix, xxxv.
Reminder, the, I, 53, 245, 254, 255; II, 26, 84, 86.
Remote Mosque, the, xxxiii.
Repetition, the seven of, I, 249, 249 n 6.
Resignation. See Islâm.
Retaliation, law of, I, 25.
Rodwell, I, 240 n 1.
Romans, ancient, II, 2 n 2.
Rosary, lxviii.
(ar-)Rû'h al Amîn, lxix.
(ar-)Rû'h al Qudus, lxix.
Rukaiyah, xxiii.
Rûm. See Greeks.
Rustam, II, 131 n.

Sa'ad ibn Waqqâz, xxiii.
Sabæans, I, 8, 107; II, 58.
Sabbath, I, 263.
— breakers punished, I, 9 n 1, 79.
— Israelites commanded to observe the, I, 93.
Sabbath, legend of breakers of, I, 158.
Sabeanism, xi.
Sab'h al Mathânî, I, 249 n.
Sacred Mosque, xxxiii.
Sacrifices, lxxiv.
— human, I, 132 n 2.
Sadaqah, lxxiii.
Sa'hîr (Chapter iv, 11), the Blaze, lxx.
Sahm, tribe of, II, 340 n.
Sâïbah, I, 112, 112 n 1.
Sakhar, a *g*inn, assumes Solomon's likeness, II, 178 n.
Sale, I, 240 n 1.
Sâleh, prophet, I, 147 n 1.
Salmân al Fârsî, xlviii.
Samaritans, the, II, 40 n 1.
(as) Sâmarîy, II, 40, 41.
Samuel, I, 37 n 3.
1 Samuel iv, v, vi, I, 38 n 3.
Sanaa, II, 341 n.
Saqar (Chapter liv, 58), the Scorching Fire, lxx.
Saracen inhabitants of Sinai, I, 147 n 1.
Satan, I, 23, 30, 50, 65, 67, 78, 81, 82, 83, 110, 120, 134, 139, 140, 159, 161 n 1, 164, 169, 223, 223 n 2, 230, 241, 256, 261; II, 6, 8, 21, 30, 75, 86.
Saul, I, 38 n 1 and 4.
Sawâliheh, I, 147 n 1.
Scriptures, I, 16.
Sebâ, II, 101.
— chapter of, II, 150, 152, 153 n.
Seil al Arim, xlviii.
Sennacherib, II, 1 n 4.
Seth, xi.
Shâh-nâmeh, II, 131 n.
Shâibân Wâil, l.
Shaqq as Sadr, the, II, 335 n.
Sheba, queen of, II, 101, 102, 103, 103 n.
Shechina, I, 38, 38 n 2, 176, 179; II, 233, 237.
Sheddâd ibn Âd, constructs a terrestrial Paradise, II, 330.
Shiahs, II, 143.
Sho'hâib, I, 149, 150, 214, 215, 249 n 3; II, 97, 121.
Si*g*dah, lxxii, lxxii n.
Si*gg*în, II, 324.
(as-)Sigill, II, 55, 55 n 1.
Simon Peter, II, 164 n.
Sinai, inhabitants of, I, 147 n 1.

Sinai, Mount, I, 57 n 1; II, 66, 336.
— Peninsula of, I, 147 n 1.
Sinaitic Peninsula, II, 152 n 1.
(as) Sirât, lxix.
Sirius, II, 254.
Slaves, II, 127.
Sleepers, Seven, II, 14 n 1, 16 n 2.
Smoke, chapter of, II, 218.
Sodom, I, 183 n 1, 249 n 4, 254; II, 298.
Solomon, I, 14, 14 n 1, 94, 125; II, 52, 52 n 1 and 3, 101, 102, 151.
— a devil assumes his likeness as a punishment for his allowing idolatry in his house, II, 178 n.
— ring of, II, 178 n.
— served by ginns, lxx.
— slays his horses, II, 178.
— taught the language of birds, II, 100.
Soul, condition of, after death, lxxi.
Spider, legend of, xxxiii.
— chapter of, II, 117.
— similitude of, I, 4 n 3; II, 121.
Spirit, li; II, 317.
— the Faithful, lxix; II, 98.
— of God, II, 53.
— Holy, lxix; I, 12, 39.
Spoils, II, 141 n, 145, 148, 274, 275.
— chapter of, I, 163.
— distribution of, I, 163.
Statues, I, 110.
Stesichorus, liv.
Strabo, I, 244 n 1.
Suhail ibn 'Amr concludes truce with Mohammed at 'Hudâibîyeh, II, 237 n.
Sunnah, lxvi.
Sunnîs, I, 110 n 3.
Sûrah, I, 182, 197, 206, 231.
— meaning of word, lvi.
Suwâ'h, xii; II, 303.
Syria, ix, xli, xliv; I, 164 n 1, 249 n 2; II, 125 n, 153 n.

Tabûk, xliii; I, 184 n 1, 190 n 1.
Tâghût, ancient Arabs, idols, and demons, I, 40, 79, 81, 82, 106, 254; II, 184.
Tâ'if, xii, xlii, xliii, lxx; II, 213, 304 n.
Tal'ha, xxiii, lxv.
Tal'h trees, II, 263.
Talmud, liv; I, 5 n 1, 57 n 1, 116 n, 121 n 1, 155 n; II, 52 n 2, 178 n.
Tâlût (Saul), I, 38.
Tamannah, meaning of word, II, 62 n 1.
Tannûr, meaning of word, I, 209 n 1.
Târah, I, 124 n.
Tarwî'h, lxxiv.
Tasnîm, II, 325.
Tawâf, ceremony of, lxxv.
Terah, I, 124 n.
Thabîr, Mount, xxii.
Thamûd, xlviii; I, 86, 146, 147 n 1, 183, 211, 212, 216, 239, 244 n 1, 249 n 5; II, 7, 61, 103, 121, 176, 242, 247, 254, 256, 298, 327, 331, 333.
(eTH) THaqalân, lxx; II, 9 n 1.
THaqîf, tribe of, xii, xlii.
THaur, Mount, xxxiii.
Tomb, examination of, lxix.
Tribes, the, I, 19, 57.
Trinity, the, xiv, lii.
Tubbâ'h, kings of the Himyarite Arabs so called, II, 219, 242.
Tuvâ, the holy valley, I, 35; II, 318.

Umm al Kitâb, xlviii; I, 2 n 2; II, 163.
Ummatun, II, 53 n 4.
— meaning of word, I, 263 n 2.
Umm Gemîl, wife of Abu Laheb, lx.
Ummîyûn, xlvii; I, 482.
Umm Salmâ, one of Mohammed's wives, I, 70 n 1.

Veiled prophet of Khorassan, xlv.
Venus, xii.
Vizîr, meaning of word, II, 36 n 2.

Wadd, xii; II, 303.
Wady, bed of a torrent, I, 191.
Wâdy as Sheikh, I, 147 n 1.
Walîd ibn 'Hugbâ wrongly accuses the tribe of Mustaleq of insubordination, II, 239 n.
(al) Walîd ibn Mughâirah, II, 295, 309 n, 320 n.
— bargains with an idolater to be relieved of the sin of apostacy, II, 253 n.
Waqf, lxxiii.
Waraqah, xv, xx, xlix.
(al) Watîyeh, I, 147 n 1.
Wazîlah, I, 112, 112 n 1.
Whisperer, the, II, 345.
Whistling reprimanded, I, 167.
Witches, II, 303.
Women, position of, lxxv.

Word, l; I, 51.
Wuzû'h, lxxii.

Yag*h*ûTH, xii; II, 303.
Yâgûg, II, 25, 54.
Yâi'as, meaning of word, I, 236 n 2.
Yamâmah, II, 86 n 3.
Y'arishûn, meaning of word, I, 153 n 1.
Yasîn, II, 173.
YaTHrib, xviii, xxx, xxxi, xxxii, xxxiii, xxxiv, xlviii; II, 140, 140 n 1.
— Jews of, xxxi.
Ya'ûq, xii; II, 303.
Yefta'h'allah, new phrase, I, 149 n 2.
Yemâmah, lvii.
Yemen, xiv; II, 150 n, 327 n, 341 n.
Yul'hidûna, meaning of word, I, 160 n 1.

Zachariah, I, 51, 125; II, 27, 27 n 1, 53, 53 n 1.
Zafâ, Mount, near Mecca, xiii; I, 22.
Zafîyah bint 'Huyâi, one of the prophet's wives, II, 240.
Zafwân ibn al Mu'hu*tt*al, causes scandal concerning 'Âyesha, II, 74 n 2.
Zâid, Mohammed's adopted son, xxix, xli, xlix; II, 144, 233 n 1.
Zâid ibn Amr, xv, xx, xxiii.
Zâid ibn THâbit, Mohammed's amanuensis, lvii, lviii, lix.
Zâinab, a widow, afterwards one of Mohammed's wives, xxix.
— divorced wife of Zâid, xxix; II, 139 n, 144 n, 233.
Zakât, lxxiii.
Zâli'h, I, 146, 147, 148 n 1, 211, 212, 215; II, 96, 103.
Zamharîr, II, 313.
Zaqqûm, II, 7 n 2, 170, 220, 264.
Zemzem, xvii.
Zingabîl, II, 313.
Zobeir, xxiii, lxv.
Zodiacal signs, II, 326.
Zoroastrianism, lxviii.
Zuhâib ibn Sinân er Rûmî, I, 30 n 1.

Transliteration of Oriental Alphabets adopted for the Translations of the Sacred Books of the East.

CONSONANTS.	MISSIONARY ALPHABET. I Class.	II Class.	III Class.	Sanskrit.	Zend.	Pehlevi.	Persian.	Arabic.	Hebrew.	Chinese.
Gutturales.										
1 Tenuis	k	...	...	क	𐬐	𐭪	ك	ك	כּ	k
2 „ aspirata	kh	...	...	ख	𐬑	𐭧	...	...	כ	kh
3 Media	g	...	...	ग	𐬔	𐭢	گ	...	גּ	...
4 „ aspirata	gh	...	...	घ	𐬖	𐬖	...	...	ג	...
5 Gutturo-labialis	q	...	...	...	...	...	ق	ق	ק	...
6 Nasalis	ṅ (ng)	...	...	ङ	{ 𐬣 (ng) 𐬧 (N) }	...	...	...	...	...
7 Spiritus asper	h	...	...	ह	𐬵 (𐬷 hv)	𐭧	ه	ه	ה	h, hs
8 „ lenis	’	...	...	...	...	...	ا	ا	א	...
9 „ asper faucalis	‘h	...	...	...	...	...	ح	ح	ח	...
10 „ lenis faucalis	’h	...	...	...	...	...	ع	ع	ע	...
11 „ asper fricatus	...	‘*ḥ*	...	...	...	...	غ	غ	ח	...
12 „ lenis fricatus	...	’*ḥ*	...	...	...	...	...	...	...	...
Gutturales modificatae (palatales, &c.)										
13 Tenuis	...	*k*	...	च	𐬗	𐭰	چ	...	...	*k*
14 „ aspirata	...	*kh*	...	छ	...	...	...	...	...	*kh*
15 Media	...	*g*	...	ज	𐬘	𐭰	ج	ج	...	...
16 „ aspirata	...	*gh*	...	झ	...	...	غ	غ	...	...
17 „ Nasalis	...	*ñ*	...	ञ	...	...	...	...	...	...

CONSONANTS (*continued*).	MISSIONARY ALPHABET. I Class.	II Class.	III Class.	Sanskrit.	Zend.	Pehlevi.	Persian.	Arabic.	Hebrew.	Chinese.
18 Semivocalis	y	...	....	य	𐬫 𐬌𐬌 𐬫 } init.	𐭉	ي	ي	י	y
19 Spiritus asper	...	(y̔)	....	...	....	...	...	...	...	...
20 ,, lenis	...	(y̓)	....	...	....	...	...	...	...	...
21 ,, asper assibilatus	...	*s*	....	श	𐬱	𐭔	ش	ش	...	...
22 ,, lenis assibilatus	...	*z*	....	...	𐬲	𐭆	ژ	...	...	*z*
Dentales.										
23 Tenuis	t	...	....	त	𐬙	𐭕	ت	ت	תּ	t
24 ,, aspirata	th	...	....	थ	𐬚	...	...	...	ת	th
25 ,, assibilata	...	...	TH	...	....	...	ث	ث	...	...
26 Media	d	...	....	द	𐬛	𐭅	د	د	דּ	...
27 ,, aspirata	dh	...	....	ध	𐬜	...	...	...	ד	...
28 ,, assibilata	...	...	DH	...	....	...	ذ	ذ	...	...
29 Nasalis	n	...	....	न	𐬥	۱	ن	ن	נ	n
30 Semivocalis	l	...	....	ल	....	۱,ط,ر	ل	ل	ל	l
31 ,, mollis 1	...	*l*	....	ळ	....	...	...	...	...	...
32 ,, mollis 2	...	...	L	...	....	...	...	...	...	...
33 Spiritus asper 1	s	...	....	स	𐬯	𐭎	س(ث)	س	שׂ	s
34 ,, asper 2	...	...	s (ʃ)	..	....	...	....	...	ס	...
35 ,, lenis	z	...	....	...	𐬰	𐭆	ز (ذ)	ز	ז	z
36 ,, asperrimus 1	...	...	z (ʒ)	...	....	...	ص	ص	צ	ʒ, ʒh
37 ,, asperrimus 2	...	...	ẓ (ʒ̣)	...	....	...	ض	...	...	...

Dentales modificatae (linguales, &c.)										
38 Tenuis	...	*t*	...	ट	...	...	ط	ط	ט	...
39 " aspirata	...	*th*	...	ठ	...	...	ظ	ظ	...	...
40 Media	...	*d*	...	ड	[illegible]	[illegible]	...	...	...	...
41 " aspirata	...	*dh*	...	ढ	...	...	...	ض	...	...
42 Nasalis	...	*n*	...	ण	[illegible]	...	...	...	...	...
43 Semivocalis	r	...	...	र	𐬭	[illegible]	ر	ر	ר	...
44 " fricata	...	*r*	...	...	...	...	...	...	...	*r*
45 " diacritica	...	...	R	...	...	...	...	...	...	...
46 Spiritus asper	sh	...	...	ष	[illegible]	[illegible]	...	...	...	sh
47 " lenis	zh	...	...	...	...	...	...	...	...	...
Labiales.										
48 Tenuis	p	...	...	प	𐬞	[illegible]	پ	...	פּ	p
49 " aspirata	ph	...	...	फ	...	...	...	...	פ	ph
50 Media	b	...	...	ब	𐬠	[illegible]	ب	ب	בּ	...
51 " aspirata	bh	...	...	भ	...	...	...	...	ב	...
52 Tenuissima	...	*p*	...	...	...	...	...	...	...	...
53 Nasalis	m	...	...	म	𐬨	[illegible]	م	م	מ	m
54 Semivocalis	w	...	...	...	[illegible]	...	...	...	...	w
55 " aspirata	hw	...	...	...	...	...	...	...	...	...
56 Spiritus asper	f	...	...	...	𐬟	[illegible]	ف	ف	...	f
57 " lenis	v	...	...	व	»	[illegible]	و	و	ו	...
58 Anusvâra	...	*m*	...	अं	[illegible] ã	...	...	...	...	...
59 Visarga	...	*h*	...	अः	...	...	...	...	...	...

VOWELS.	MISSIONARY ALPHABET. I Class.	II Class.	III Class.	Sanskrit.	Zend.	Pehlevi.	Persian.	Arabic.	Hebrew.	Chinese.
1 Neutralis	0	. . .	. . . .	. . .	. . . .	. . .	. . .	. . .	ְ	ă
2 Laryngo-palatalis	ĕ	. . .	. . . .	. . .	. . . .	. . .	. . .	. . .	. . .	. . .
3 „ labialis	ŏ	. . .	. . . .	. . .	. . . .	𐭠 fin.	. . .	. . .	. . .	. . .
4 Gutturalis brevis	a	. . .	. . . .	अ	𐬀	𐭠 init.	َ	َ	ַ	a
5 „ longa	â	(*a*)	. . . .	आ	𐬁	𐭠	َا	َا	ָ	â
6 Palatalis brevis	i	. . .	. . . .	इ	𐬌	. . .	ِ	ِ	ִ	i
7 „ longa	î	(*i*)	. . . .	ई	𐬍	𐭉	ِي	ِي	ִי	î
8 Dentalis brevis	*li*	. . .	. . . .	ऌ	. . . .	. . .	. . .	. . .	. . .	. . .
9 „ longa	*lî*	. . .	. . . .	ॡ	. . . .	. . .	. . .	. . .	. . .	. . .
10 Lingualis brevis	*ri*	. . .	. . . .	ऋ	. . . .	. . .	. . .	. . .	. . .	. . .
11 „ longa	*rî*	. . .	. . . .	ॠ	. . . .	. . .	. . .	. . .	. . .	. . .
12 Labialis brevis	u	. . .	. . . .	उ	𐬎	. . .	ُ	ُ	ֻ	u
13 „ longa	û	(*u*)	. . . .	ऊ	𐬏	𐭅	ُو	ُو	וּ	û
14 Gutturo-palatalis brevis	e	. . .	. . . .	. . .	𐬆(e) 𐬇(*e*)	. . .	. . .	. . .	ֶ	e
15 „ longa	ê (ai)	(*e*)	. . . .	ए	𐬉, 𐬈	𐭉	. . .	. . .	ֵ	ê
16 Diphthongus gutturo-palatalis	âi	(*ai*)	. . . .	ऐ	. . . .	. . .	َيْ	َيْ	. . .	âi
17 „ „	ei (ĕi)	. . .	. . . .	. . .	. . . .	. . .	. . .	. . .	. . .	ei, êi
18 „ „	oi (ŏu)	. . .	. . . .	. . .	. . . .	. . .	. . .	. . .	. . .	. . .
19 Gutturo-labialis brevis	o	. . .	. . . .	. . .	𐬊	. . .	. . .	. . .	ָ	o
20 „ longa	ô (au)	(*o*)	. . . .	ओ	𐬋	𐭅	. . .	. . .	וֹ	. . .
21 Diphthongus gutturo-labialis	âu	(*au*)	. . . .	औ	𐬀𐬎 (*au*)	. . .	َوْ	َوْ	. . .	âu
22 „ „	eu (ĕu)	. . .	. . . .	. . .	. . . .	. . .	. . .	. . .	. . .	. . .
23 „ „	ou (ŏu)	. . .	. . . .	. . .	. . . .	. . .	. . .	. . .	. . .	. . .
24 Gutturalis fracta	ä	. . .	. . . .	. . .	. . . .	. . .	. . .	. . .	. . .	. . .
25 Palatalis fracta	ï	. . .	. . . .	. . .	. . . .	. . .	. . .	. . .	. . .	. . .
26 Labialis fracta	ü	. . .	. . . .	. . .	. . . .	. . .	. . .	. . .	. . .	ü
27 Gutturo-labialis fracta	ö	. . .	. . . .	. . .	. . . .	. . .	. . .	. . .	. . .	. . .